Higher Education in Scotland and the UK

HIGHER EDUCATION IN SCOTLAND AND THE UK

Diverging or Converging Systems?

Edited by Sheila Riddell, Elisabet Weedon and Sarah Minty

EDINBURGH
University Press

© editorial matter and organisation Sheila Riddell, Elisabet Weedon and
Sarah Minty, 2016
© the chapters their several authors, 2016

Edinburgh University Press Ltd
The Tun – Holyrood Road
12 (2f) Jackson's Entry
Edinburgh EH8 8PJ
www.euppublishing.com

Typeset in 10 on 12pt Ehrhardt by
Servis Filmsetting Ltd, Stockport, Cheshire,
and printed and bound in Great Britain by
CPI Group (UK) Ltd, Croydon CR0 4YY

A CIP record for this book is available from the British Library

ISBN 978 1 4744 0458 7 (hardback)
ISBN 978 1 4744 0459 4 (webready PDF)
ISBN 978 1 4744 0460 0 (epub)

Contents

Figures

Tables

Acknowledgement

This book is based on research carried out as part of ESRC's Future of the UK and Scotland Programme. The project, entitled Higher Education in Scotland, the Devolution Settlement and the Referendum on Independence (ES/K00705X/1), was conducted by researchers at the University of Edinburgh between March 2013 and July 2014. We are indebted to the ESRC for the project funding and to the School of Education for supporting Susan Whittaker's doctoral studentship. We would like to thank the members of our advisory committee for their sound guidance throughout the project and to the university sector key informants. Particular thanks are due to the international students and the young people from Scotland and the north of England who agreed to be interviewed about their future higher education plans.

The Contributors

Sheila Riddell is Director of the Centre for Research in Education Inclusion and Diversity (CREID) at the University of Edinburgh (www.creid.ed.ac.uk) and was previously Director of the Strathclyde Centre for Disability Research at the University of Glasgow. Her work explores themes of social justice and equality across a range of policy fields including education, social care and employment.

Lucy Hunter Blackburn is a freelance writer and researcher specialising in student funding within the UK. She has twenty years' experience of working in public policy in local and national government, mainly in Scotland, including four years as Head of Higher Education in the Scottish Executive. Her recent work includes publications on student funding as part of the ESRC's *Future of the UK and Scotland* programme and for the Higher Education Policy Institute.

Linda Croxford is an honorary research fellow of the Centre for Educational Sociology (CES) at the University of Edinburgh (www.ces.ed.ac.uk). She has wide interests in education and youth transitions, and specialises in quantitative analysis of survey and administrative datasets.

Chung-yan (Grace) Kong is a research assistant and the academic coordinator of CREID. Her recent research focused on the experiences of Chinese students studying at Scottish universities. Grace previously tutored at the Open University of Hong Kong and worked for the Information Services Department of the Hong Kong Government. She recently obtained her PhD in Translation Studies at the University of Edinburgh.

Sarah Minty is a Research Fellow at CREID. She has particular interests in social justice and policy evaluation and has undertaken research in the school, vocational and higher education sectors. Sarah is currently working on a number of projects relating to higher education funding and access, and exploring how student finance affects young people's higher education choices.

David Raffe was a member of CES at the University of Edinburgh from 1975 and was its director for many years until his death in February 2015. He conducted research on numerous aspects of secondary and post-secondary education and training in Scotland and elsewhere, and served on committees of the Scottish and UK governments and public educational bodies in the UK and Europe.

Elisabet Weedon is Deputy Director and a Senior Research Fellow of CREID. Her main research interests are in the area of further and higher education, equality and social justice in education. She has worked on a range of research projects including studies of lifelong learning across Europe, disabled students in higher education and workplace learning.

Susan Whittaker is a PhD student at Moray House School of Education, University of Edinburgh, researching cross-border mobility of university students in the UK and equality of access. She has previously worked as a researcher within the fields of lifelong learning and school education.

This book is dedicated to David Raffe who passed away in February 2015 just before the completion of the manuscript. David was a scholar of great integrity and insight. He was widely respected both nationally and internationally and did much to help to shape the modern sociology of education in the UK. His highly influential research covered an impressive breadth of work including the comparative study of education systems, within which field he pioneered 'home international' comparisons within the UK – to which this book is testimony.

1

Scottish Higher Education and Devolution

Sheila Riddell

INTRODUCTION

This book focuses on the challenges and opportunities faced by Scottish higher education following the outcome of the referendum on independence in September 2014. Whilst 55 per cent of votes cast were in favour of remaining within the UK, a significant minority of the electorate voted for independence, leading to a general endorsement of the idea that further devolution was needed. The precise nature and scale of future constitutional change, and how this will impact on higher education in Scotland and the rest of the UK, is unclear at the time of writing. However, a central theme of this book is to track the ebb and flow of policy convergence and divergence across a range of domains such as tuition fees, widening access and internationalisation. Throughout the book, comparisons are drawn with higher education systems in other parts of the UK and, where relevant, Europe and the developed world. The book considers whether we are witnessing the demise of a common UK higher education system and the emergence of a new system in Scotland, based on different social values and reflecting wider social policy drift across the UK.

This question is important not just for political reasons, but also because Scottish universities make up an essential element of the country's economic infrastructure (Universities Scotland, 2010). According to Universities Scotland in its submission to the Smith Commission, universities contribute £6.7 billion in gross value added to the Scottish economy (Universities Scotland, 2014). This implies that every £1 of public investment leads to £6 of economic impact. Whilst these numbers may be disputed, it is evident that much employment in Scotland depends on the higher education infrastructure either directly or indirectly; universities employ over 39,300 people and support over 142,000 jobs in areas such as catering, rentals, construction and so on. At the same time, as is evident in recent policy discourse, Scotland's higher education system plays a major role in the formation of national identity and the assertion of difference from systems operating in the rest of the UK, particularly England.

The book draws on findings from a project on higher education within the ESRC's *Future of the UK and Scotland Programme*, which ran from March 2013 to July 2014 and aimed to contribute independent and reliable evidence to inform the debate in the run-up to the referendum. The project featured here, entitled *Higher Education in Scotland, the Devolution Settlement and the Referendum on Independence* (ES/K00705X/1) involved both primary research and knowledge exchange activities. It included the following elements: (i) a review of policy and statistical data to explore the ongoing effects of administrative and political devolution on higher education in Scotland and the other countries of the UK; (ii) an analysis of Higher Education Statistics Agency (HESA) data to investigate the impact of devolution on cross-border student flows; (iii) key informant interviews with policy makers to illuminate the implications of devolution and/or independence for present and future higher education policy; (iv) interviews with young people in schools in Scotland and England to explore their view of current government higher education policy; and (v) interviews with international students. Knowledge exchange activities, carried out over the entire course of the project, included a series of seminars and the production of a film aimed at 16- and 17-year-olds. Research methods employed in different parts of the project are explained more fully in Appendix 1.Throughout the book, we use the shorthand 'the ESRC project' to refer to this work.

This chapter begins by outlining the key themes which run throughout the book, beginning with a brief account of the countervailing pressures within higher education in the developed world, as the homogenising forces of globalisation are countered by localising forces seeking national, regional and local solutions to global economic challenges. We then provide a recent history of higher education in Scotland, focusing on drivers of divergence with the rest of the UK, in particular approaches to undergraduate tuition fees. Subsequently, we discuss areas of common concern across the UK, in particular efforts to widen participation and reduce social inequalities in access to universities. We then consider drivers of convergence, in particular the salience of cross-border student flows, participation in common UK, European and international research areas, and the recruitment of international students. Finally, we provide an overview of the dominant policy discourses in recent government documents and statements on higher education, which tend to emphasise growing differences across the UK. We conclude with an outline of the book chapters, which develop these central themes in greater depth.

GLOBALISATION, LOCALISATION AND HIGHER EDUCATION

As noted above, the central concern of this book is to chart the contradictory pressures shaping Scottish higher education and, as Raffe (2013) has argued, this requires an understanding of the literatures relating to globalisation on the one hand and devolution on the other. The internationalisation of higher education has been fostered by a number of trans-national bodies, including the EU. For a decade and a half, national signatories to the Bologna Process have been encouraged to expand higher education participation rates, harmonise qualification frameworks

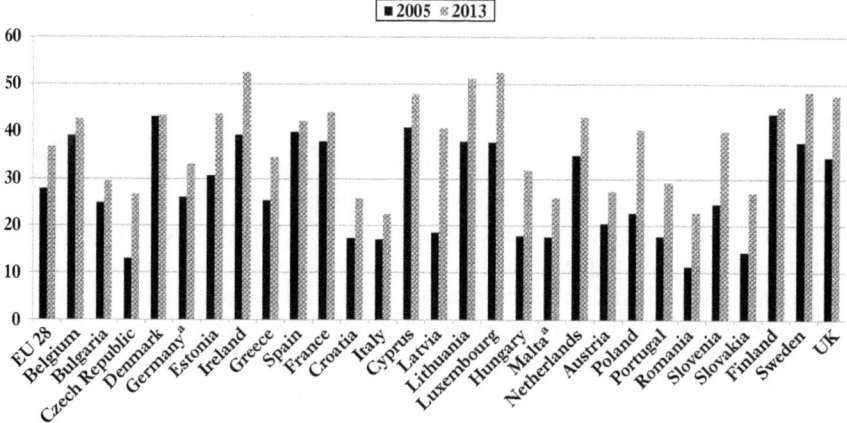

Figure 1.1 Changes in the proportion of 30–34-year-olds with tertiary education in EU28 countries between 2005 and 2013

a break in data series in 2005

Source: Eurostat, 2014

and promote social mobility by reducing the link between social background and higher education participation. Across the EU, the proportion of 30–34-year-olds with tertiary level education has increased (see Figure 1.1), and in 2010 the EU set a target of 40 per cent participation in all countries by 2020, a goal which has already been reached by many member states including the UK.

The assumption underpinning the Bologna Process is that the majority of new jobs created across Europe and the developed world will require higher-level skills, with a projected shortfall of workers with qualifications in areas such as science, technology and engineering. At the same time, there is believed to be an over-supply of workers competing for low-skill jobs, which is driving down wages and increasing economic inequality (Nicaise, 2010; Riddell and Weedon, 2012). In addition to the EU, the Organisation for Economic Co-operation and Development (OECD) has been an active promoter of the case for an expanded and harmonised higher education system across the developed world as a means of countering growing levels of inequality which threaten social cohesion (OECD, 2008, 2011).

At the same time as developed countries have been urged to smooth over national differences within higher education systems, political discourse in Scotland has tended to emphasise growing divergence between Scotland and England (see below for further discussion). This is in line with predictions made by political scientists, who have characterised devolution as a 'fragile divergence machine', which, once set in train, would inevitably lead to the rupture of the UK as a nation state (Greer, 2007). According to Jeffery (2007), UK devolution has been handled so far in a piecemeal and uncoordinated manner, with a tendency to ignore central problems such as the non-devolved unit of England. Despite the lack of an English parliament, the sheer size of England compared with the devolved nations means that it is able to exert a disproportionate influence on the political decisions of the devolved governments, including within the field of higher education. The lack of a devolution master plan, Jeffery argued, would continue to threaten the coherence and stability of the devolution process. Discussion of growing differences in social and political values between Scotland and England featured prominently in the independence debate, with some commentators, such as Riddoch (2014), suggesting that Scotland is in the process of developing a social welfare regime more closely aligned to that of the Nordic countries than the heavily marketised regime which holds sway in England.

Overall, it is evident that Scottish and UK higher education systems are subject to both convergent and divergent pressures. In order to understand these shifting currents, the various chapters in this book draw on the literature of both devolution and globalisation. In the following section, we provide a brief overview of changes in the Scottish higher education system, particularly in relation to student funding, which are explored in greater depth in future chapters.

DEVOLUTION, DIVERGENCE AND UNDERGRADUATE TUITION FEES

Across the four jurisdictions of the UK, a formerly unitary higher education system funded by a single body has been reconfigured over time with particular contrasts emerging between Scotland and England. Following the Browne Review (2010) and the subsequent White Paper (BIS, 2011), the cap on tuition fees in England was raised to £9,000 per annum, with most universities charging the full amount. Since the abolition of the graduate endowment in 2007, fees of Scottish and EU students studying in Scottish universities have been paid by the Scottish Government. Below, we provide a brief historical overview of the emergence of this wide difference in citizenship entitlement.

Between 1919 and 1989, UK universities were funded directly by the University Grants Committee (later Council), which also allocated student numbers. Policy differences began to emerge in different parts of the UK following administrative devolution in 1992, when the funding councils established in each jurisdiction adopted responsibility for resource distribution. During the 1990s, despite emerging differences in the allocation of research funds and the use of colleges as higher education providers, there continued to be strong similarities across the systems, with the Dearing Report in England and the Garrick Report in Scotland, both published in 1997, recommending that the rapid expansion of higher education should be funded in part by students themselves, with the state continuing to play a major role in university funding. These reports reflected a view of higher education as both a public and a private good, thus warranting a cost-sharing approach.

Following political devolution and the establishment of the Scottish Parliament in 1999, far greater differences in approaches to student funding have emerged between the four nations, particularly between England and Scotland. Table 1.1 summarises emerging differences in undergraduate student funding in relation to fees, loans and grants.

Table 1.1 Student support in the UK before and after devolution

1945–7	First national legislation empowering local authorities and Ministers to support students in higher education. Greater provision of national and local state scholarships ensured many students received grants and had full fees paid, but no absolute entitlement. Separate primary legislation for Scotland and Northern Ireland, both showing some variation in the detailed approach, including more emphasis in Scotland on studying locally.
1961–2	Following the Anderson Committee report, the introduction of full payment of fees (partially subject to means-testing until 1977) and means-tested grants, as an automatic entitlement on the award of a university place for the first time in any part of the UK. Separate primary legislation, regulations and administrative arrangements for Scotland and for Northern Ireland, but student entitlements essentially the same as for England and Wales.
1990	Introduction of student loans to supplement living cost grants across the UK. 'Mortgage-style' repayment with only link to earnings the ability to seek twelve months' suspension of repayments.
1998–9	Means-tested fee payment of up to £1,000 introduced across the UK. No liability below £23,000; full liability from £30,000. Grants reduced, loan entitlements increased and extended at higher incomes. Loans become 'income-contingent', payable at 9 per cent of all earnings over a threshold, initially £10,000.
1999–2000	Grants abolished completely across all of the UK and replaced with higher loans.
2000–1	Fee payments abolished for Scottish students studying in Scotland. Fee of £1,000 continues for all other students in the UK.
2001–2	Introduction in Scotland of post-graduation payment (the 'graduate endowment') of £2,000, supported by income-contingent loan. National means-tested grants reintroduced for young Scottish students, up to £2,000. Institutionally administered grants introduced for Scottish students.
2002–3	In Wales and Northern Ireland, means-tested grants of up to £1,500 reintroduced (for young and mature students).
2004–5	In England, means-tested grants of up to £1,000 reintroduced (for young and mature students).

Table 1.1 (continued)

2006–7	In England and Northern Ireland, variable fees of up to £3,000 introduced, with dedicated income-contingent fee loan. Grant maximum increased to £2,765. No change to fee arrangements in Wales. Income-contingent fee loan made available for Scottish and Welsh students studying in the rest of the UK. Annual fee payable by students from the rest of the UK in Scotland increased to £1,700 (£2,700 for medicine).
2007–8	Graduate endowment abolished in Scotland. In Wales, £3,000 fee introduced, backed by income-contingent loan, but with an additional non-means-tested grant towards fees of £1,845 to all Welsh students studying in Wales, reducing de facto fee liability. Grants increased to a maximum of £2,700.
2010–11	Fee grant abolished in Wales and means-tested maintenance grant increased to £5,000. National means-tested grant of up to £1,000 reintroduced in Scotland for mature students.
2012–13	In England, variable fees of up to £9,000 introduced, as before with dedicated income-contingent loan. Loan-repayment threshold increased to £21,000 and loan interest rates increased. Grants increased to £3,250. In Wales, variable fees of £9,000 also introduced, but with a dedicated fee grant covering all fee costs over £3,465 for Welsh students studying in any part of the UK, effectively capping fees at that level. Maximum grant raised to £5,161. New loan rules adopted, as for England. In Scotland, variable fees with no legal maximum introduced for students from rest of the UK; loan increased to £9,000 for Scottish students in rest of UK; free tuition retained for Scots in Scotland. In Northern Ireland, fees capped at £3,465 for Northern Irish students in Northern Ireland, maximum fee loan increased to £9,000 for NI students in the rest of the UK. Variable fees of up to £9,000 introduced for students from the rest of the UK.
2013–14	Maximum grant for young students reduced from £2,640 to £1,750 in Scotland. Mature student grant reduced to £750 and income threshold for grant reduced; tapered system replaced with steps. Minimum loan increased from £940 to £4,500.

In the aftermath of the first Scottish Parliamentary election in 1999, student fees featured prominently in coalition negotiations between Labour and the Liberal Democrats. In order to prevent the derailing of the coalition, the Cubie Committee was set up to review student funding. This led to the removal of upfront fees in Scotland, which were initially replaced by a one-off graduate endowment (set at £2,289 in 2006–7) which was to be repaid after the student had left university and was in employment, with exemptions for disabled students and those from poorer backgrounds. In 2007, following the election of a minority SNP administration, all graduate contributions were abolished. Since that point, the absence of tuition fees north of the border has been presented as one of the defining features of the Scottish education system and wider polity, exemplifying the principles of universalism rather than marketisation (see Chapter 2 for further discussion). In the Scottish Government White Paper on independence (Scottish Government, 2013) and during the course of the referendum debate, frequent reference was made to the distinctiveness of Scottish higher education as based on 'the ability to learn rather than the ability to pay'. In November 2014, a memorial stone to Alex Salmond's tenure at the Scottish political helm was unveiled at Heriot-Watt University, engraved with the First Minister's pronouncement that: 'The rocks will melt with the sun before I allow tuition fees to be imposed on Scotland's students'. This clearly throws down the gauntlet to political parties and universities who might regard some form of student contribution as both socially just and economically prudent.

Senior managers in the university sector who were interviewed during the course of the project underlined the significance of tuition fees policies north and south of the border and the dilemmas thrown up in both countries. As noted by one interviewee, undergraduate student funding represented one of the most significant areas of divergence post-devolution:

> I think I would characterise the divergence in higher education policy as probably the most extreme difference in citizen entitlement across borders of anything. If you have to put it bluntly, if my son fell over and broke his leg in Oxford, you'd expect it to be mended for free even though the health service there is organised very differently. If my son decided to go to Oxford University, he'd be incurring a deferred fee of £9,000 in contrast with not incurring a fee here at all for undergraduate full time study. I think that's probably the most divergent citizen entitlement of any policy between England and the devolved administrations. (Manager, university lobby group, Scotland)

Despite this divergence, he believed that 'within a highly divergent policy environment, a genuinely UK wide university eco system has managed to subsist'. Scottish university managers welcomed the fact that the Scottish Government had been able to fund universities from the public purse and some believed the policy was sustainable provided the government was willing to prioritise higher education over other areas of public expenditure:

> [The policy of free undergraduate tuition] is sustainable so long as the Government is prepared to make difficult decisions. And at the end of the day this is very simply just

an allocation of resource. And the Scottish Government at the moment is prepared to say that it wishes to fund higher education as a free good. And therefore not to fund other things. This is entirely sustainable as long as the Scottish Government maintains a commitment that it wishes to prioritise higher education for the benefit of the Scottish economy. (Senior manager, post-92 university, Scotland)

However, the majority of university managers in Scotland were not opposed in principle to some form of student contribution or graduate tax and believed that the issue of tuition fees in Scotland was 'dormant' rather than permanently resolved. However, it was recognised that the introduction of some sort of graduate contribution was off the political agenda for the time being, although this might be to the detriment of the Scottish university sector:

It'll be so difficult for any Scottish government to introduce fees that they will not do so until a spending review too late. And that means three years at least and maybe more of Scottish universities actually being underfunded in comparison with their English counterparts. (Senior manager, post-92 university, Scotland)

Whilst many university managers believed that fiscal challenges might make some form of student contribution necessary in the future, some managers believed the Scottish tuition fees system made university education accessible to students from diverse backgrounds and that the English system would prove unsustainable:

I think in the long term [free tuition] will promote access. It will promote more inclu-sivity and fairness . . . I think in the long run what we're doing in Scotland is sustain-able and what they're doing in England isn't. I think the funding system that is going to crash against the buffers and just be revealed to be unworkable is the English one. That's because of the way they've handled the student loan and the student debt. And they are suddenly going to find themselves with a massive government debt because they will move to, 'Oh gosh 50 per cent aren't going to repay or whatever but we've doled out all these loans on the basis that 25 per cent or 30 per cent would not repay'. So I just think the Scottish way of doing it is better . . . And I think ten years from now we will see that in England they made a massive mistake when they introduced the £9,000 fees. (Senior manager, post-92 university, Scotland)

University managers in England generally believed that higher education was both a public and a private good and therefore should be co-funded. However, some academics disagreed strongly and felt that funding for higher education should come from a progressive taxation system:

In principle, yes [I think that the state should fund higher education]. I don't think it's ever going to happen now. In principle I would go for a progressive tax regime which then funds higher education and adult education and further education . . . I don't have kids who are benefiting from school education, but I accept that as part of a civilised society, my taxes contribute to school education . . . I would rather pay more taxes and have a decent public and social system that includes education. (Academic, post-92 university, England)

Concerns were expressed by English interviewees over levels of student debt in England, but also about the territorial injustice associated with different tuition fees regimes operating across the UK:

> in the end it's the same pool of taxpayers paying for very different life experiences. But there you are. I'm for fees in principle and I think the Scots are wrong really. I think they're wrong actually and they also deter their students from coming south. And actually it weakens the university system. And I personally think that where we were pre the rise in fees was about right. Maybe you could lift a little bit more. The good thing is it has insulated the university sector from what would otherwise have been serious cuts. But the taxpayer is going to pay in the end. I think the student loan book is going to be worth 35 or 40p for every pound that's been borrowed. So I think that the impact of the £9,000 fees is toxic on the education system. Toxic on academic life in the medium term. And the Scottish system is very different . . . I understand why they've done it. But it's profoundly inequitable. (Senior manager, post-92 university, England)

The views expressed above suggest that university managers north and south of the Border are well aware of dilemmas surrounding university fees and regard the issue as subject to future change rather than permanently resolved. Whilst tuition fees policy has dominated the debate, as noted in Chapter 3, far less attention has been paid to the structuring of student maintenance debt in Scotland, where non-repayable grants have largely been replaced by repayable loans. These decisions have had a particularly adverse impact on students from poorer backgrounds, who are least likely to go to university in the first place. An additional significant consequence of the emergence of the different fees regimes across the UK is the extent to which these arrangements tend to encourage or disincentivise cross-border student flows, arguably an important feature of a common UK higher education area. In some Scottish universities, for example St Andrews and Edinburgh, about a third of undergraduate students are incurring high levels of personal debt to cover tuition fees, whereas the fees of Scottish and EU students are being paid by the Scottish Government. The impact of such arrangements on students' perceptions of funding arrangements is discussed in Chapter 4, whilst Chapter 5 provides an analysis of patterns of cross-border flows over time.

HIGHER EDUCATION, WIDENING PARTICIPATION AND SOCIAL JUSTICE

Whilst the funding of undergraduate tuition can be seen as an area of marked policy divergence, widening access is characterised by much greater policy accord, at least at the rhetorical level. Since the Second World War in western democracies, there has been a strong belief that achieving equality of educational opportunity is essential to the maintenance of social and political cohesion (David, 2008; Trench, 2009). More recently, the Child Poverty and Social Mobility Commission (2014) has emphasised the role of universities in supporting social mobility, and the importance of such mobility to social and economic well-being. In the post-war years, a relatively low proportion of the age group (about 4 per cent) gained a university place. Fifty years after its publication, the Robbins Report (1963) is recognised as a groundbreaking document. The report reflected the belief that all who are qualified by ability and attainment should be entitled to a place in higher education, supported by a national system of grants. The recommendations for university expansion were accepted by the UK Government and a wave of new universities was established, leading to an increased participation rate of about 12 per cent by 1980. The next spike in university participation took place in the 1990s following the abolition of the binary divide between the universities and polytechnics/central institutions. By the mid-1990s, about 32 per cent of 17–30-year-olds across the UK had experienced some form of higher education. By 2005, 42 per cent of 17–30-year-olds were entering higher education (although not necessarily completing a degree).

Across the UK, there is a broad commitment to increasing the number of students participating in higher education, with England declaring its intention to lift the cap on student numbers by 2016, whilst in Scotland student numbers continue to be centrally controlled. There is also a desire to increase the proportion of students from poorer backgrounds, with the Office for Fair Access regulating activity in England and the Scottish Funding Council fulfilling a similar role in Scotland. In order to enforce widening access agreements, the techniques of new public management have been adopted in both jurisdictions, with institutions threatened with financial penalties for failing to meet their widening access targets.

Even before the cap on student numbers is lifted in England, Scotland appears to have lower rates of participation by 18-year-olds compared with other parts of the UK, with a reduction between 2010 and 2013 despite a higher proportion of students leaving school after S6 over this period (see Table 1.2). However, it is important to note that some students with appropriate Highers are able to progress to university at age 17 in Scotland. The shape of the higher education systems also differ between Scotland and England, with articulation between college and university a significant feature of the former. Figure 1.2 illustrates the relatively high proportion of higher education students on sub-degree programmes in Scotland compared with England, and also the fact that Scottish students are more likely to be older when they first enter higher education, compared with their English counterparts.

There is clearly a link between widening participation and improving access for students from socially disadvantaged backgrounds since, as argued by Iannelli (2011), those from poorer backgrounds are more likely to increase their rates of participation when the system is expanding, as is likely in England with the forthcoming lifting of the student numbers cap. As noted above, the absence of tuition fees in Scotland has contributed to a political discourse which assumes that access to higher education in Scotland is 'fair'. Throughout this book, we examine the evidence underpinning this assumption. Recently published data from the Scottish Funding Council, for example, show that in 2012–13, only 9.7 per cent of those from the most socially deprived backgrounds entered higher education compared to 32.5 per cent of the most advantaged. Over half of students from the most deprived backgrounds (51.1 per cent) undertook higher education

Table 1.2 Number of acceptances and entry rates of 18-year-olds to end of cycle, by country of domicile

	2010	2011	2012	2013	2013 v 2010
England					
Acceptances	359,005	367,150	342,755	367,900	2.48%
18-year-old entry rate	27.4%	29.4%	28.7%	30.3%	
Scotland					
Acceptances	32,250	30,800	30,900	31,495	−2.34%
18-year-old entry rate	24%	22.9%	23.8%	24.2%	
Wales					
Acceptances	18,670	18,325	19,305	19,665	5.33%
18-year-old entry rate	24.8%	24.9%	26.2%	26.6%	
Northern Ireland					
Acceptances	13,505	13,790	13,285	14,555	7.77%
18-year-old entry rate	33.7%	34.1%	33.7%	36.2%	

Source: Universities and Colleges Admissions Service, 2014

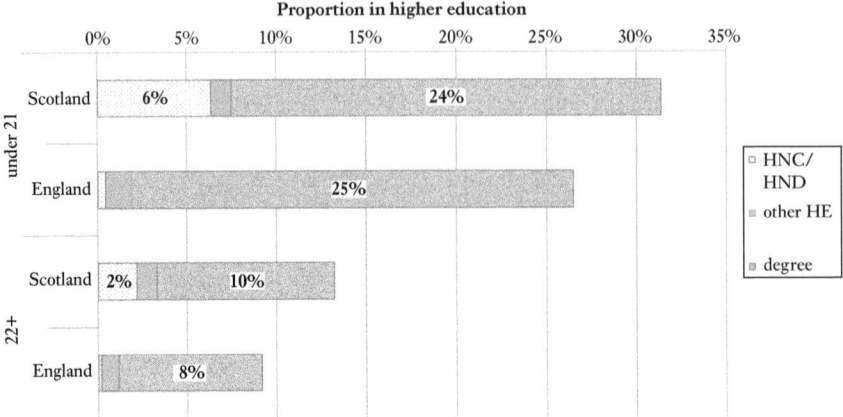

Figure 1.2   Higher education participation in England and Scotland, 2013

Source: Labour Force Survey 2011, quoted in Wyness, 2013

in college, and 8.2 per cent of students from the most deprived backgrounds studied in ancient universities, an increase of only 0.3 per cent since 2004–5 (see Table 1.3).

The relationship between student tuition fees, participation rates and widening access is explored more fully in Chapter 6.

INTERNATIONALISATION AND CONVERGENCE: RESEARCH AND INTERNATIONAL STUDENTS

We have so far referred to areas where there appears to be at least some degree of difference in approaches to higher education policy between Scotland and the rest of the UK. However, there are also areas where there appears to be strong similarity in approaches, specifically with regard to the recruitment of international students (Chapter 7) and research (Chapter 8). These are areas where the operation of some type of global higher education market, albeit not of a conventional variety, is most apparent (Marginson, 2008, 2013; Watson and Carasso, 2013). Interestingly, during the course of the referendum debate, the importance of retaining a common UK research area was agreed upon by all parties, although there was less agreement over the Scottish Government's tentative proposal for the establishment of a Scottish Research Council to run alongside the UK Research Councils. Issues surrounding the recruitment of international students were used in the referendum debate to illustrate the unwelcome constraints placed by UK immigration policy on Scottish institutions, although there is also tension in this area between English universities and the UK Government. A central theme explored in Chapters 7 and 8 is the nature of international competition in student recruitment and research, the way in which this is currently shaping the mission and culture of Scottish universities, and how this varies by type of institution.

Table 1.3 Scottish-domiciled entrants from deprived areas to higher education in the UK by institution type, 2004–5 to 2012–13

Type of institution	Percentage of higher education entrants from deprived areas								
	2004–5	2005–6	2006–7	2007–8	2008–9	2009–10	2010–11	2011–12	2012–13
Colleges	21.3%	21.7%	21.8%	21.8%	21.7%	22.6%	22.3%	22.4%	22.8%
Ancient Universities	7.9%	7.6%	7.7%	7.3%	7.8%	7.6%	7.9%	7.4%	8.2%
Newer Universities	11.6%	11.7%	11.7%	11.1%	11.0%	11.1%	11.2%	10.7%	11.1%
Post-92 higher education institutions	13.9%	14.4%	14.6%	14.8%	14.7%	14.6%	14.8%	13.9%	15.3%
Specialised higher education institutions	7.3%	7.7%	6.5%	7.5%	6.6%	7.9%	7.2%	8.6%	7.4%
Open University	13.7%	13.2%	13.7%	13.2%	14.0%	14.0%	14.7%	14.7%	15.4%
Universities outside Scotland	6.3%	6.8%	6.3%	6.9%	7.4%	7.0%	9.0%	7.5%	5.8%
All entrants from deprived areas	14.9%	15.0%	15.0%	14.8%	14.9%	15.1%	15.4%	15.1%	15.8%
% of Scottish population living in deprived areas	19.8%	19.7%	19.6%	19.3%	19.2%	19.1%	19.0%	19.0%	19.3%
% of Scottish working-age population living in deprived areas	19.5%	19.4%	19.4%	19.0%	19.0%	18.9%	18.8%	18.8%	19.3%
Under-representation of total population from deprived areas	−5.0%	−4.7%	−4.6%	−4.5%	−4.3%	−4.1%	−3.6%	−3.9%	−3.5%
Under-representation of working-age population from deprived areas	−4.6%	−4.4%	−4.4%	−4.2%	−4.1%	−3.8%	−3.4%	−3.7%	−3.5%

Sources: Higher Education Statistics Agency and Scottish Funding Council

The extent to which this is tending to promote a greater degree of homogenisation across universities in different UK jurisdictions is also discussed.

THE STRUCTURE OF THE BOOK

Having outlined the cross-cutting themes, in the following section we summarise each chapter in slightly more detail to provide the reader with a sense of the overall structure of the book. Chapter 2 considers changing forms of governance in Scottish universities. Devolution was expected to redistribute power within each 'home country' of the UK as well as between the country and the UK centre, heralding a more open, participatory and inclusive form of democracy. Universities in Scotland – if less evidently in Wales – appear to have taken advantage of this policy style. They have not only had the ear of government, but they have often played an active role in shaping policy for higher education, one that would have been inconceivable before devolution. This role has been facilitated on the one hand by the perception that Scottish higher education is an asset and a source of comparative advantage, and on the other hand by the capacity of Scottish universities to find common cause and to present a united front.

At the same time, devolution has also brought government closer to the universities, and it has increased expectations of what universities can and should do. It has led to the expectation that universities should be closely engaged with other stakeholders, and that they should contribute more actively to the economic, social and cultural development of their host societies. Universities are expected to see themselves as part of a lifelong learning system, developing more coherent links with other sectors of education and training and leading the drive to promote social equality. In pursuit of these aims, devolved governments have been tempted to tighten their controls over universities – in the eyes of some, threatening institutional autonomy.

Drawing on policy documents and key informant interviews, this chapter reviews these tensions as they have played out in the years since devolution, with a primary focus on Scotland. It argues that Scottish higher education has so far managed to strike a balance between institutional freedom and engagement with the host society, but that the future of this balance cannot be guaranteed.

Chapter 3 explores student funding in Scotland, looking not just at university tuition fees, but also at maintenance grants and loans. As noted above, the development of a more socially just approach to student funding is often claimed to be a distinctive achievement of devolution. This chapter examines the distinctive features of student support in Scotland with other parts of the UK. The chapter also examines how changes in England have affected the resources available to the devolved administrations through the Barnett formula and how that has constrained policy-making in Scotland, Wales and Northern Ireland. It is argued that the clearest beneficiaries of policy-making in Scotland in recent years have been students from better-off homes, who can now expect to leave university with the least debt of any group in the UK. As well as analysing the content of student funding, the chapter considers how the issue is commonly reported and discussed in Scotland, including in the White Paper on independence and the wider consti-tutional debate. It argues that it is Scotland's internal politics, rather than consti-tutional or financial considerations, which set the most severe constraint on the ability of any future Scottish government to move away from the current model of student support, with its clearly regressive effects.

In Chapter 4, the consequences of different funding regimes are further explored, based on an analysis of school pupils' attitudes towards higher education funding and debt in Scotland and England. Drawing on interviews with 16- to 19-year-olds in Scotland and the north of England, the chapter assesses how young people make decisions in relation to higher education, including choice of institution and whether to study at an institution close to home or one which involves living in a different location. Views of the merits and drawbacks of different funding regimes in England and Scotland are discussed, as well as attitudes towards debt.

Patterns of cross-border student flows and their significance is the focus of Chapter 5. Data from the Higher Education Statistics Agency (HESA) are used to describe the cross-border flows of students in relation to country of residence, institutional sector and subject, and the demographic, social and educational char-acteristics of movers and stayers. In particular, the chapter considers the extent to which cross-border movement is associated with inequalities in participation, and the implications for measures to widen participation. The impact of the rise in tuition fees in 2012 on the cross-border movement of students is considered, with a particular focus on the way in which it changed the relative costs of study in the rest of the UK compared with the home country. We conclude with a discussion of the value of leaving home to study, and the potential difficulties which arise if the movement of students is restricted by different fees regimes, with a focus on the particular implications for Scotland.

Social justice and widening participation is the topic addressed in Chapter 6. Widening access to higher education for under-represented groups has become increasingly important in higher education policy since the publication of the Dearing and Garrick Reports in 1997. These reports led to the development of a range of performance indicators to measure the nature and performance of the higher education sector in the UK. These were initially developed by the Higher Education Funding Council for England (HEFCE) but responsibility was later transferred to HESA. This chapter provides an overview of policy and initiatives in relation to widening participation for students from lower socioeco-nomic backgrounds in Scotland and the rest of the UK and questions whether different approaches have produced distinctive outcomes. Challenges in making cross-border comparisons and developing reliable performance indicators are considered.

Chapter 7 deals with the growing importance of the international higher edu-cation market and the extent to which UK immigration rules are perceived as a challenge to Scotland's ambitions in this area. Within the context of the knowledge economy, higher education is characterised as a major UK and Scottish export and is relatively more important to the Scottish economy than is the case in the rest of the UK. This chapter begins with an analysis of HESA data, exploring the expansion of the international student market and changing patterns of participation by students from different countries. A case study of Chinese students in a Scottish ancient university is used to explore the motivation and experience of this group of international students. Interviews were conducted during the pre-referendum period and the analysis highlights factors that attracted this group of international students to apply to a Scottish university. Their accounts draw attention to the importance of international league tables and of the UK, rather than specifically Scottish, brand. The chapter also highlights the extent to which the students would be attracted by the reinstatement of a post-study work visa.

Research policy, the subject of Chapter 8, is another area where the impact of a UK and international market is keenly felt. The chapter uses HESA data on research funding, policy documents and key informant interviews to explore the development and future of science and research policy in Scotland and the rest of the UK. This is an area where Scottish and UK policy has sometimes differed, with the Scottish Government traditionally seeking to distribute funding more evenly across different types of institutions, whereas the UK Government has emphasised research selectivity and different university missions. More recently, the Scottish Government also appeared to be concentrating resources on research-intensive universities, although funding decisions following REF2014 suggest that there is a swing back to the distribution of research funding across the sector. Given its importance to the Scottish economy as well as individual institutions, it is not surprising that the future of science and research was debated extensively during the course of the referendum campaign. Academics opposing independence suggested that a common research area would be impossible to sustain in an independent Scotland, whilst supporters of constitutional change suggested that Scottish research would flourish, attracting a higher proportion of EU and international funding. This chapter considers possible future directions of science and research policy in Scotland and the rest of the UK, and the overall implications for systemic convergence or divergence.

In the concluding chapter of the book, we return to the central themes identified above. We consider the extent to which Scottish higher education is diverging from systems in the other parts of the UK, and, if this is indeed the case, whether this signals the emergence of a new type of social policy underpinned by different core values. Within the UK context, we summarise the impact of different fees regimes in relation to levels of student debt, widening access and cross-border student flows. A key question is the extent to which, by avoiding upfront tuition fees, Scotland has indeed produced a 'fairer' higher education system. The influence of the international higher education market in areas such as international student recruitment and research is also considered. Before the referendum, Mooney and Scott (2012) argued that even though Scotland portrayed itself as a bastion of older egalitarian and collectivist culture, the campaign for independence tended to prioritise issues of territorial justice and neglected issues of social justice. In the wake of the referendum and the outcome of the Smith Commission, we consider the way in which debates on territorial and social justice are likely to play out within the Scottish higher education system of the future.

REFERENCES

Brown, R. and H. Carasso (2013), *Everything for Sale: The Marketisation of UK Higher Education*, London: Routledge.

Browne Review (2010), *Securing a Sustainable Future for Higher Education: An Independent Review of Higher Education Funding and Student Finance*, London: Her Majesty's Government.

David, M. (2008), *Widening Participation in Higher Education: A Commentary by the Teaching and Learning Research Programme*, London: Institute of Education.

Department for Business, Innovation and Skills (BIS) (2011), *Higher Education: Students at the Heart of the System*, London: BIS.

Eurostat (2014), http://epp.eurostat.ec.europa.eu/tgm/table.do?tab=table&init=1&language=en&pcode=t2020_41&plugin=1 (accessed 10 March 2015).

Greer, S. (2007), 'The fragile divergence machine: citizenship, policy divergence and intergovernmental relations', in A. Trench (ed.), *Devolution and Power in the United Kingdom*, Manchester: Manchester University Press, pp. 136–59.

Iannelli, C. (2011), 'Educational expansion and social mobility: the Scottish case', *Social Policy and Society*, 10: 2, 251–64.

Jeffery, C. (2007), 'The unfinished business of devolution: seven open questions', *Public Policy and Administration*, 22: 1, 92–108.

Marginson, S. (2008), 'National and global competition in higher education', in B. Lingard and J. Ozga (eds), *RoutledgeFalmer Reader in Education Policy and Politics*, London: RoutledgeFalmer, pp. 131–53.

Marginson, S. (2013), 'The impossibility of capitalist markets in higher education', *Journal of Education Policy*, 28: 3, 353–70.

Mooney, G. and G. Scott (2012), *Social Justice and Social Policy in Scotland*, Bristol: Policy Press.

Nicaise, I. (2010), 'A smart social inclusion policy for the EU: the role of education and training', paper presented at the Belgian Presidency Conference on Education and Social Inclusion, Ghent, 28–9 September 2010.

Organisation for Economic Co-operation and Development (OECD) (2008), *Growing Unequal? Income Distribution and Poverty in OECD Countries*, Paris: OECD.

Organisation for Economic Co-operation and Development (OECD) (2011), *Divided We Stand: Why Inequality Keeps Rising*, Paris: OECD.

Raffe, D. (2013), 'Was devolution the beginning of the end of the UK higher education system?', *Perspectives: Policy and Practice in Higher Education*, 17: 1, 11–16.

Riddell, S. and E. Weedon (2012), 'Lifelong learning and the wider European socioeconomic context', in S. Riddell, J. Markowitsch and E. Weedon (eds), *Lifelong Learning in Europe: Equity and Efficiency in the Balance*, Bristol: Policy Press, pp. 17–38.

Robbins Report (1963), *Higher Education: Report of the Committee Appointed by the Prime Minister under the Chairmanship of Lord Robbins 1961–3*, London: Her Majesty's Stationery Office.

Scottish Government (2011), *Building a Smarter Future: Towards a Sustainable Scottish Solution for the Future of Higher Education*, Edinburgh: Scottish Government.

Scottish Government (2013), *Scotland's Future: Your Guide to an Independent Scotland*, Edinburgh: Scottish Government.

Social Mobility and Child Poverty Commission (2014), *State of the Nation 2014: Social Mobility and Child Poverty in Great Britain* https://www.gov.uk/government/

uploads/system/uploads/attachment_data/file/367461/State_of_the_Nation_-_sum mary_document.pdf (accessed 11.03.15)

Trench, A. (2009), 'Un-joined-up government: intergovernmental relations and citizenship rights' in S. L. Greer (ed.), *Devolution and Social Citizenship in the UK*, Bristol: Policy Press, pp. 117–36.

Universities and Colleges Admissions Service (2014), *2013 Application Cycle: End of Cycle Report*, http://www.ucas.com/sites/default/files/ucas-2013-end-of-cycle-report.pdf (last accessed 10 March 2015).

Universities Scotland (2010), *Independent Budget Review: Submission from Universities Scotland*, Edinburgh: Universities Scotland.

Universities Scotland (2014), *Submission to Smith Commission*, Edinburgh: Universities Scotland. http://www.universities-scotland.ac.uk/uploads/Universities%20Scotland %2029%20Oct%2014%20-%20Smith%20Commission%20Submission.pdf (accessed 11 March 2015).

Wyness, G. (2013), 'Education in a devolved Scotland: a quantitative analysis of attainment and inequality', presentation at seminar on educational attainment and inequality in Scotland: How does Scotland compare with the rest of the UK? University of Edinburgh, 28 August 2013.

2

Higher Education Governance and Institutional Autonomy in the Post-devolution UK

David Raffe

INTRODUCTION

Devolution was expected to redistribute power within each 'home country' of the UK as well as between each country and the UK centre. It was to herald a more open, participatory and inclusive form of democracy. It would bring government closer to public institutions such as universities, and help these institutions to contribute to the economic, social and cultural development of their host societies.

Devolution thus presented both opportunities and threats for universities. It brought higher education closer to government, and closer to the centre of national life. It made higher education more visible as an area of public policy, and strengthened its claim on the public purse as a core institution and contributor to society. It gave universities more influence over policy debates, especially in a country such as Scotland where trust in professionals and providers of public services remained relatively high. It enabled the leaders of higher education – both institutional leaders and representatives of the sector as a whole – not only to have the ear of government but also to play a more active role in shaping policy than would have been conceivable beforehand. But devolution also presented threats. It brought higher education closer to government, but by the same token it brought government closer to higher education. It exposed universities to greater legislative and executive scrutiny than had been possible under the Westminster regime. It encouraged and enabled devolved governments to take a closer interest in the day-to-day activities of universities, in the interests both of democratic accountability and of maximising their economic, social and cultural contributions. And it tempted governments to tighten their controls over universities – in the eyes of some, threatening institutional autonomy.

In this chapter I review these tensions as they have played out in the years since devolution, with a primary focus on Scotland. The chapter starts with a narrative of the governance of Scottish higher education following administrative devolution in 1992 and especially parliamentary devolution in 1999. The narrative focuses on the relations between universities and government. The internal governance of institutions is of interest primarily as a test of this relationship: if the government takes an interest in how universities are run, is this a legitimate expression of its democratic mandate or an unwanted interference in the internal affairs of autonomous institutions (Murray et al., 2013)? The narrative covers the shifting balance between institutional autonomy and government control, and the development of what some have seen as a Faustian bargain between universities and a centralising Scottish Government. The chapter then adopts a more analytical perspective, and asks to what extent the trends described earlier can be attributed to devolution. It suggests three ways in which devolution has created additional threats to the institutional autonomy of universities, and three factors that have helped to minimise such threats. The analysis focuses on Scotland but the analytical framework can be applied to the devolved administrations in Wales and Northern Ireland and it explains some of the differences across the home nations. The chapter focuses on universities and other higher education institutions, although in Scotland a significant share of higher education is delivered in the college sector. I draw attention to the striking contrast between the relative success of Scottish universities in defending their shared sectoral interests and their institutional autonomy, and the Scottish colleges' less successful record: a contrast which our analytical framework helps to explain.

GOVERNMENT AND SCOTTISH HIGHER EDUCATION SINCE 1992

The Further and Higher Education (Scotland) Act of 1992 transferred the responsibility for funding Scottish universities from the UK-wide Universities Funding Council to a new Scottish Higher Education Funding Council (SHEFC), which in turn reported to the Scottish Office of the UK Government. The new Council's remit covered existing universities as well as the former central institutions – Scotland's closest equivalents of the English polytechnics – which were already under Scottish Office control. The Act introduced a significant measure of administrative devolution, but it was more a by-product of English policy than an expression of national self-determination. The decision had been taken to end the binary divide between universities and polytechnics, but it would have been politically unacceptable to transfer the central institutions from Scottish to British control so a separate Scottish body was created to oversee all Scottish higher education institutions. The new English, Welsh and Scottish Funding Councils were all 'arm's-length' bodies mediating between central government and higher education institutions; they applied somewhat different funding formulae, reflecting different priorities, but they embodied the same basic model of governance. However, the SHEFC helped to re-establish a Scottish frame of reference for higher education policy, which in previous decades had increasingly been subsumed within wider UK discourses. By 1996, when the Dearing Committee was appointed to review the purposes, shape, structure, size and funding of higher education in the UK, it was natural to appoint a separate sub-committee for Scotland, the Garrick Committee. The curricular and institutional factors which contributed to a distinct Scottish frame of reference included the role of the colleges, which accounted for a substantial fraction of higher education provision, much greater than in England or Wales. A Scottish Further Education Funding Council (SFEFC) was created at the same time as the SHEFC; the two councils had distinct memberships but shared an executive.

In 1999 a Scottish Executive, accountable to the new Scottish Parliament, inherited the main administrative responsibilities of the Scottish Office, including oversight of the SHEFC. The role of the SHEFC as an arm's-length body mediating between government and institutions continued much as before. There was similar continuity in the SHEFC's engagement with several UK-wide arrangements for accountability or support for universities, such as the Quality Assurance Agency and the Research Assessment Exercise. However, one exception to 'business as usual' following parliamentary devolution was the decision to place universities and colleges in a new lifelong learning department of the Scottish Executive, along with enterprise (and later transport), separate from school education.

Elections to the Scottish Parliament were based on proportional representation and no party gained an overall majority in the first elections in 1999. The Liberal Democrats agreed to enter a coalition with Labour, one of the conditions for which was the early appointment of an independent committee to review the future of tuition fees. This committee, chaired by Andrew Cubie (now Sir Andrew Cubie), recommended the replacement of upfront fees by a means-tested graduate endowment to which graduates would contribute once their earnings reached a certain threshold. A modified version of this recommendation was swiftly implemented.

Devolution was an occasion for national stocktaking, and in 2001 both the Executive and the Parliament initiated strategic reviews. The Scottish Executive's multi-stage review of higher education generated a series of reports between 2002 and 2004 (for example, Scottish Executive, 2003). These reports asserted the importance of higher education's economic and social contributions, appraised funding options, rejected a further large increase in participation and reviewed a number of issues of governance. They called for a new relationship between the higher education institutions, the Executive and the Funding Council which was expected to develop a strategic and coordinating role. The Parliament's review, conducted by the Enterprise and Lifelong Learning Committee, was more wide-ranging and covered all post-school learning (Scottish Parliament, 2002). It stressed the importance of the social, cultural and individual development aims of higher education alongside its economic functions. A theme of both reviews was the need for a lifelong learning perspective. Among other things this meant that higher education institutions had to work more closely with colleges and schools to ensure a coherent set of opportunities with progression between them. This perspective led, in 2005, to the merger of the SHEFC and the SFEFC to form a single Scottish Funding Council (SFC). This merger extended the logic of the previous arrangement, under which the two Councils had been served by a single executive, and its immediate implications were relatively modest. Universities were concerned that future Councils might be tempted to equalise the levels of funding for the two sectors, although these concerns were not substantiated.

In an article written in 2007, published the following year, David Caldwell, director of Universities Scotland, wrote:

> The increase in attention and scrutiny from both government and parliament can be perceived as presenting a threat of excessive political interference which might undermine the autonomy of higher education institutions. It would be reckless to say that this could not happen; but to date it has not. Ministers have concentrated on broad strategic direction, resisting the temptation to become involved in the detailed management of the sector. The outcome has been positive: we have parliamentarians, ministers and senior officials who are better informed about higher education than their predecessors, and whose improved understanding of its potential has benefited the sector. (Caldwell, 2008: 65)

In the 2007 election to the Scottish Parliament the Scottish National Party (SNP) won the greatest number of seats and formed a minority administration. It restructured the Scottish Executive – renamed the Scottish Government – on the basis of directorates and directorates-general. These were intended to encourage 'joined-up' decision-making across policy areas. The different sectors of education were reunited within the same branch of government.

Top-up fees had been introduced in the rest of the UK in 2006 (2007 in Wales) and student funding, once again, was an issue in the 2007 Scottish election. The SNP campaigned on a promise to abolish all student debt. Although this promise was never fulfilled, soon after the election the new government announced the abolition of the graduate endowment with effect for graduates in 2007. It promised to make up any funding gaps from its central budget. This commitment was soon tested in 2007 when lower than expected budget allocations were perceived to threaten the viability of Scottish universities. Anxious lobbying by the Scottish universities persuaded the Scottish Government to set up a Joint Future Thinking Task Force on Universities, with a remit to consider how to optimise the universities' contributions to the Scottish economy, culture and society and the political priorities of the Scottish Government, and to identify the resources needed to achieve this and how to provide them. Its report, *New Horizons*, called for a new relationship between the Scottish Government, SFC and the university sector, and established a Tripartite Advisory Group to promote this (Scottish Government, 2008). Regulation by the SFC would adopt a lighter touch, with an increased focus on the outcomes of higher education. *New Horizons* committed the Scottish Government to maintain funding parity with England, in return for the universities' acceptance of a closer alignment with the government's national purpose and strategic objectives. The universities thus not only secured a significant increase in funding; they also cemented their role as partners in the development of national higher education policy.

Concerns over funding were as much to do with relative as with absolute levels of funding. UK-wide competition for staff, students and resources meant that the viability of any financial settlement depended on the resulting 'funding gap' with higher education in the rest of the UK, and especially England. In contrast to Wales and Northern Ireland, Scotland had maintained relatively favourable levels of funding (Trench, 2008). However the introduction and increase in fees in England put this at risk. A study by the Institute for Fiscal Studies concluded that funding levels for 2007–8 undergraduates were about the same in Scotland and England, allowing for compositional differences, but that England pulled ahead in subsequent years (Dearden et al., 2012). The gap threatened to widen further following the Browne Review of fees in England and the subsequent decision by the UK Government to raise the cap on top-up fees to a maximum of £9,000 p.a. This could make it difficult for Scottish higher education institutions to maintain their competitive position if they continued to be supported by central funding alone. Partly as a result, there was a growing acceptance among Scottish universities and many stakeholders of the principle of a graduate contribution to the cost of higher education, if not at the level proposed by Browne. However, an accident of timing – the forthcoming Scottish election in May 2011 – kept the reintroduction of tuition fees off the policy agenda for the time being. The SNP government promised to maintain free tuition if re-elected, a promise then repeated by the two largest opposition parties (Labour and Liberal Democrats). Once again universities' anxieties were stilled by incorporating them into the policy process. A technical working group drawn from the government, universities and the SFC was set up to review the funding options; its report, published early in 2011, estimated the additional central funding that would be required to close the funding gap under certain scenarios, which included charging high fees for students from the rest of the UK (Scottish Government, 2011). The government committed itself to provide the additional funding, a commitment it was to honour over the following year but at the expense of the colleges whose budgets suffered severe cuts.

The SNP continued in power after the 2011 election, this time with a one-seat majority. This did not lead to any major change in policy, but the shift from minority to majority government coincided with a change in policy style. A large number of key informants interviewed for the ESRC project entitled *Higher Education in Scotland, the Devolution Settlement and the Referendum on Independence* perceived an increasingly 'centralising' role of the Scottish Government (Riddell, 2014). Many informants also associated this with a relative decline in the status and role of the SFC. As the government's own expectations for higher education institutions became more urgent and more precise, there was less scope for an intermediary body to interpret and mediate its demands.

In 2011 the Scottish Government established a Review of Higher Education Governance under Professor von Prondzynski to consider whether current arrangements delivered 'an appropriate level of democratic accountability given the level of public funding institutions receive'. The Review's recommendations (Scottish Government, 2012) included a Code of Good Governance for higher education institutions, subsequently developed on a voluntary basis, and an improved gender balance on university courts, which was pursued through SFC guidance rather than legislation, as equality legislation was reserved to the UK Parliament. In November 2014 the Scottish Government (2014) consulted over proposed legislation to implement further recommendations of the Review, including the transfer of responsibilities from the UK Privy Council to a Scottish Committee, the election of chairs of governing bodies and arrangements for making these bodies more representative. It also proposed to establish a new and more precise definition of academic freedom. The consultation paper stressed that the aim of the changes was 'not to increase Ministerial control over our institutions, but to support them to develop and refine their own governance systems' (p. 3). However, the boundary between interference and support remains a sensitive issue. Shortly after the von Prondzynski Review was published, a British Council study found that senior staff and stakeholders in Scottish universities 'clearly considered that the Scottish government [was] seeking to involve itself too directly in how universities are run, and that the prescriptions of the governance review [were] inconsistent with university autonomy' (Kemp and Lawton, 2013: 6). This view was not shared by the staff and student representatives interviewed for the study, who supported the proposed changes.

However, the more significant changes affecting relationships between universities and government were the outcome agreements, which had been introduced in 2012 and were placed on a statutory basis, along with wider access outcome agreements, by the Post-16 Education (Scotland) Act of 2013. Each year the SFC agrees a set of outcomes with each institution. The outcomes express the broad goals which the higher education institution expects to achieve over the following years in such areas as access, innovation, research and graduate employability. They are supported by measures of performance at national and institutional levels. The outcomes are linked to funding; in principle a failure to achieve them could result in a reduction of funding.

Among the key informants interviewed for the ESRC project, '[t]he majority of senior managers [in higher education institutions] believed that the Scottish Government had centralising tendencies, and saw outcome agreements as a new form of governance which was likely to impinge on their autonomy' (Riddell, 2014). However, in practice the concerns have been relatively muted, partly because of the flexible way in which outcome agreements have been implemented by the SFC. The negotiations over outcome agreements have enabled each institution to shape its own agenda and, up to a point, the means by which its performance is judged. Rather more heat has been generated over the choice of indicators – especially the Scottish Index of Multiple Deprivation (SIMD) – than over the principle of accountability which the indicators are used to support. Outcome agreements might be used less flexibly in future, and they could come to represent a more substantial threat to institutional autonomy. But in 2014 the general feeling was that this had not happened and it did not threaten to happen in the near future. One key informant was critical of the Scottish Government's approach but accepted that 'compared to other European models we have good autonomy in Scotland. So I think in fact it's a small relative decline in autonomy.' (Riddell, 2014: 15). Another felt, of the Post-16 Act, 'I'm not sure it's going to make a huge difference.'

This contrasts with more drastic changes to the governance of colleges, which were required to merge on the basis of thirteen regions, each of which was to be served by a single college or, in a few cases, a consortium of colleges. Compared to the universities, the colleges experienced the 'double whammy' of severely reduced funding and a major programme of restructuring imposed from above.

The British Council study cited above found that

> a (surprisingly) relaxed view prevailed [among senior higher education staff and stakeholders] over the 'outcome agreements' . . . With a few exceptions, they are seen as an acceptable *quid pro quo* for the government which maintained public funding for higher education in Scotland when it was cut in other jurisdictions. (Kemp and Lawton 2013: 6).

Interviewed for the ESRC study, a Universities Scotland spokesman pointed out: 'So to be in a situation where in the worst financial crisis in living memory we achieved a 15 per cent uplift of university funding I would say is the best you could expect' (p. 16). At least in the short term, the Scottish universities traded a relatively minor loss of autonomy for a huge benefit in terms of funding. It remains to be seen whether this verdict will hold for the longer term, or whether Scottish universities have contracted what proves to be a Faustian bargain with the Scottish Government.

HOW HAS DEVOLUTION MADE A DIFFERENCE?

So far I have shown how devolution, by bringing Scottish universities closer to government, has both increased the political influence of higher education institutions, individually and collectively, and increased the perceived threats to institutional autonomy. However, similar tensions may be observed in other countries, not only those affected by devolution. To what extent can the trends described above be attributed to devolution? Below I suggest three ways in which devolution has helped to increase the threats to the institutional autonomy of universities. I then suggest three ways in which such threats have been minimised. These two sets of factors are connected; to some extent they can be seen as two sides of the same coin, a reflection of the ambiguities inherent in the new political relationship. The discussion focuses on Scotland but the analytical framework could be applied to all three devolved countries in the UK.

DEVOLUTION AND THE THREAT TO INSTITUTIONAL AUTONOMY

First, devolution has increased the threat to institutional autonomy by bringing universities more closely within reach of government. It has made the missions, achievements and failings of individual higher education institutions much more visible to government, and consequently more likely to be the subject of government intervention. In contrast to England, the minister in one of the devolved governments is likely to know, and meet on a regular basis, with most if not all university and college principals. While this proximity may be a source of opportunity and strength (Hodgson et al., 2011), it can also be a source of threat.

A friendly interest on the part of the minister may soon turn into unwanted interference.

The proximity of government and higher education institutions is partly a matter of simple arithmetic: fewer institutions means greater proximity. The dynamics of governance are inevitably different in a polity with only nineteen higher education institutions – or fewer, in Wales and Northern Ireland – than in one with well over a hundred. The role of a funding council as a buffer between government and institutions becomes harder to sustain; instead of a clear separation of government, Funding Council and higher education institutions there are pressures to develop a tripartite relationship in which all participate simultaneously. It is similarly harder to maintain the anonymity of formula-based funding or of policy priorities expressed in general terms. In a system with very few institutions a policy which prioritises certain subject areas, steers research activity or promotes institutional restructuring cannot help but visibly favour particular institutions at the expense of others.

The second way in which devolution increases the threat to institutional autonomy relates to a more qualitative aspect of the relationship between government and higher education institutions. One of the expected benefits of devolution was to enable the devolved administrations to tailor policies that would better address the distinctive needs of each territory. Higher education was and is a natural focus for this aspiration. An early assessment of the impact of devolution on higher education perceived 'a strong sense that the devolved administrations want and expect more from "their" higher education institutions' (Court, 2004: 151). A few years later Tapper (2007: 83) noted that higher education institutions in England 'are not perceived as quite so integral to the nation's future welfare as they are in Scotland and Wales and thus face somewhat less pressure to deliver tightly prescribed policy goals'. A more recent review of policy divergence following devolution concluded:

> To the extent that policies have diverged, the main contrast is between England on the one hand and the three devolved governments on the other . . . [T]here are distinctive emphases in the policy rhetoric, and to some extent the actions, of the devolved governments. These include an emphasis on the economic development role of higher education, on lifelong learning and the development of more coherent education systems, on the social and cultural functions of higher education and on coordination at a regional level. Higher education in the devolved nations is expected to be more active in engaging with, and supporting, the social, cultural and economic needs of its host society, and to be more closely integrated with the education system and the other institutions which perform complementary roles within that society. (Raffe, 2013: 5–6)

If the devolved administrations want and expect more from 'their' higher education institutions, higher education is higher on their policy agendas and they face a stronger temptation to intervene in order to ensure that these higher expectations are fulfilled. As Tapper (2007: 87–8) notes, a more inclusive policy process could either create a consensus on the basis of equally respected inputs, or merely legitimate the policy goals of the state and the values that underlie them. A more recent analysis perceived a move towards 'a more traditional European model' of higher education governance within the three devolved territories of the UK, characterised by government intervention to ensure that higher education serves a wider set of economic and social objectives (Bruce, 2012: 99). Paradoxically, as key informants to the ERSC study pointed out, the Scottish Government's willingness to maintain the funding for higher education has increased its consequent power. Conversely, the higher education institutions which perceive least threat to their autonomy tend to be those who receive the greatest share of funding from non-government sources.

The third way in which devolution has increased the threat to institutional autonomy relates to the politics of devolution. In all three devolved administrations, education is one of the most important policy areas to have been devolved. Wales provides the exception that proves the rule: although the powers that were initially devolved (notably over tuition fees) were found to be inadequate, they were very quickly expanded. Education, and especially higher education, tends to be highly valued in the devolved territories, where it is associated with national identity as well as with opportunities for social ascent (albeit often linked to emigration). It is politically visible and an area where devolved governments can make their mark: tuition fees and student support have been prominent issues in every Scottish election since 1999. Free tuition is the Scottish policy of which the former First Minister Alex Salmond claimed to feel most proud. Analysts of globalisation argue that education – in contrast, say, to economic policy areas more directly affected by global interdependencies – is one of the areas of public policy where national sovereignty has been least eroded. A very similar argument can be made with respect to devolution: that education has been a policy area where the freedom of manoeuvre of the devolved governments has been least constrained by reserved powers, and where there is scope for distinctive policies even without significant economic powers and with relatively fixed budgets. However, in practice there are significant interdependencies between the higher education policies of the home countries, particularly with respect to fees, which have limited policy divergence (Gallacher and Raffe, 2012) and had implications for institutional autonomy which I discuss in the next section.

Devolved governments are consequently more likely to be active in policy-making in education than in many other policy areas. Whether this poses a threat to universities depends on the extent to which governments recognise the principle, and the value, of institutional autonomy. What it does mean, however, is that autonomy will not be maintained by default, as a result of the indifference or inactivity of governments.

DEVOLUTION AND THE DEFENCE OF INSTITUTIONAL AUTONOMY

I now suggest three reasons why Scottish higher education institutions have been able to preserve a large measure of institutional autonomy.

The first reason is the perception, widely shared among policy-makers and opinion-formers, that Scotland's higher education system is a global success story and a national asset. In 2006–7 the Labour–Liberal Democrat coalition conducted a wide-ranging stocktake to assess the country's strengths and weaknesses and the potential for future development. This identified higher education as one of the country's principal assets and as a source of national comparative advantage. A similar perception informed the SNP administrations after 2007. The Cabinet Secretary, interviewed in 2014, said: 'We believe that it's a societal good and the sector produces enormous profits and benefits – it's the third largest sector in our economy, the multiplier is pretty good for us' (Riddell, 2014: 17). *Scotland's Future*, the Scottish Government's White Paper on independence, introduced the section on higher and further education with the claim that 'Higher Education is one of Scotland's major strengths with more universities in the *Times Top 200 World Universities* per head of population than any other nation' (Scottish Government, 2013: 188). Later on the same page the document referred to another commonly cited international comparison: 'Scotland ranks third in the world (after Switzerland and the Netherlands) and ahead of all the G8 countries in terms of citations per researcher'.

No devolved government would want to earn a reputation for having put this valuable national asset, with its enormous potential contribution to the country's economic, social and cultural development, at risk. It is hardly surprising that successive governments have been responsive to warnings from the sector that budget cuts may harm its international competitiveness. And the contrast with colleges, whose budgets faced severe cuts notwithstanding warnings from the sector, is instructive. Although the colleges' role in promoting access and social inclusion is widely recognised, they have had a harder task in arguing that their contribution to economic growth and development is critical. In 2009 Universities Scotland published a report by a team of economists which argued that the Scottish economy needed to move up the value chain in order to develop new areas of competitive advantage. This meant focusing on high-level skills and innovation supported by higher education, not the intermediate-level vocational skills delivered by the colleges. 'The current debate on the need for more "vocational" education is not based on economic evidence and has the potential to become the biggest inhibiting factor on economic growth in Scotland' (Universities Scotland, 2009: 33). Moreover, the colleges do not have access to the same types of global comparisons which have so helped the case of the universities. It is much harder for colleges to use comparative data either to assert their global excellence or to argue that their competitiveness is threatened by inadequate budgets.

This leads to the second reason why it has been relatively easy for universities to protect their institutional autonomy: the internationalisation of higher education. I use this term somewhat loosely to refer to the range of factors which contribute to the interdependence of universities across the globe and/or to their shared dependence on similar pressures or policy 'drivers'. It includes interdependences and commonalities within the UK as well as globally: the position of Scottish universities within UK higher education raises similar issues to those raised by the position of UK (including Scottish) universities in relation to higher education across the globe (Gallacher and Raffe, 2012).

Internationalisation, thus defined, restricts the power of the Scottish Government in four respects. First, higher education's values, priorities and criteria of quality are increasingly determined internationally. They are implicit in the indicators which underpin international comparisons and league tables such as the *Times Top 200 World Universities* so proudly cited by the Scottish Government. Within the UK, these values are implicit in the criteria for competitive funding and in assessments of research quality as well as in UK-wide university rankings. Scottish universities therefore need to play by 'rules of the game' that are determined internationally, or at least at a UK-wide level, in order to maintain their successful position. The corollary is that the Scottish Government has limited power to change these 'rules of the game', and if it tries to direct the behaviours of Scottish universities too closely it risks either infringing these rules or, at least, undermining the competence of institutions which have proved themselves to be adept at playing by them. Second, competitive pressures encourage national higher education systems to combine within 'higher education areas' which provide critical mass, favourable conditions for collaboration, a more level playing field for institutional competition, the exchange of students and staff, the joint provision of infrastructure, enhanced quality assurance, and so on. Europe has sought to emulate the critical mass of US higher education by creating a European Higher Education Area (EHEA). The UK, with its wide range of organisations to support such functions as research funding, quality assurance, infrastructure and student admissions, and its common tax and legal environment, is a more complete albeit smaller example of a common higher education area. All sides in the debates leading up to the referendum on Scottish independence agreed on the value of this 'eco-system' of UK higher education, even if they disagreed on how easily it could be maintained if Scotland became independent. But whether independent or not, a Scottish Government needs to surrender or pool sovereignty in order to participate in a wider UK area, and Scottish institutions would need to participate on terms that may not wholly reflect the Scottish Government's own priorities. Third, as institutions in different countries compete more closely, parity of funding becomes more critical. The international comparisons of higher education funding conducted by organisations such as the OECD have been influential. The pressure for funding parity does not, of course, make it impossible for national governments to cut university budgets, but it increases the political cost of doing so. This has been particularly true within the UK, whose more developed higher education area makes institutions much more vulnerable to differences in resources compared with their competitors. The funding gap with England has long dominated the policy agendas in Wales and Northern Ireland (Trench, 2008). For many years Scottish universities enjoyed a relatively favourable level of funding, but successive fee increases in England, contrasted with the commitment to free tuition, put this at risk. The fear of a funding gap precipitated the appointment of both the Joint Future Thinking Task Force in 2007 and the Joint Technical Group in 2010; both resulted in a much more favourable financial settlement for the universities and a significant input by universities to strategic policy-making for higher education. Once again the comparison with colleges is instructive: although it is easier to compare levels of college funding across the UK than internationally, there is less direct competition between institutions in different parts of the UK, so the concept of a funding gap is less likely to arise. Fourth and finally, the value of institutional autonomy is itself one of the 'rules of the game'. In debates over the Post-16 Bill the Scottish universities were quick to point out that the most successful higher education systems, including the US and the UK, were characterised by higher levels of 'responsible autonomy', and that other OECD countries were seeking to emulate their example.

These implications of internationalisation have been recognised by the SNP government, and help to explain why it has been restrained in its challenges to institutional autonomy. As we have seen, it has accepted the legitimacy of global university rankings and, by implication, of the values and priorities that underpin them. It has recognised the value of international collaboration, and in *Scotland's Future* it placed considerable emphasis on the need to maintain the UK's higher education area with its eco-system supporting research and teaching. The debate that followed was solely about the political and financial feasibility of Scotland's continued participation in a UK research area, never about its desirability. Successive governments have recognised that a viable higher education system must not incur a funding gap vis-à-vis the rest of the UK. And the government has repeatedly affirmed its belief in the benefits of responsible autonomy.

So far in this section I have suggested that the institutional autonomy of Scottish universities has been protected both by the perceived success of Scottish higher education and by the implications of internationalisation, which requires national authorities to surrender some of their autonomy and to allow universities freedom to compete within a wider area. In both cases I have assumed a degree of rational policy-making on the part of government: that a Scottish government would not jeopardise the performance of a successful higher education system and that it recognises the implications of internationalisation for institutional autonomy. But governments do not always act rationally. The third reason why Scottish universities have managed to protect their institutional autonomy is that they have been effective as a political force. Key informants in the ESRC study agreed that Universities Scotland, together with the National Union of Students, had exerted a powerful influence on Scottish policy. The colleges, by contrast, were perceived by many key informants to have lost influence.

How have universities maintained their political strength? University leaders have recognised that their influence is much greater when they speak with a common voice, and the relatively small scale of the Scottish sector, with just nineteen higher education institutions, has enabled them to do so.

Mission groups, a focus for intra-sectoral division in England, play a negligible role within Scotland. However, similar conditions applied in Wales where, at least in the early years of devolution, higher education institutions were less united. Two further considerations are cultural and policy-related. Working in partnership is claimed to be 'part of the DNA of the Scottish sector' (Kemp and Lawton, 2013: 38), and the willingness to reach agreement is rewarded in a policy culture which values consensus, or at least the appearance of consensus. And in contrast to Wales, Scottish governments have (mostly) avoided the divisive issue of institutional reconfiguration.

CONCLUSION

The relationship between universities and the devolved governments is still evolving. Some institutions may continue to feel threatened by these governments' rising aspirations, especially perhaps smaller and more vulnerable institutions and those in Wales. And they may feel further threatened when high aspirations are counterbalanced by drastic cuts in government budgets, potentially leading to the tight day-to-day control of university spending recently seen in the Republic of Ireland. But where universities can show that they already contribute to the economic, social and cultural well-being of their home country, and especially in the context of the internationalisation of higher education, they have a strong bargaining position in their relations with the devolved governments, if they also have the political skill to use it.

REFERENCES

Bruce, T. (2012), *Universities and Constitutional Change in the UK: the Impact of Devolution on Higher Education*, Oxford: Higher Education Policy Institute.

Caldwell, D. (2008), 'Scottish higher education: character and provision', in T. Bryce and W. Humes (eds), *Scottish Education, Third Edition: Beyond Devolution*, Edinburgh: Edinburgh University Press, pp. 59–68.

Court, S. (2004), 'Government getting closer: higher education and devolution in the UK', *Higher Education Quarterly*, 58: 2/3, 151–75.

Dearden, L., A. Goodman and G. Wyness (2012), 'Higher education finance in the UK', *Fiscal Studies*, 33: 1, 73–105.

Gallacher, J. and D. Raffe (2012), 'Higher education policy in post-devolution UK: more convergence than divergence?', *Journal of Education Policy*, 27: 4, 467–90.

Hodgson, A., K. Spours and M. Waring (eds) (2011), *Post-Compulsory Education and Lifelong Learning Across the United Kingdom: Policy, Organisation and Governance, Bedford Way Papers*, London: Institute of Education Publications.

Kemp, N. and W. Lawton (2013), *A Strategic Analysis of the Scottish Higher Education Sector's Distinctive Assets*, Edinburgh: British Council.

Murray, C., R. McAlpine, A. Pollock and A. Ramsay (2013), *The Democratic University: a Proposal for University Governance for the Common Weal*, Jimmy Reid Foundation, http://reidfoundation.org/wp-content/uploads/2013/11/Democratic-Universities.pdf (accessed 20 April 2015).

Raffe, D. (2013), *Devolution and Higher Education: What Next? Stimulus Paper*, London: Leadership Foundation for Higher Education.

Riddell, S. (2014), *Working Paper 5 – Key Informants' Views of Higher Education in Scotland*, Edinburgh: University of Edinburgh, Centre for Research in Education Inclusion and Diversity (CREID).

Riddoch, L. (2014), *Blossom: What Scotland Needs to Flourish*, Edinburgh: Luath Press.

Scottish Executive (2003), *A Framework for Higher Education in Scotland: Higher Education Review Phase 2*, Edinburgh: Scottish Executive.

Scottish Government (2008), *New Horizons: Responding to the Challenges of the 21st Century. Report of the Joint Future Thinking Taskforce on Universities*, Edinburgh: Scottish Government.

Scottish Government (2011), *Report of the Scottish Government – Universities Scotland Technical Group on Higher Education*, Edinburgh: Scottish Government.

Scottish Government (2012), *Report of the Review of Higher Education Governance*, Edinburgh: Scottish Government.

Scottish Government (2013), *Scotland's Future: Your Guide to an Independent Scotland*, Edinburgh: Scottish Government.

Scottish Government (2014), *Consultation Paper on a Higher Education Governance Bill*, Edinburgh: Scottish Government.

Scottish Parliament, Enterprise and Lifelong Learning Committee (2002), *Report on Lifelong Learning*, Norwich: The Stationery Office.

Tapper, T. (2007), *The Governance of British Higher Education: The Struggle for Policy Control*, Dordrecht: Springer.

Trench, A. (2008), *Higher Education and Devolution: Impact and Future Trends*, London: Universities UK.

Universities Scotland (2009), *What Was/What Next? What the Evidence Tells Us About the Next Steps for Scotland's Economic Strategy*, Edinburgh: Universities Scotland.

3

Student Funding in the UK: Post-Devolution Scotland in a UK Context

Lucy Hunter Blackburn

INTRODUCTION

This chapter examines the common claim that the development of a more socially just approach to student funding is a distinctive achievement of devolution in Scotland. It compares how the funding for students in full-time undergraduate higher education has developed in Scotland and the other devolved administrations since 1999 and what now distinguishes the arrangements for such students in Scotland from those in other parts of the UK. It shows that when systems are compared in terms of their distributional effects between students within each jurisdiction, it is the Scottish system alone which demonstrates a clearly regressive pattern, calling into question widely held beliefs about which students have benefited most from Scottish policy-making in this area since 1999.

THE CLAIM MADE FOR SCOTLAND

In August 2014 Michael Russell, then Cabinet Secretary for Education, said, 'Scotland is the only country in the UK to ensure young people, our workforce of the future, can go to university based on ability, not the ability to pay' (Russell, 2014). Over recent years, this has become the central claim distinguishing the Scottish approach to student support from that elsewhere in the UK. It draws on a belief often found in wider Scottish debate that Scotland is more egalitarian in its approach to higher education than England, in particular. Thus one commentator, a newspaper columnist who is a high-profile supporter of free tuition and a former Rector of Edinburgh University, stated that there is:

> a feeling among MSPs that Scottish university principals are out of sympathy with the educational traditions of Scotland, summed up by the phrase the 'democratic intellect' . . . The choice is between an essentially privatised system of higher education, which is the English model, and the Scottish tradition of open access. (MacWhirter, 2011)

Behind such statements there lies a strong implication that the model of student funding adopted in Scotland is more socially just than those now found elsewhere in the UK.

FREE TUITION: A SCOTTISH TRADITION?

The assertion that university tuition fees are inherently at odds with a specifically Scottish tradition has been a prominent feature of political debate over nearly two decades, with fee charging presented as alien to the history of the Scottish education system, including, importantly, its higher education system.

Scottish universities have, however, traditionally charged their students fees. The privately endowed Carnegie Trust for Universities in Scotland was established in 1901 'to render attendance at the Universities of Scotland and the enjoyment of their advantages more available to the deserving and qualified youth of Scotland to whom the payment of fees might act as a barrier'. The Trust played an important role in facilitating access to university in Scotland in the first half of the twentieth century. However, as already seen in Chapter 1, in the years prior to 1962, Scots had no more entitlement to publicly funded tuition on the award of a university place than students elsewhere in the UK. Indeed, the characterisation of the Scottish higher education system of the nineteenth and much of the twentieth century as essentially open and egalitarian has been more generally challenged by T.C. Smout (1986) and others. The discretionary post-war arrangements for student funding preceding the changes introduced in 1962 appear to have been more uniformly applied in Scotland than elsewhere. However, the entitlement to a free university place so often cited as specifically traditional to Scotland was a product not of the country's distinctive system of higher education, but of the post-war UK welfare state.

Turning to more recent history, it can be argued that in 1999 a particular combination of the timing of the initial elections to the devolved legislatures, more powers than were initially granted to Wales and fewer distractions than in Northern Ireland, led to Scotland alone reversing a tuition fees policy which was controversial across the UK. Moreover, while there may be room to disagree about how far policy divergence since 1999 has resulted from differing values rather than local political dynamics, recent differences are by definition not evidence of a tradition.

Indeed, the focus on locally domiciled full-time, first-time undergraduate students often obscures the continuing significance of fee income to Scottish universities. Over half the students in Scottish universities are not covered by the policy of free tuition, a group comprising overseas students, those from other parts of the UK, part-time students above a particular income, those caught by 'previous study' rules and most postgraduates. Overseas and rest-of-UK students have provided a growing amount of income to universities in recent years, a process encouraged by the Scottish Government.

DEVOLUTION AND THE INITIAL DEBATE OF STUDENT SUPPORT IN SCOTLAND

Scottish higher education does have a distinctive history unrelated to fee policy, visible in such differences as the four-year degree. This was acknowledged in the initial, pre-devolution debate about university funding. The Dearing Committee set up a Scottish Standing Committee ('the Garrick Committee'). This, like the main committee, recognised the case for the introduction of a graduate contribution, albeit in more cautious terms: while Dearing recommended this 'on a balance of considerations', Garrick 'recognised [it] with reluctance'. The government responded to the Dearing Committee's recommendations by introducing a UK-wide means-tested fee of £1,000 a year. At the same time, it increased living cost support by raising loan entitlements and abolishing grants.

It was in this period that the Scottish National Party (SNP) began to lay down the rhetoric which still dominates in Scotland, linking its opposition to the introduction of tuition fees and the abolition of grants to a narrative of Scottish distinctiveness. Speaking in Parliament in 1998, Andrew Welsh MSP, the SNP's education spokesman, said:

> I hope that hon. Members will understand that there is a distinct and different Scottish education system which should be dealt with in a distinct and different way . . . I stand by the traditional Scottish view of access to education available for all, irrespective of wealth, to allow each person to develop to the fullest of their abilities for the benefit of all in society. (Hansard, 1998)

These arguments were built on during the 1999 Scottish elections, although the argument about fees tended to be pursued with more rhetorical power and financial commitment than that about grants. The 1999 SNP manifesto stated that:

> one of the first shameful acts of New Labour was to end the right to free education by imposing tuition fees. We will restore the principle of free education in Scotland . . . In a move which hit poorest students hardest, New Labour are also abolishing student maintenance grants . . . We propose to re-introduce a maintenance grant of £500 per annum for the poorest 20,000 Scottish students.

While free tuition was to be wholly reinstated, the commitment on grant fell far short of restoring it to pre-1998 levels. In 1997–8, almost 80,000 students in Scotland had received the Standard Maintenance Allowance, the maximum value of which had been £1,685.

Commitments to abolish fees were also included in the manifestos of the Liberal Democrats and the Conservatives. In March 1999 the *Times Higher Educational Supplement* (THES) reported that Professor David McCrone 'said he did not believe the three parties were targeting the student vote. But they were capitalising on an issue in which Labour could be presented as "less Scottish", lacking autonomy from London'.

The incoming Labour–Liberal Democrat coalition quickly set up a committee of inquiry chaired by Andrew Cubie (the 'Cubie Committee') to review student funding. Coverage and debate of the Committee's work was dominated by the issue of fees. As time passed, grants struggled to command the same degree of media attention or political heat. In July 1999 a spokesperson for the Committee of Scottish Higher Education Principals (now Universities Scotland) told the THES:

> Misunderstanding has been the defining factor of this whole debate. We need to get the message across that fee abolition is not about helping the poorest students. The public and political parties are worried about access and student hardship and want to ensure that that's put right. Tuition fees are only a tiny part of this, but have become shorthand for all the ills.

This focus on fees followed a trend already evident in wider UK debate and established a pattern in Scottish political and media discourse that would endure, with important consequences for those at lower incomes.

The Committee proposed the reintroduction of grants, to be funded by a new earnings-related post-graduation contribution (the 'graduate endowment'). In scrutinising the Scottish Government's response to this, the Scottish Parliament focused on the repayment threshold for the endowment, much lower than Cubie had proposed, a function of the decision to use the existing student loan scheme as the mechanism for linking repayment to earnings. The reintroduction of a national student grant (for young students only: mature students were exempt from the endowment) passed relatively unremarked by comparison. The new system of an annual £2,000 maximum grant plus a one-off endowment payment of £2,000 (also lower than Cubie had recommended) was worth more to students from low incomes than the pre-election SNP proposal of free tuition plus £500 in grant. This comparison was however rarely, if ever, made. The principle of free tuition had already become a more significant issue than how the detailed mathematics affected poorer students, in what would become a further recurring feature of the debate in Scotland.

THE MOVE TO DEFERRED FEES IN THE REST OF THE UK AND THE IDEA OF 'ABILITY TO PAY'

In 2006 fees rose to a maximum of £3,000 in England, Wales and Northern Ireland (this change had been announced shortly before the second set of Scottish and Welsh elections, in May 2003). At this point, Wales lacked the legal powers to legislate otherwise and Northern Ireland had temporarily returned to direct rule. For the first time a dedicated non-means-tested loan, repayable in proportion to future earnings, was made available to cover the upfront cost of fees. Means-tested grants had already been reintroduced for all full-time students in Wales and Northern Ireland in 2002 and in England in 2004, leaving mature students in Scotland the only group without access to national grant.

Using student loans to defer the cost of fees marked a critical shift, as it removed 'ability to pay' as an issue for full-time, first-time students, the group whose treatment dominates most political discussion. From 2006–7 onwards, fees ceased to be an issue of immediate access to private sources of cash and became one of debt, to be repaid once graduates were earning, relative to their income. It could no longer be accurately argued that an inability to find cash upfront of itself might impede access for first-time students. Debt aversion (specifically, willingness to borrow against future earnings) became the point at stake.

The debate in Scotland has struggled to adjust to this change. As already seen, the central differentiator of the Scottish system in government rhetoric has remained that it is based on 'ability to learn, not ability to pay'. As a result, it is now regularly suggested in Scotland that entry to university in England now depends both on access to private resources and on accumulating large debts. Media coverage in Scotland has not challenged the implication that 'ability to pay' is the central characteristic of the systems south of the border.

The persistent emphasis on 'ability to pay' indeed may explain an apparently common misunderstanding in Scotland, witnessed in Chapter 5, about the situation of low-income students south of the border. For example, material produced for the independence referendum by the campaign body Yes Scotland noted [emphasis in original]:

> The amazing thing about free tuition fees is that no matter what your family background, you can go to university and not have to worry about finding the money . . . Compare [the system in England] to up here where some of my friends from my football club just wouldn't be able to go to university if they had to pay. (Yes Scotland, 2014)

THE CHANGING ATTITUDE TO DEBT AND GRANT IN SCOTLAND

As in 1999 and 2003, changes in England formed the backdrop to the 2007 elections to the Scottish Parliament.

In July 2006, Nicola Sturgeon MSP, then leader of the SNP Parliamentary party in opposition at Holyrood, drew again on the narrative of Scottish distinctiveness, in launching the SNP's 'Dump the Debt' campaign. She said:

> Access to education based on the ability to learn rather than the ability to pay is one of the oldest and most cherished public policy principles in Scotland. But it is a principle that is under considerable threat . . . Our higher education system, today, is predicated on the accumulation of debt . . . If you believe – as we do – that academic ability alone should determine access to university, then a system that prices anyone out of education in that way is simply not acceptable. (Scottish National Party, 2006)

She went on to make a series of commitments that were later reflected in the 2007 SNP manifesto, which stated:

> Access to education should be based on the ability to learn, not the ability to pay. An SNP government will abolish the Graduate Endowment tuition fee and replace the expensive and discredited Student Loans system with means-tested student grants. We will remove the burden of debt repayments owed by Scottish domiciled and resident graduates.

These strongly expressed commitments contrasted with the far more cautious and general statements made in the 2003 manifesto about living cost support.

The other main parties offered voters a mixture of proposals relating to student funding. The Liberal Democrats offered a package most like that of the SNP, but less dramatically framed. They promised to abolish the endowment, with a further commitment to raise bursaries by 10 per cent. The Labour Party by contrast remained committed to the endowment 'as a means of financing young people from the poorest families to study in higher education'. It undertook to increase living cost support through raising the amount of loan available and to 'build upon the introduction of student bursary grants'. The Conservatives promised a 'root and branch review' of higher education funding, including student debt and finance. They noted they did not have 'any particular difficulty with the idea of a student contributing towards the cost of their education', describing student borrowing with income-contingent repayment as 'the basis of a sound system for student finance', provided a higher repayment threshold was introduced. The SNP's commitments on loans and grants were criticised by opponents as unaffordable, with an ill-tempered exchange conducted between politicians through the media in the months leading to May 2007.

The SNP emerged as the largest party in May 2007 and formed a minority government. A bill to abolish the graduate endowment was prioritised and quickly introduced. In the Policy Memorandum to the draft Bill, the new Scottish Government declared that:

> The GE [graduate endowment] has burdened many graduates and their families with additional debt and has acted as a disincentive to accessing higher education . . . It is essential that education in Scotland is as accessible as possible and that students are not presented with a financial bill from government for their participation in higher education. (Scottish Government, 2007a: 3)

The Bill was passed with the support of the Liberal Democrats. Abolition of the endowment took effect for all those graduating after 1 April 2007.

Events took a different course with student grants and loans. The Scottish Government's *Programme for Government*, published in September 2007, promised to issue a consultation paper seeking the views on the proposal to replace student loans with 'a fair and affordable system of means-tested grants' and on 'measures to tackle graduate debt' (Scottish Government, 2007b: 5). By spring 2008, with the consultation paper still to issue, opponents were accusing the government of pulling back from its original commitments. When the paper was finally published, in December 2008, it repeated that 'we believe that it is wrong for students to be put into debt by the state' (Scottish Government, 2008: 5). However, it also listed three 'restrictions, outside this Government's control, which may prevent us fully delivering on all of our commitments'. These were: having 'no control over a large proportion of the loans budget' as loans were funded directly by the Treasury; the 'toughest spending review for Scotland since devolution' as a result of which the Government has been forced to make hard choices on its spending priorities . . . we will need to consider whether existing funds could be used more effectively . . . While [replacing loan with grant] remains our preferred option, we are aware that there are a range of views on how best to support students . . . [and] . . . the final constraint is political. As a minority Government, we know that there is no consensus of support from other parties for our proposals, therefore, we have to concentrate our limited resources on areas that we can deliver within existing legislative frameworks. (ibid.: 3)

The paper sought views on how best to use £30 million of new cash which had been found for investment in student support, against a loans budget at that point worth £150 million a year.

Meantime, the National Union of Students (NUS) Scotland was placing increased emphasis on student hardship and the general support, whether as loan or grant, available to students for living costs. As a result of discussion with the NUS, the consultation resulted in some of the available cash being converted into further loan subsidy, releasing a larger volume of upfront funding. It was from this point that the Scottish Government ceased to describe student loans as intrinsically problematic and began to reserve its criticism of loans for those used for fees in other parts of the UK, while still emphasising that systems elsewhere in the UK rested on 'ability to pay'.

By 2010 there were signs that opinion was softening in some quarters in Scotland towards the principle of student contributions. Indeed, a Scottish Government consultation paper issued in December of that year included questions on how a contribution scheme might work, even while declaring the government's own opposition to fees. The paper noted that NUS Scotland supported some sort of earnings-based scheme 'in principle, considering the current financial pressures, as long as it were progressive and tied to genuine financial benefit, but only if the funds raised were channelled into increasing levels of student support' (Scottish Government, 2010: 35). Just a week earlier, however, Iain MacWhirter had reported that that within the Scottish Government 'attitudes [were] hardening' towards any kind of graduate contribution, in the light of the Browne Review (MacWhirter, 2010a) and that a clear commitment to maintaining free tuition could be the 'Big Idea' needed by an administration which he described as 'rudderless and outvoted', having had to abandon various high-profile policies (MacWhirter, 2010b). The following April, with the debate about fees once again dominating the UK media, and weeks ahead of an election at Holyrood, the First Minister Alex Salmond famously announced to an SNP party conference that 'the rocks will melt with the sun before I allow tuition fees to be imposed on Scotland's students'.

In 2011 the Holyrood elections were therefore once again dominated by fee policy in England. The SNP manifesto repeated its opposition to tuition fees, as its sole policy commitment on student funding. Labour and the Liberal Democrats now also both committed themselves to having neither tuition fees nor a post-graduation payment. The Conservatives alone argued for introducing a 'graduate contribution facilitated through student loans'. They linked this to 'enhanced bursary support', making them the only one of the four parties to make an explicit reference to grants. The Liberal Democrats promised only 'a student-led review of student support', while this time it was Labour's turn to suggest a general 'root and branch review of Scottish higher education'. Between 2007 and 2011, grants had therefore all but vanished from mainstream political discussion in Scotland. The SNP went on to gain an outright majority.

THE IMPACT OF THE 2012 FEE RISE IN ENGLAND ON THE DEVOLVED ADMINISTRATIONS

In Northern Ireland and Wales, where there were also elections in 2011, the devolved governments similarly resisted the move to higher fees. In Wales, taking advantage of new legislative powers in this area, all parties but the Conservatives promised to shelter students from Wales from the change taking place in England. As in Scotland, grants were barely mentioned (although this may reflect in part that there had been a very large increase in grant levels in Wales in 2010). With the Northern Irish Assembly reconvened, no party there proposed following the English model, with Sinn Féin maintaining its absolute opposition to tuition fees. Again, student grants did not attract much attention. In both these nations, as in Scotland, the incoming administrations had a clear mandate to reject the English model. All three nations were, however, faced with a significant financial challenge in implementing their responses.

In 1999 and 2006 the new income from fees had not been used to substitute for existing investment in universities in England. By contrast, the 2012 changes in England led to a large reduction in the government higher education teaching grant there. In 2011–12, the last financial year fully under the old system, total funding for teaching provided through the Higher Education Funding Council for England (HEFCE) was £4.339 billion. For 2015–16, with the new arrangements more or less fully in place, the indicative figure is £1.418 billion. The budget for student grants rose over the same period, although by much less than the fall in teaching grant: the increase was around £0.3 billion. Research funding through HEFCE was meantime held at the same cash value, meaning a real-terms reduction over the period.

At the same time a very substantial increase in student loans was planned in England to underwrite the new higher fees which would compensate universities for their lost government teaching grant. Fee income supported through loans was expected to rise from £2.6 billion in 2011–12 to £8.2 billion in 2015–16, implying a real-terms rise in total income to universities from HEFCE and regulated fee income of over 20 per cent over the period (Bolton, 2014: 6), before taking account of student number growth.

These changes had a large impact on the budgets of the three devolved admin-istrations, through the operation of the Barnett formula. Under this, the devolved administrations currently receive each year a population-based share of changes in relevant, comparable UK Government spending in England (around 10 per cent for Scotland, and 5.8 per cent and 3.5 per cent for Wales and Northern Ireland respectively). These calculations produce a total amount of additional funding which is applied to the previous year's baseline for each devolved nation, adjusted as necessary for changes in responsibilities. The baselines are in turn the product of the accumulated changes applied to an initial spending allocation, dating from when the Barnett formula was first introduced in the late 1970s. The devolved administrations are free to allocate their total resources between the services for which they are responsible as they wish, except in a few cases where the resources are ring-fenced. The cost of student loan funding is among the ring-fenced categories of funding.

From 2012 the substantial reductions to the HEFCE budget meant that for the first time fee increases caused cash allocations under the Barnett formula to be lower than they would otherwise have been (although reductions in HEFCE funding may have prevented cuts to other spending programmes relevant to Barnett: the extent of that effect is hard to assess). Although the devolved administrations' access to loans increased sharply, their only available discretion over that element of their budget was to increase, or not, the use of loans by their students: they could not convert this funding into cash support for students.

Faced with such significant changes, each of the devolved administrations took action to respond to the impact on their budgets. While all three protected locally domiciled students studying in their home nation from any increase in fees, they permitted their universities to charge students from other parts of the UK up to £9,000 and removed controls on the recruitment of cross-border students. Students going to another part of the UK from Scotland had always had to pay, or from 2006 borrow, the cost of the fees charged by their host university. This remained the case. Students from Northern Ireland studying elsewhere were also limited to additional loan to cover their higher fees. In Wales, by contrast, the decision was taken to treat funding for fees as a portable citizen entitlement, not tied to study within the jurisdiction. Thus in Wales the notional maximum fee rose to £9,000, but all Welsh students, wherever they studied in the UK, were provided with a fee grant which brought the cost down to the previous headline fee, then around £3,500. This meant that fee costs were unchanged even for those crossing the border. A flat-rate bursary of £600 additional to main student grant, and available to all Welsh students from households with incomes up to £34,000, was abandoned only a year after it had been introduced, although this still left Wales with a significantly higher maximum grant than other parts of the UK.

In Scotland and even more so in Wales, the decision to apply the fee rise to incoming students created a substantial new income stream for institutions, at no cost to the devolved government. Around 15 per cent or so of full-time UK undergraduate students in Scotland are from other parts of the UK and were already being charged a smaller amount. The additional income from this group appears likely to equal around one-quarter of the loss to the Scottish block grant due to the HEFCE budget cut. In Wales around 40 per cent of full-time, first-degree students come from other parts of the UK. In the spring of 2014 the Higher Education Funding Council for Wales (HEFCW) predicted that once all fee income was included there would be an 11 per cent increase in funding for Welsh institutions between 2013–14 and 2014–15, even though its own grant-in-aid funding was reducing (HEFCW, 2014: Table 6). In Northern Ireland, by contrast, which imports relatively few students from other parts of the UK, there was little scope to make up for reductions in the block grant by increasing cross-border income.

While direct grant funding from government to higher education institutions fell in Wales and Northern Ireland between 2012–13 and 2015–16, it was originally planned to rise in real terms in Scotland over the same period, to demonstrate that the government's commitment to free tuition was not at the universities' expense. This coincided with plans for a substantial reduction in the budget for colleges (later partially reversed) and also with reductions in the budget for student support from that year, the effects of which are discussed below. However, in November 2014 the Scottish Government asked the Scottish Funding Council (SFC) to hold back £21 million of its 2015–16 allocation for higher education institutions, to provide more 'flexibility' in the 'post-16 budget'. At the time of writing, it is not clear what will happen to this money. Removing it from higher education institutions would convert the previously announced increase over the period from 2012–13 to 2015–16 into a real-terms standstill.

From the perspective of students, the most obvious effect of the changes which took effect from 2012 was the expectation of much higher borrowing for those from England (and border crossers from Scotland and Northern Ireland) as the new fee regime was implemented. It was widely noted in Scotland that average borrowing would now be highest in England and lowest in Scotland. However, it went unobserved that within Scotland students at the lowest incomes were now borrowing significantly more in practice than their better-off peers. This was a product of relatively low means-tested grants compared to other jurisdictions, while at higher incomes the 'minimum loan' for living costs was smaller than elsewhere and, following the abolition of the graduate endowment, there was no longer any pressure to borrow to fund a contribution. The main means-tested grant for young students had been frozen in value from 2010, so that equivalent grants elsewhere in the UK had overtaken it. A new grant for Scottish mature students had been introduced in 2010, but at a lower rate than for younger students. Official statistics implied that 70 per cent of total borrowing was accounted for by a group of borrowers drawn from the poorest 45 per cent of students, while those from homes with incomes over £50,000 appeared to account for less than 10 per cent of all loan debt (Hunter Blackburn, 2014a: 38). In the other UK jurisdictions, average borrowing by income was, by contrast, quite evenly spread, except that in Wales and Northern Ireland it was lowest at the lowest incomes (Hunter Blackburn, 2014b). Within the UK by 2012–13 only the Scottish system was producing in practice a regressive distribution of student loan debt, so that those from lower-income backgrounds were the most likely to leave university owing the government the largest sums.

SCOTTISH CHANGES FROM 2013–14

In August 2012 the Scottish Government announced changes to student support from 2013–14 which increased the total value of upfront support, describing the resulting arrangements as the 'best in the UK'. It later emerged that the new

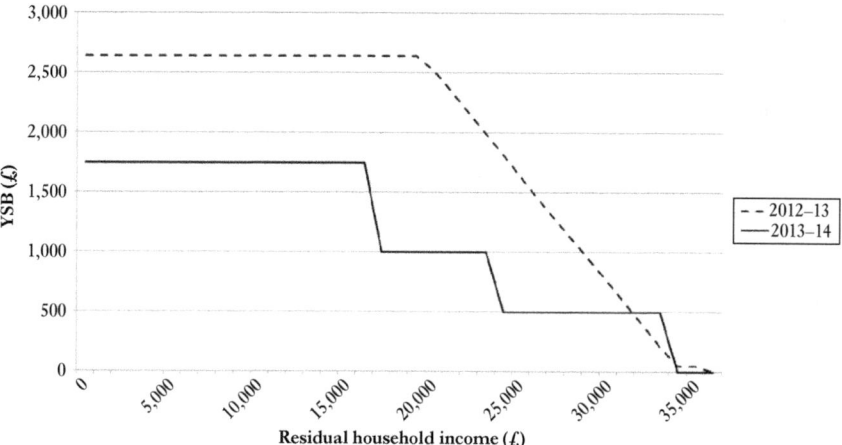

Figure 3.1   Young Student Bursary in Scotland in 2012–13 and 2013–14

Source: Student Awards Agency for Scotland

arrangements would mean a substantial reduction in grants, as more reliance was placed on loans to support living costs. In 2013–14 spending on means-tested student grants fell by 40 per cent, from £89.4 million to £53 million (Student Awards Agency for Scotland, 2014: 63). Figure 3.1 shows how the reduction affected grant levels for young students studying in Scotland.

This was the first time basic grant entitlements had been reduced anywhere in the UK since 1999: Scotland was the only jurisdiction to use some of the additional sums becoming available as student loan to substitute for existing grant. Further loan was used to increase students' total living cost support at all incomes. The draft 2013–14 budget projected a near-doubling in net student lending, from £241.3 million in 2012–13 to £468.3 million in 2014–15. These changes meant that the system was now explicitly designed on the assumption that those at the lowest incomes would borrow the largest amounts, a model unique within the UK.

The new system reduced the scale of the imbalance in borrowing at different incomes, as a substantial increase in the minimum non-means-tested loan to £4,500 led to higher borrowing by students from middle- to high-income families. However, average borrowing also increased among students at lower incomes, among whom higher loan take-up rates also persisted. Seventy per cent of students on Young Student Bursary borrowed the maximum amount available at low incomes (£5,500), with a further 5 per cent borrowing a smaller sum, while 83 per cent of students on the Independent Student Bursary had borrowed the maximum for that group (£6,500), and a further 2 per cent something less (Constance, 2015). This compared with a borrowing rate of 70 per cent across the Scottish-domiciled student population as a whole. These figures suggest that up to 25 per cent of younger students at low incomes, and 15 per cent of mature students, may have been seeking to complete their higher education debt free, most probably by living in the parental home: however, in doing so they were limited to very little help with their living costs from the state. Among those taking out a loan, average borrowing was £5,780 among the group entitled to means-tested grant or loan, that is from households with incomes below £34,000: for the remainder, it was £4,140 (Student Awards Agency for Scotland, 2014: 65). As a result, a final debt of well over £20,000 could be confidently predicted for the majority of low-income four-year degree students, while many of those from better-off backgrounds could still be expected to leave university with little or no debt.

This regressive effect, under which both on paper and in practice those who started from the households with the least resources become in time the graduates paying back the largest amount from their earnings to the state, sits uneasily with claims that the Scottish system is intrinsically socially just.

THE UK IN 2014–15: SYSTEMS IN DETAILED COMPARISON

In practice, claims for greater social justice in the Scottish system have not been based on how it distributes costs and benefits within Scotland, but generally depend entirely on comparisons with the rest of the UK, and specifically with fee levels in England.

Comparisons between systems based only on fee levels are problematic, however, because they exclude other factors relevant to students. The comparisons below therefore look at systems in the round, in particular (i) how much students are given in total by the state towards their living costs while they study, referred to below as spending power; (ii) the total amount of final debt students face on graduation for fees and living costs; and (iii) how repayments are collected. When systems are compared in this way, the claim that Scotland stands out as being unusually socially just within the UK also becomes more open to question.

The discussion below considers how systems are designed to work rather than the actual borrowing patterns discussed above. It excludes the effect of the institutional bursaries and fee waivers which form part of the English system, the availability of which is variable and unpredictable. Readers should however bear in mind that at the lowest incomes especially, the figures for England in particular will tend to understate spending power and overstate debt, compared to what students may experience in practice. Figures have been derived from the relevant official student finance government calculators.

Spending Power

Spending power is the combined value of grant and loan provided to support living costs. Although more work needs to be done to establish a relationship between any particular aspect of student support and patterns of participation and retention, immediate help with living costs might be empirically expected to be at least as relevant for access as levels of long-term debt.

By 2012–13 spending power for Scottish students had fallen significantly behind that in England or Wales and the case for an increase was strong. The Scottish

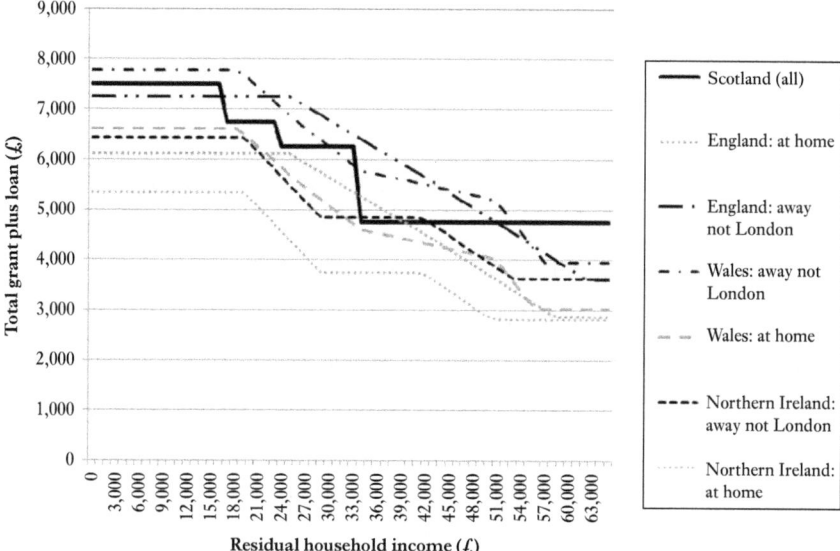

Figure 3.2 State support for student spending power across the UK, 2014–15

Source: Relevant government student finance calculators and Student Awards Agency for Scotland; detailed calculations by author

Government highlighted an increase in spending power as a significant element of its new arrangements from 2013. The new maximum package of support available of £7,250 (£7,500 in 2014–15) was described as providing a 'minimum income guarantee'.

Figure 3.2 compares spending power for students across the UK in 2014–15. The additional support available for students studying in London is excluded, as is the additional support available to some students, such as lone parents, under the English and Welsh Special Support Grant arrangements and other supplementary grants in Scotland and Northern Ireland.

In all parts of the UK the majority of full-time undergraduate students live away from the parental home. For this group, which faces the highest living costs, the greatest spending power is generally provided by either the English or Welsh system. Northern Ireland has the least generous level of support, with Scotland between the two extremes. Only at incomes above £54,000 does Scotland offer the most support. For those living at home, Scotland generally offers the most, as alone in the UK the Scottish Government now offers the same level of support to students regardless of whether they live away or at home. The Scottish Government has explained this as a function of its decision to simplify the system. It similarly provides no additional funding for students who study in London.

Despite the claims made for the relatively strong performance of the Scottish system for poorer students, it emerges from this particular comparison that for students living away from home, families in Scotland at low-to-middle incomes receive less assistance upfront than in one, two or all three other parts of the UK. In effect, the Scottish system tends to assume greater 'ability to pay' on the part of such families, particularly at household incomes between £17,000 and £50,000.

The Scottish system is in addition stepped rather than tapered. The change creates sudden falls in entitlement for students with incomes at £17,000, £24,000 and £34,000. This has made the system simpler to describe, predict and operate, but has the disadvantage of creating sharp 'marginal rates' of benefit withdrawal at each step.

As Table 3.1 shows, within living cost support, Wales makes the largest use of grant, while Scotland makes the least. As a result, Scottish students at lower incomes are expected to have substantially more living cost debt than those from other jurisdictions, affecting the calculation of total final debt discussed below.

Final Debt

Debt is less straightforward to compare than spending power. As Figure 3.2 showed, the debt associated in each system with students claiming their full package of support can mask considerable variation in how much spending power that borrowing supports. The total final debt comparison below therefore removes variability in spending power, by setting it at the same level in all cases as applies in Scotland. It shows the resulting total debt expected at the point students become liable to repay, in the April after they leave their course, for those undertaking the shortest commonly available honours degree in each jurisdiction, that is, three years in England, Wales and Northern Ireland and four years in Scotland. This set of calculations comes closest to giving a true like-for-like comparison of expected debt for the commonest group of degree students in each country.

The comparison takes into account that a lower interest rate applies in Scotland and Northern Ireland than in England and Wales while students study. Fee loans for English students and Scottish and Northern Irish border crossers are assumed to be £9,000, which will tend to produce slight over-estimates: the provisional average fee loan reported by the Student Loans Company for English-domiciled students under the new arrangements in 2014–15 was £8,100 (Student Loan Company, 2014: Table 4(c)(i)). A flat-rate write-off of £1,500 of debt available to most Welsh-domiciled students on commencing repayment is taken into account.

In 2014–15, the comparison shows that, rather than a division between Scotland and the rest of the UK, for those studying the commonest form of honours degree in their home nation there is instead more clearly a division between:

1   a lower debt group covering students from Scotland, Northern Ireland and Wales, where expected debt falls roughly in a range from £20,000 to £30,000. The figures fall within near-identical upper and lower limits. The only difference is that in Scotland debt goes from high to low as income rises, while in the other two nations the opposite happens. Scotland as a result has relatively high figures among the devolved nations for low-income degree students, particularly mature students; and

2   a higher debt group covering English students, where debt falls roughly within a range from £40,000 to £50,000.

Table 3.1 Student grant in the UK in 2014–15

Non-repayable means-tested grant for full-time undergraduate students in the UK: 2014–15		Maximum grant	Available up to residual household income	Thereafter
Domicile	*Category*	£	£	
England	All	3,387	25,000	Tapers to £0 at £42,621
Northern Ireland	All	3,475	19,203	Tapers to £0 at £41,065
Scotland	Young	1,750	16,999	£1,000 at incomes up to £23,999; £500 at incomes up to £33,999; £0 at higher incomes
	Independent (mature)	750	16,999	£0 at incomes over £16,999
Wales	All	5,161	18,370	Tapers to £0 at £50,020

Source: Relevant government student finance calculators and Student Awards Agency for Scotland 2014

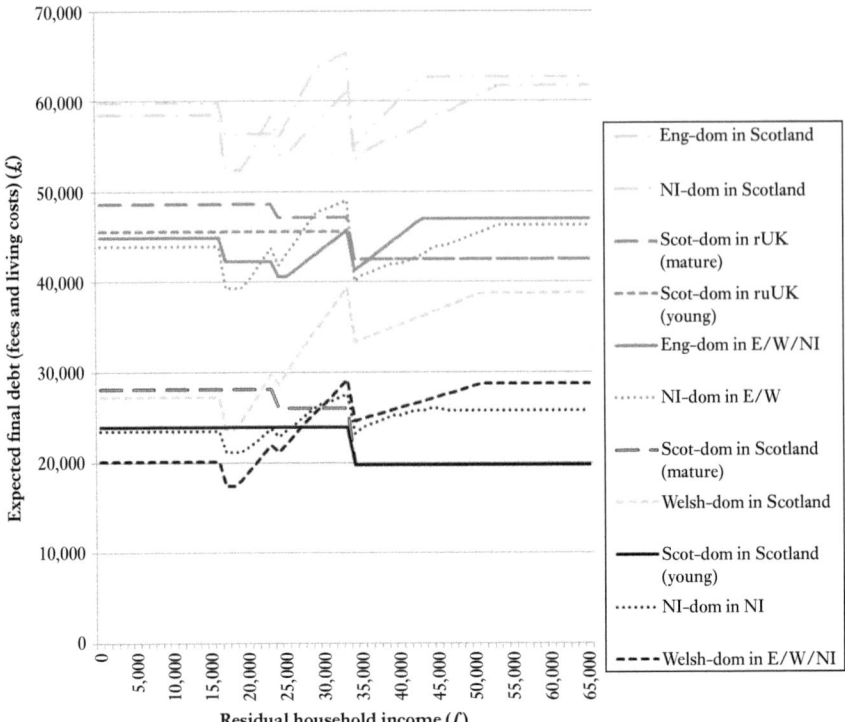

Figure 3.3   Expected final debt for commonest length degree, by domicile and place of study in the UK estimated assuming Scottish spending levels, using 2014–15 figures

Source: Relevant government student finance calculators and Student Awards Agency for Scotland; detailed calculations by author

Cross-border Welsh students also fall into the low debt group, except for those from middle-to-high incomes who study for an additional year in Scotland: those students fall somewhere in between the two. Scottish and Northern Irish border crossers fall into the higher debt group. Scottish students in the rest of the UK, particularly mature students, are expected to have the highest annual borrowing of any group, but gain from studying for three years rather than four. English and Northern Irish students in Scotland face the highest final debt of all, as they are liable for full fees for four years. The comparison with Wales brings out that the higher debt for cross-border students from Scotland and Northern Ireland results from policy choice.

It turns out that no-fee systems do not automatically generate the least debt for all students. For Welsh students, and Northern Irish students who study in Northern Ireland, higher debt for fees than in Scotland can be compensated for by lower borrowing for living costs. At the lowest incomes, standard honours degree students from Wales are expected to emerge with the least debt. Shorter degrees help, but high grant, combined with debt write-off, is the more critical difference. Even on courses of equal length many low-income students from Wales are still expected to have less debt (Hunter Blackburn, 2014c).

Moreover, Wales stands out as the only country which seeks to limit debt within what might be termed 'devolved' levels for all its students, at all incomes, wherever they study. England is the only one which offers its students no possibility of lower debt, beyond what can be achieved through lower-fee courses, fee waivers or institutional bursaries. Higher-income Scots studying in Scotland emerge as the group expected to borrow least, relative to all other UK students.

Repayment Regimes

Various authors have demonstrated that higher repayment thresholds and shorter write-off periods for income-contingent student loans tend to benefit low earners, while lower interest rates tend to benefit higher earners (see, for example, Chowdry et al., 2012). This is because the interest rate charged is irrelevant to graduates who do not earn enough to pay off their whole initial debt before it is written off.

In all parts of the UK, student loan is collected at the rate of 9 per cent of all earnings over a threshold. In Northern Ireland and Scotland the governments have chosen to remain with the model which applied prior to 2012. In both cases, student loan becomes repayable at a lower threshold than now applies for England or Wales (£17,335 compared to £21,000 from April 2015) and the interest is also lower. The period after which debt is written off also varies, at thirty-five years in Scotland and thirty elsewhere.

The combined effect of these differences is that the Scottish loan repayment system has the least progressive combination of factors of any in the UK. Scottish students are more likely to repay any given amount of debt, as they will pay more back at lower incomes and be expected to continue paying for longest. In 2013 researchers in the Scottish Parliament's Information Centre identified that at the lowest two lifetime earnings deciles, the total value of lifetime repayments would be higher for a debt of £16,000 under Scottish rules than one of £36,000 in England or Wales (MacPherson and Liddell, 2013: 14). The Scottish repayment threshold has since risen slightly, so this precise effect may no longer hold. It demonstrates, however, that the repayment threshold and write-off period can be as significant as final debt on graduation, in determining the actual eventual cost to individuals. At the time of writing, the Scottish Government is subject to calls from NUS Scotland and the Scottish Liberal Democrats to increase the repayment threshold to the same level as in England and Wales.

In summary, whether considering spending power, final debt or loan repayment rules, the Scottish system does not stand out as exceptional for lower-income students or low-earning graduates, and is often outperformed by one or more of the other jurisdictions. Wales in particular often produces more favourable results at low incomes on all measures. It is only at higher incomes that the Scottish system offers consistently better outcomes, compared to the other home nations, calling into question the presentation of the Scottish arrangements as being socially just in comparison with those found elsewhere in the UK. Even the English system, with its much higher overall debt, does not distribute that debt regressively between students from different backgrounds and limits the impact of repayment on lower earners more effectively.

THE DEBATE IN SCOTLAND SINCE 2013

Even as evidence began to emerge over 2013 of the regressive long-term impacts of Scottish policy, the dominant narrative in Scotland in relation to student funding remained one of social justice, contrasted with other parts of the UK, turning as ever on an isolated comparison between fee levels in England and Scotland. Criticism by the opposition parties of the effects of grant reductions on students from low-income backgrounds was dismissed by the Scottish Government as inauthentic and merely concealing a desire in principle to introduce fees. This was well illustrated in the response from the government benches to an opposition motion criticising grant reductions put forward for debate in the Scottish Parliament in June 2013 (Official Report, 2013).

As the debate on independence came increasingly to dominate Scottish political discussion during 2013 and 2014, fees continued to receive considerable attention, while grants and debt were persistently absent. In October 2013 the White Paper on Scottish independence said, 'Access to higher education will be based on ability, not wealth; this Government will protect free tuition fees for Scottish students' (Scottish Government, 2013: 182), adding:

> on independence, Scottish domiciled students will continue to have free access to higher education. This guarantee will save Scottish students up to £9,000 a year compared with the cost of studying in England. Free education for those able to benefit from it is a core part of Scotland's educational tradition and the values that underpin our educational system. (ibid., p. 198)

The White Paper's comments on wider student support were by contrast limited to a commitment to 'continue to provide appropriate support for living costs' (ibid., p. 182), with no reference to the role envisaged for student grants or loans or even to the potential for more radical alternatives, such as a graduate tax. Discussion in the mainstream media and online did not touch on these topics.

The wider debate about student indebtedness had fallen away, just as actual debt levels had risen sharply. Whereas in 2007 abolishing the graduate endowment had been described by the Scottish Government as 'the first step' towards its 'aspiration of having a higher education system in Scotland that is free for all' (Scottish Government, 2007a: 3), in the June 2013 parliamentary debate, the then Cabinet Secretary for Education, Michael Russell MSP, argued that the government needed to 'continue to deliver free education, because that is the only way – along with the legislation that we have – that we will genuinely widen access'. It was sometimes asserted that 'free education' might be included in the constitution of an independent Scotland, with the clear implication that this included free university tuition, not the return of full grants.

Over the period, 'free education' had moved, therefore, from meaning the absence of debt to just the absence of fee payments. Living cost debt had been repositioned by government, and at times also by the student movement in Scotland, as a pure public good, the distribution of which was therefore not relevant to the questions of social justice or equity.

A further persistent narrative in popular debate over the period was that fees had damaged access to higher education in England. However, as this became increasingly difficult to justify from the data, for younger students at least, an overt link between the policy of free tuition and widening access became less common in the official lines, which rested on the more general claim that Scotland's system was 'best in the UK' and based on 'ability to learn, not ability to pay', providing an implicit message of greater social justice, without making a specific, testable claim about effects on access.

David McCrone's observation that concentrating on tuition fees had been a way of presenting Labour, but now also the Liberal Democrats and the Conservatives, as 'less Scottish' and lacking autonomy from London remained relevant. It was a regular assertion of pro-independence campaigners that a 'No' vote would mean the introduction of fees: meanwhile, those on the other side identified risks to free tuition under independence as an ironic weakness of the Scottish Government's position. The SNP's apparently successful association of supporting free tuition with having authentically Scottish values was well exemplified in a tweet from Iain MacWhirter on 21 August 2014 that stated '#YesBecause Tuition fees, Ukip, Bullingon [sic], benefits cap' (MacWhirter, 2014). While some earlier polling data on the subject of free tuition had suggested that many Scottish voters would in fact support a system in which graduates made some contribution, according either to parental or post-graduation income, the Scottish Conservatives were the only political party in Scotland critical of the progressive claims made for free tuition as a policy. In late 2014 Scottish Labour repeated its 2011 commitment not to introduce tuition fees, although it did follow this in March 2015 with a commitment to restoring the cuts made to grants for young students, tying this to additional funding it said would flow from the election of a Labour government at UK level. NUS Scotland, meantime, in contrast to its reported position in 2010, was now very critical of any suggestion that fees might be introduced in Scotland, even on the loan-based model used elsewhere in the UK. It had strongly supported the changes introduced in 2013, which it had helped to formulate, and appeared unconcerned about the long-term regressive effects of Scottish policy (although by autumn 2014 it was arguing that any further increases in support for those at low incomes should be through grant rather than loan).

The NUS position, and perhaps also the political power of arguments about authentic Scottishness, may explain in part why there was relatively little critical scrutiny of the detail of student finance in the Scottish media over 2013 and 2014. As at spring 2015, BBC Scotland appeared still not to have run a story dealing with the issue of grant cuts, for example. Relatively little pressure was applied over the period within the Scottish Parliament, where a government majority in the main chamber was reflected on the relevant parliamentary committee, which was chaired by a member of the governing party. Such exposure as there was of the distribution of student debt, and the reversal of the Scottish Government's attitude to grant and loan, caused no political damage to the SNP. While references to the Liberal Democrat reversal on fees at Westminster remained common in Scottish politics and the Scottish press, the change in the SNP's position on debt was rarely mentioned there, despite its more direct impact on Scottish students. Scottish Liberal Democrat support for abolition of the graduate endowment in 2007 went equally unacknowledged.

Indeed, by early 2015 it appeared that the party least likely to sustain political damage in bringing forward a system of student contributions in Scotland, particularly if linked to increased support for those at low incomes, might arguably be the SNP itself, able to command considerable loyalty from its supporters, being least vulnerable to criticism of 'lacking autonomy from London' and perhaps using similar arguments to those it deployed successfully to explain its radically altered position on student debt in the period after 2007. The rhetoric on fees has been exceptionally strong, but so once was the rhetoric on ending student debt. Certainly the SNP appears at present to be the party most likely to be in government in Scotland up to 2020 and dealing with whatever challenges that may present.

FUTURE DEVELOPMENTS

The systems in the devolved nations can be expected to come under a variety of pressures over the coming years. All are likely to see real-terms reductions in their block grant, as further Westminster austerity measures take effect through the Barnett formula. The planned lifting of the cap on student numbers in England could cause a fall in university income in Scotland or Wales, if it reduces the numbers travelling out of England to study, although any such effects may be gradual. There would be cross-border implications in any further changes to student funding in England, whether an increase or a decrease in fees for all or some students. A decrease in fees as promised by the Labour Party in February 2015 would reduce cross-border income but would also, presumably, have positive Barnett consequentials for the devolved administrations which would more than compensate. Indeed, it was the prospect of this which Scottish Labour suggested in March 2015 would enable it to restore grant levels.

In Wales, a further review of student finance is already underway, though at such an early stage that it is difficult to tell how radical its proposals may be. There has been no indication to date that there is an appetite among politicians in the Welsh Assembly Government for a substantial rise in fee levels, for example. In Northern Ireland general budget pressures and limited capacity to raise income from students from the rest of the UK are already putting significant strain on higher education funding. In Scotland, the establishment of a new Commission on Widening Access is likely to lead to greater scrutiny of Scotland's record there.

Universities and Colleges Admissions Service (UCAS) figures in addition suggest that Scotland's more tightly capped system, coupled perhaps with the high cost of cross-border study, has led to lower acceptance rates for Scottish applicants to university than those seen elsewhere in the UK.

A further significant issue will be how the devolved nations choose to use any new revenue-raising powers generated by the planned extension of devolution. Greater freedom over tax raising ought in theory to make it easier for them, if they wish, to reject relying so heavily on loans and choose instead to increase their cash spending on students. However, in practice student loans seem likely to remain a significant element of funding in all three devolved nations, given that the opportunity was not taken during the recent independence campaign in Scotland to make any commitment to reducing the use of student loans, there is no sign of a strong political (or indeed public) desire to revert to a fully cash-funded student support system in Wales or Northern Ireland and the probability that other areas will be a high priority for any new resources in all three countries.

CONCLUSION

Every set of elections to the Scottish Parliament and its sister devolved assemblies has been held relatively soon after a controversial decision has either been announced or implemented at Westminster to increase tuition fees. It should therefore be no surprise that fee policy has been a repeatedly high-profile electoral issue in all three devolved nations and used repeatedly to demonstrate distinctiveness and independence in devolved policy-making. Although the debate in Scotland tends to emphasise its difference from the rest of the UK, in practice an equally clear distinction can be made between England and the rest. Even there, it bears remembering that none of the plans for fee increases in England have been endorsed by voters at an election. They have always been developed and enacted by governments once in office, sometimes in direct contravention of manifesto commitments.

While Scotland has preserved free tuition, it has not given the same priority to protecting cash support for living costs. As a result, within Scotland the highest debt levels are now expected for, and experienced by, those from the poorest backgrounds, a situation unique in the UK. Although comparisons are most often made with England, setting the Scottish arrangements beside those in Wales and Northern Ireland shows that the two latter countries assume similar levels of debt to Scotland and indeed can offer as low, and sometimes lower, debt for the poorest students. Scotland also currently does least to shelter low-earning graduates from loan repayment. The clearest beneficiaries of policy-making in Scotland in recent years have in fact been students from better-off homes, who can now expect to leave university with the least debt of any group in the UK. The comparison with Wales and Northern Ireland shows that the regressive effects seen in Scotland are a product of political choice, not an inevitable effect of the operation of the devolution settlement. From this a rather different story of Scottish distinctiveness emerges. Looking at the material effects of policy, rather than the dominant rhetoric, Scotland stands out as the part of the UK where the interests of those at higher incomes have been most protected, even as students from poorer backgrounds have seen the non-repayable cash provided to support their participation in higher education decrease.

Yet the Scottish system continues to be successfully presented as a model of equity, with free tuition positioned as an expression of what are asserted to be specifically Scottish values. With selective comparisons with fee levels in England commanding more interest than the actual effects of student funding policy in total, the prominence of fees obscures the role of grant in preventing long-term regressive effects in the distribution of graduate debt. Such effects might be disregarded as marginal, could it be demonstrated that using resources in this way is clearly more effective in widening access. However, there is no evidence for that. The long-term regressive effect of the Scottish approach to student support requires to be considered as an issue of social justice in its own right.

With the party dominant in Scottish politics strongly opposed to using graduate contributions to generate any new funding for student support, facing little challenge to that position and under pressure to direct its cash to other areas of public spending, the current distribution of student borrowing in Scotland seems likely to hold for some time to come. In that case, whether considered in its own right or in comparison with other parts of the UK, Scotland's claim to having a system of student funding strongly characterised by social justice will continue to be very much open to question.

REFERENCES

Bolton, P. (2014), *HE in England From 2012: Funding and Finance*. House of Commons Library Standard Note SN06206, London: House of Commons Library.

Chowdry, H., L. Dearden, A. Goodman and W. Jin (2012), 'The distributional impact of the 2012–13 higher education funding reforms in England', *Fiscal Studies*, 33: 2, 211–36.

Constance, A. (2015), *Written Answers S4W–24400 and S4W–24402*, 23 February 2015, Edinburgh: Scottish Parliament.

Hansard (1998), *House of Commons Debates*, 16 March 1998, Vol. 308 Col. 1019, London: Hansard.

Higher Education Funding Council for Wales (HEFCW) (2014), *HEFCW's Funding Allocations 2014/15*, Cardiff: HEFCW.

Hunter Blackburn, L. (2014a), *Working Paper 3 – The Fairest of Them All? The Support For Scottish Students in Full-Time Higher Education in 2014*, Edinburgh: University of Edinburgh, Centre for Research in Education Inclusion and Diversity (CREID).

Hunter Blackburn, L. (2014b), *Actual Average Borrowing by Income in Each Part of the UK*, http://adventuresinevidence.com/2014/04/28/actual-average-borrowing-by-income-in-each-part-of-the-uk (accessed 2 October 2014).

Hunter Blackburn, L. (2014c), *Wales/Scotland Debt Comparisons in Detail*, http://adventuresinevidence.com/2014/04/29/walesscotland-debt-comparisons-in-detail (accessed 2 October 2014).

MacPherson, S. and G. Liddell (2013), *Student Loans and Repayments Briefing 13/78*, Edinburgh: Scottish Parliament Information Centre (SPICe).

MacWhirter, I. (2010a), *Students United*, http://opinion.publicfinance.co.uk/2010/12/students-united-by-iain-macwhirter (accessed 2 October 2014).

MacWhirter, I. (2010b), *Tuition fees CAN be Stopped in Scotland*, http://iainmacwhirter2.blogspot.co.uk/2010/12/tuition-fees-can-be-stopped-in-scotland.html (accessed 2 October 2014).

MacWhirter, I. (2011), *Tuition Fees – the Argument Continues*, http://iainmacwhirter2.blogspot.co.uk/2011/03/tuition-fees-argument-continues.html (accessed 1 December 2014).

MacWhirter, I. (2014), #YesBecause Tuition fees, Ukip, Bullingon [sic], benefits cap, https://twitter.com/iainmacwhirter/status/502385601631756288 (accessed 7 October 2014).

Official Report (2013), *Meeting of the Parliament*, 5 June 2013 cols 20744–20770, Edinburgh: Scottish Parliament.

Russell, M. (2014), *Scottish Student Numbers 'On Course' for Record 19 August 2014*, http://www.bbc.co.uk/news/uk-scotland-19305260 (accessed 1 December 2014).

Scottish Government (2007a), *Graduate Endowment Abolition (Scotland) Bill: Policy Memorandum*, Edinburgh: Scottish Government.

Scottish Government (2007b), *Principles and Priorities: The Government's Programme for Scotland*, Edinburgh: Scottish Government.

Scottish Government (2008), *Supporting a Smarter Scotland: A Consultation on Supporting Learners in Higher Education*, Edinburgh: Scottish Government.

Scottish Government (2010), *Building a Smarter Future: Towards a Sustainable Scottish Solution for the Future of Higher Education*, Edinburgh: Scottish Government.

Scottish Government (2013), *Scotland's Future: Your Guide to an Independent Scotland*, Edinburgh: Scottish Government.

Scottish National Party (2006), *Sturgeon Unveils £100m Student Plans*, http://snp.org/media-centre/news/2006/jul/sturgeon-unveils-%C2%A3100m-student-plans (accessed 2 October 2014).

Smout, T. C. (1986), *A Century of the Scottish People, 1830–1950*, London: Collins.

Student Awards Agency for Scotland (2014), *Higher Education Student Support in Scotland 2013–14: Statistical Summary of Financial Support Provided to Students by the Students Awards Agency for Scotland in Academic Session 2013–14*, Edinburgh: Student Awards Agency for Scotland.

Student Loan Company (2014), *Student Support Awards (Loans and Grants) Academic Year 2013–14*, Glasgow: Student Loan Company.

Yes Scotland (2014), *Keeping University Tuition Fees Free*, http://www.yesscotland.net/reasons/keeping-university-tuition-fees-free (accessed 20 September 2014).

4

Young People's Attitudes towards Student Debt in Scotland and England

Sarah Minty

INTRODUCTION

Whilst participation rates in higher education have increased rapidly since the 1960s, the most selective universities across the UK continue to be dominated by young people from the most socially advantaged backgrounds (Raffe and Croxford, 2015). Successive Scottish and UK Governments have stressed the need for increased participation in higher education in order to meet the needs of a knowledge economy, but have also emphasised the need for fairer access in order to increase social mobility. Since 1997 there has been a growing expectation that students and their families will make a significant contribution to the cost of higher education by shouldering part of the burden of tuition fees and living expenses. This policy has led to anxiety that students from poorer backgrounds, who are already under-represented, may be deterred from accepting a university place. Indeed, as discussed in Chapter 3, the danger of deterring poorer students was the main justification for the abolition of the graduate endowment in Scotland in 2007. However, we know very little about Scottish young people's views of this important issue, and whether their views are distinctively different from those of young people living in England.

This chapter begins with an overview of the literature on UK attitudes to tuition fees and student debt. It then draw[s] on interviews with young people in Scotland and England, undertaken as part of the ESRC project, to explore views of fees regimes in different parts of the UK, contrasting the attitudes and awareness of those from more and less socially advantaged backgrounds.

As described more fully in Appendix 1, interviews were conducted with 121 young people aged 14 to 19 from across Scotland and twenty-seven from the north of England (148 interviews in total). Most young people who agreed to be interviewed were planning to enter higher education, either via university or college routes. All interviewees were asked for the postcode of their family home, which was classified according to the Scottish Index of Multiple Deprivation

(SIMD) or the Income Deprivation Affecting Children Index (IDACI). SIMD and IDACI are measures of neighbourhood rather than individual deprivation, with 1 being the most deprived and 5 being the least deprived area. There is a strong association between individual and neighbourhood deprivation, although of course not all families living in areas of deprivation are low income and vice versa.

The chapter explores young people's views on the distribution of higher education costs between the individual student and the state, the association between social class background and attitudes to debt and the extent to which young people are aware of student finance arrangements in different parts of the UK.

PUBLIC ATTITUDES TO THE FUNDING OF HIGHER EDUCATION: MESSAGES FROM THE LITERATURE

Student Debt and Participation Rates

Since the publication of the Dearing and Garrick Reports in 1997, researchers have investigated the impact of growing levels of student debt on patterns of participation. In 2002 Callender and colleagues conducted a survey of more than 2,000 prospective students across the UK, using a stratified random sample of schools and colleges (Callender, 2003; Callender and Jackson, 2005; Callender and Jackson, 2008). The study found that students from lower social class backgrounds were more debt averse than those from other social classes, and were far more likely to be deterred from going to university because of fear of debt. Furthermore, fear of debt appeared to have a strong impact on the choices of students from lower social class backgrounds, causing them to apply to universities where they were likely to incur lower living costs and good term-time employment opportunities. However, fear of debt did not appear to influence their choice of qualification and subject. Students from low-income backgrounds were more likely to perceive the costs of higher education as a debt rather than an investment. Callender and Jackson (2005) concluded that Westminster government policy on student funding, predicated on the accumulation of debt, was likely to deter the very students at the heart of widening access policies. The challenge for government was to move from a model of student funding which actively deterred students from disadvantaged backgrounds, to one which had a positive impact on participation rates. This was likely to involve the targeting of financial support on those from low-income backgrounds via grants and bursaries.

Developing this analysis further, Dearden et al. (2011) used historical data to examine the combined impact of tuition fees and student support on rates of participation in the UK. Writing before the 2012 tuition fee increases, they noted that the UK had seen two dramatic changes to higher education finance, the first occurring in 1998 following the Dearing and Garrick Reports and the second taking place eight years later in 2006–7. Maintenance grants for the poorest students were also increased substantially at this time. Labour Force Survey data from 1992 to 2007 were used to examine the effect of these changes on entry to university. The study attempted to benchmark the combined impact of both fees and grants, and concluded that a £1,000 increase in tuition fees reduced university participation by 3.9 percentage points, while a £1,000 increase in maintenance grants increased participation by 2.6 percentage points. These findings, the researchers noted, are consistent with US studies using similar methods, but inevitably miss out some of the fine detail, including the relative impact of a cluster of support mechanisms (including means-tested bursaries) on students from different social class backgrounds. Furthermore, the study did not make cross-UK comparisons. It is noted that, following the decision to abolish tuition fees in 2000, Scotland would have provided an interesting point of comparison with the rest of the UK. However, the researchers argue, the introduction of the graduate endowment and grants at this point means that there was not a 'clean' policy change, making analysis difficult.

It should be noted that the majority of research exploring the link between student debt and participation rates has been undertaken in England. Within the Scottish context of free tuition for Scottish-/EU-domiciled students, the question of how the cost of higher education impacts on participation remains under-explored despite the fact that the majority of Scottish students take out maintenance loans and those from lower-income backgrounds incur the greatest debt.

Who Should Pay for Higher Education?

Despite the Scottish Government's abolition of tuition fees in 2000 and the graduate endowment in 2007, public attitudes towards the funding of higher education in Scotland and England are, perhaps surprisingly, broadly similar, with a majority in both countries believing that better-off individuals should make a contribution to the overall cost. Data from the Scottish and British Social Attitudes Survey (Curtice and Ormston, 2011; Curtice, 2014) show that in 2000 about a third of people (38 per cent of Scottish and 30 per cent of English respondents) agreed that no one should have to pay towards the cost of university tuition. By 2010 support for free tuition had fallen, with just 20 per cent of people in Scotland and 18 per cent of people in England believing that university education should be free for all students regardless of family income. In 2013 about two-thirds of both Scottish and English respondents supported the proposition that some students or their families should make a contribution towards the cost of tuition, depending on their financial circumstances. About a quarter of Scottish respondents believed that no student should pay (that is, the cost should be entirely borne by the state), and 8 per cent said that all should pay (ScotCen, 2013). Despite the strong political support for free tuition within the Scottish Government, this does not appear to be backed up by public attitudes. Indeed, in 2014, 38 per cent of those surveyed by Panelbase (2014) said that it was likely that in the next ten years students in Scotland would have to pay for university tuition. Just over a third (35 per cent) said that the introduction of tuition fees was unlikely, whilst 27 per cent were unsure.

Surveys of student attitudes reveal lower levels of support for tuition fees compared with public attitudes more generally. Purcell et al.'s *Futuretrack* survey (2008) found that just over half (54 per cent) of students agreed with the statement that 'students in higher education should contribute to its cost if they can afford to'. Young people in Scotland were less likely to agree that students should make a contribution compared with those in the rest of the UK. Scottish students were also more likely to disagree with the statement that 'student loans are a good idea' and that 'all universities should charge the same annual fees'.

Higher Education Policy and Family Finances

Relatively little attention has been paid to the impact of higher education policy changes on the private world of the family. As noted by West et al. (2015), the existence of means testing to determine access to various forms of student support assumes that parents are responsible for the financial maintenance of the student/child throughout their higher education. This contrasts with the situation in Sweden, where students are assumed to be financially independent of their parents, thus requiring support from the state rather than the family. Across the UK, Ahier observed, parental contributions to students' living expenses are 'based upon notions of what good parents are expected to contribute to their children's higher education' (Ahier, 2000: 686). Drawing on interviews with twenty-eight parent/student dyads, West et al. (2015) investigated the extent to which such support was occurring in practice and the impact of these financial assumptions on family relations. The study found that more affluent families felt responsibility for their children's financial situation, acting to avoid, minimise or cushion the debt. By way of contrast, less affluent families were unable to support their children, thus creating a new form of intra-generational inequality. Whilst Willetts (2010) has argued that those born after 1980 have been affected by new forms of inter-generational inequality, West et al. suggest that the picture is more complex, with those from more affluent backgrounds benefiting from the transfer of accumulated wealth from parents to children, whereas those from poorer backgrounds, without access to inherited wealth, experience both escalating inter- and intra-generational inequality.

Student Finance and the Growth of Consumerism in Higher Education

In the light of escalating student debt and the expectation that students will act as critical consumers, there is growing emphasis on access to reliable financial information by students and their families. Survey and interview studies have shown that many prospective students do not understand the full extent of study-related costs and the various forms of financial support to which they may be entitled (Hutchings, 2003; Christie and Munro, 2003; National Union of Students, 2009; Mangan et al., 2010). There is also some evidence that students from low-income families, who are most in need of reliable information, may be particularly poorly informed (Purcell et al., 2008; National Union of Students, 2009). In recognition of the new role of the student as the driver of the higher education market, since 2012 the consumer affairs organisation Which? has published annual reviews of the value for money of different universities and courses, based on a range of metrics including postgraduate employment rates and student satisfaction surveys

(Which?, 2014). The growing emphasis within UK universities on 'the student experience' indicates the extent to which the ideology of consumerism is now firmly embedded.

To summarise, young people, particularly those from low-income families, report negative attitudes to tuition fees, but paradoxically this is not reflected in the increase in student numbers, including the growing proportion of those from less socially advantaged backgrounds. Some qualitative data suggest that middle-class families are likely to provide significant levels of financial support to their offspring during their university years, in contrast to lower-income families who are less able to support their children. This suggests that the growth in student debt is likely to have a particularly adverse effect on those from poorer backgrounds, exacerbating intra-generational as well as inter-generational inequality. Young people and their families, particularly those with fewer economic resources, tend to be poorly informed about tuition fees and student support. Despite escalating levels of student debt, about two-thirds of people in Scotland and England appear to support the principle that, depending on their financial circumstances, students and their families should contribute to the cost of higher education. Students, on the other hand, are fairly evenly divided between those who believe that the state should bear the cost of higher education and those who think that individual beneficiaries should contribute to the cost. Scottish students are less likely to endorse the idea of a student financial contribution compared with those in the rest of the UK. In the following sections, I outline findings from the ESRC project on the attitudes of young people in Scotland and the north of England towards the funding of higher education.

FINDINGS FROM STUDENT INTERVIEWS

Young People's Views of Higher Education Funding Policy

Young people in Scotland and the north of England expressed different views with regard to whether students should be expected to contribute to the cost of higher education. The majority of Scottish interviewees (around three-quarters) believed tuition should be free for all with funding provided entirely by the state, while the majority of English interviewees supported the principle that students should contribute towards the costs of higher education.

Scottish interviewees were supportive of government policy, perceiving free tuition as a means of ensuring participation by young people from low-income backgrounds. In both Scotland and, to a lesser extent, the north of England, interviewees saw higher education as 'a right, not a privilege' because of its capacity to improve life chances and assist social mobility. Young people pointed out that a growing number of jobs required degree-level qualifications and the state should ensure that labour market needs were addressed.

Young people in Scotland suggested that prospective students in England, especially those from disadvantaged backgrounds, might be deterred from participating in higher education by tuition fees and the fear of greater debt. Young people from low-income families commented that without free tuition they would not have applied to university. Steven from Glasgow said:

> It's easier for us because we've got the tuition fees covered. But if I was going down to study in England, the tuition fees would definitely put me off because I'm no' in a financial situation where I could afford it. I know you can take loans and all that. But it's the tuition fees that you receive here, it makes your life easier in the future 'cause you don't have to pay back all these loans and have debt on your shoulders. (Steven, 16, SIMD 1, Scotland)

Young people's views of who should pay for higher education were informed by ideas of 'fairness'. There was a strong view that everyone should be treated 'the same' or 'equally' regardless of their background. Consequently, many interviewees in both countries believed that it would be 'unfair' to charge pupils from better-off families if others were exempt from tuition fees. Others believed that student support should be redistributive, so those from higher-income families should pay more. Some young people, particularly those from the most deprived neighbourhoods, suggested that it would be 'fairer' if those from richer backgrounds were asked to contribute so that higher education tuition remains free for the poorest. Similarly, and perhaps more surprisingly, some of those from more advantaged areas also believed that the better off should pay:

> I think it's a good system [free tuition in Scotland] but whether I agree with it is different because I feel that there are some people out there who could definitely easily pay for higher education. If they keep taking money off the government to go to the university then eventually they might have to stop because we can't fund it. And that would be a shame because then all of a sudden you're going back to the previous [situation] where only the rich could go to university. (Ross, 16, SIMD 4, Scotland)

In contrast, interviewees in the north of England were more likely to believe that all students should contribute to the cost of tuition and regard it as an 'investment'. They emphasised the individual benefits of higher education, referring to the graduate premium for example, with little recognition of the wider social benefits. Harry, from a deprived area in the north-west of England, said he supported tuition fees because 'it's your choice to go to university', noting that 'if you want a job that's a bit higher qualified you should have to pay for it'. Another pupil, David, who lived in an area of high deprivation in the north-east, said 'it's like an investment into your future. The more you spend on your tuition, the more it should return'. Many interviewees in England, and to a lesser extent Scotland, felt that students were more likely to value a university degree if they had contributed to its cost. They believed that students should use their time wisely and not 'waste time' with degrees which might not lead to employment. A number of interviewees in the north of England felt great pressure to do well at university given the debt they were accruing, while some Scottish interviewees said free tuition encouraged young people to go to university 'for the sake of it'. This was seen as particularly likely where young people studied non-vocational subjects:

I feel like some people don't necessarily really want to go to university. And they don't know what they'd study but they'd feel like they should, and then they end up going. And especially when it's free tuition fees, it's almost a waste of money cause they either drop out and once they've finished they don't do anything related to that or they don't really get a job that's benefited from them having that degree. (Christina, 17, SIMD 4, Scotland)

A report based on a University Lifestyle Survey (Sodexo, 2014) stated that 'students in Scotland are less job-focused when choosing their course than those at English institutions – an idealistic streak arguably linked to the absence of tuition fees for Scottish residents'. However, Scottish interviewees in this study had a strong focus on finding employment after university and both English and Scottish students described higher education in instrumental terms. These utilitarian attitudes may be indicative of a wider cultural shift not necessarily related to the payment of fees.

The majority of young people regarded gaining a degree as a route to employment, and were concerned about graduate employment opportunities, particularly in light of higher education expansion and credential inflation. This led a sixth form student from the north of England to argue that charging tuition fees retains an element of 'elitism', ensuring degrees retain their value in the labour market.

Amongst those who supported the principle of tuition fees, there was a general view that the current fees level of £9,000 a year was too high. Instead, £3,000–£4,000 a year was seen to be more manageable and unlikely to deter prospective students. Some English interviewees expressed anger at the trebling of fees in 2012, questioning its necessity. They called for greater transparency in showing how the fees were used by universities, suggesting that young people are increasingly embracing the role of consumer and demanding better information on how funds are being spent. This change was noted by John, a working-class pupil from the north-east, who argued that the rise in fees has meant universities are now much more like businesses where 'the product's the education'. In his view, 'university is becoming a luxury [. . .] for people with more money'.

Understandings of Student Finance

In both England and Scotland, understandings of student finance, including arrangements for loan repayments, were sketchy, particularly amongst those from more deprived areas who were likely to be the first in their family to go to university. Scottish young people believed that in England tuition fees were paid upfront, and they were unaware of the different loan repayment thresholds. While understanding was somewhat better in England, pupils nonetheless had poor knowledge of grants and bursaries available to them.

In both countries, young people had little understanding of the costs of studying outside their country of residence and struggled to understand why funding systems across the UK were so widely different. They were aware that tuition was free in Scotland for Scottish students whilst those from the rest of the UK had to pay. However, few interviewees in either country realised that tuition was also free for students from the European Union studying in Scotland. On hearing that this was the case, they expressed surprise:

> It's a bit annoying because why do Scottish citizens get it free and we don't when we're in the same country? What makes Scottish [students] special, and we have to pay? And especially with EU students coming across, how come they don't have to pay and we do? Are we paying for them? I'm not sure how it works. (John, 17, IDACI 1, England)

A minority of Scottish interviewees sympathised with the rationale behind the policy and suggested that if tuition in Scotland was free for students from the rest of the UK then it might threaten Scottish students' places:

> I think it's quite good that people from England that come up have to pay because I think it sort of discourages them from just coming up because it's free up here, which means there's more places for Scottish people. (Graham, 16, SIMD 1, Scotland)

In the following sections, I categorise Scottish and English students' attitudes towards debt.

Scottish Students' Attitudes to Debt

Despite the fact that free tuition means that the average level of debt in Scotland is significantly lower than in the rest of the UK, the majority of Scottish interviewees could be categorised as debt averse. They were apprehensive about getting into debt, feeling 'worried', 'daunted', 'stressed' and 'scared' by it. Many said they would take out loans only as a 'last resort', and planned to avoid student loans either completely or by keeping their debt to a minimum.

Students who planned to avoid debt tended to come from families with intermediate or lower occupational backgrounds where neither parent had been to university and were living in the most deprived neighbourhoods. These young people intended to avoid loans by attending a local university and living at home to avoid the costs of accommodation. They planned to work part-time during term time and anticipated some family financial support. Data from the Department for Business, Innovation and Skills confirm that more than 50 per cent of Scottish-domiciled students live at home (compared with 30 per cent of other UK students) and that these students are more likely to come from lower-income families (Department for Business, Innovation and Skills, 2014). They may prioritise minimising debt over obtaining a degree from a higher-status institution, which might lead to a higher-paying job in the long term. For example, Joanne was a first-generation entrant who had applied to study at a local post-92 institution and intended to live at home while studying. Her father was self-employed whilst her mother did not work outside the home. She saw university as a route to employment and had carefully investigated which degree would bring the best employment outcomes:

> The [benefits] have to [outweigh the costs] because . . . jobs are so tight at the moment I think this is the only way you're going to get a good job. (Joanne, 17, SIMD 2, Scotland)

She planned to live at home while studying and hoped that by relying on family support she could avoid taking out a student loan. Her family was a key influence on her plans and on her attitude towards debt:

> My family, they don't see the idea of student loans and getting into debt at the end of it, so it's just that if you stay at home you've got a lesser chance and it's going to be a minimal [loan] even if you do have to get a debt or whatever. We've got the facilities here to be able to stay here so if you have the opportunity why not stay here instead of moving away and getting just the same education? (Joanne, 17, SIMD 2, Scotland)

Some debt avoiders in Scotland came from higher-earning families and planned to rely almost entirely on family support to cover the costs of going to university. These pupils tended to come from managerial and professional backgrounds and from the most affluent SIMD neighbourhoods. In contrast to those who intended to live at home to reduce costs, these young people planned to move away from home but remain in Scotland, with parents and other family members agreeing to cover substantial amounts or all of their living costs. Some independent school pupils spoke of the benefits of studying in Scotland rather than England because they would not incur any student debt as a result. Other pupils from state schools explained that their parents or extended family members had been saving towards the costs of them going to university for some time, and that this would allow them to avoid or reduce the amount of debt they would incur. One pupil planned to take out a student loan but place the funds in a savings account as her family had said that they would support her through university. Another pupil's parents were so keen for their children to avoid student debt that they had taken out commercial loans to support them through university, although this was likely to be a poor financial choice because of relatively high interest rates.

Possibly as a result of their disinclination to take out student loans, most Scottish students were unaware of how the repayment system operated. Christina, who planned to study at an ancient university, was unusual in understanding that student loans attracted interest:

> And it compounds interest 'cause that's what I'd worry about, 'cause what if you can't pay it off for ages, but then suddenly you can? Like, not so long that it gets cancelled or whatever, but I don't know how much you're going to end up owing, 'cause it depends how much time you take [to repay]. So . . . I'd like to avoid it if I can. (Christina, 17, SIMD 4, Scotland)

The third group of Scottish interviewees were more relaxed about student debt and pointed to the benefits of having loans to support them through their studies. They tended to have more realistic estimates of levels of debt they might incur and a better understanding of the student finance system. Most of the pupils in this group came from managerial and professional backgrounds and lived mainly in the least deprived SIMD quintiles. They also tended to come from families where parents or siblings had been to university and therefore had prior knowledge of the loan system, leading them to believe that debt repayment would be manageable. Like English students, they were able to distinguish between low-interest student debt and 'real' or commercial debt and believed that student debt should be seen as an 'investment'.

By way of illustration, Lucy, 17, came from a managerial and professional background and lived in the most affluent SIMD quintile. Her mother had been to university as had her siblings. She planned to study at a Russell Group university in England and estimated she would incur debts of £45,000 which would include tuition fee loans and maintenance loans. Lucy believed students should contribute something towards the costs of going to university:

> I feel everyone's saying 'oh my goodness, it's £9,000 a year' but . . . English students have no problem with that, I have English cousins, they have no problem. It's not that big a deal 'cause everyone has to do it. I don't see why it should be such a big deal for me. If they can cope doing that and we worked it out that actually a lot of people see it as a debt, but if you look at it as just an extra tax of about £30 a month, once you're earning over £22,000 [in fact, the repayment threshold at that time was £16,910], £30 a month just over the course of your life is not [that great] . . . Everyone's expecting that you have to pay the £9,000 there and then, but if you do it in a sensible way then I don't feel it's any different than if I was going to a Scottish university. (Lucy, 17, SIMD 5, Scotland)

English Students' Attitudes to Debt

Interviewees in the north of England were on the whole less debt averse than their Scottish counterparts, despite average debt in England being substantially higher than in Scotland. Young people acknowledged the inevitability of taking out student loans, and saw it as a necessary aspect of student life. Some, however, were more resistant to this idea than others. The following paragraphs illustrate the range of attitudes amongst this group of students.

The majority of interviewees in the north of England, many of whom came from working-class backgrounds, were resigned to student debt and their views could be characterised as 'pragmatic acceptance' (Brennan et al., 2005). When asked how they felt about the debt, young people frequently replied 'I'm not bothered'. They recognised the need to get a degree and were determined to go to university whatever the cost. While worries were expressed about the level of debt they would incur, these concerns were outweighed by optimism about future employment prospects, the graduate salary premium and the chance to study a subject they loved. Fears about debt were also allayed by an understanding of the tuition fee and student loan system. Interviewees were reassured by the income contingent nature of debt repayment and the fact that the debt would be cancelled after thirty years. Some interviewees believed that they would never have to repay their loan in full.

Despite this, few young people were able to estimate the level of debt they would have when they graduated, and frequently said 'I don't want to think about it'. Additionally, some did not know what fees were charged by the universities they had applied to and were not interested in 'shopping around' to find the best value for money. Choice of higher education institution was based on reputation of the institution and course, as well as distance from home. A number of interviewees were likely to have been entitled to grants, but few had investigated eligibility and the extent to which a grant or bursary would reduce the funds they would need to borrow to cover living expenses.

Mark, 19, was a working-class pupil living in the most deprived IDACI quintile and was the first member of his family to go to university. He had originally chosen Medicine but had failed to achieve high enough AS Level grades and therefore planned to study Biomedical Science at a Russell Group university with a view to transferring to Medicine at a later point. He estimated that he might leave university with a debt of up to £100,000:

> if I was to stay in England, if I was to do Biomedical Science and then Medicine, it would probably be approaching £100,000. I seem to take it considerably less seriously than my friends do, in that it doesn't go on my credit record, and it's just going to be a bit of money each month. [. . .] Yeah perhaps I'm just being naive. But I'm trying to avoid worrying about it because I don't think it's going to have too much effect. (Mark, IDACI 1, England)

His concerns were mitigated by the monthly repayments which would reflect his income:

> I wasn't too bothered about [the loan] because it'll get paid off gradually over decades . . . some people liken it to student tax. It's just going to be a little thing that I don't see every month – so not really. Although I am slightly envious of Scottish people who don't pay anything. (Mark, 19, IDACI 1, England)

A minority of interviewees in the north of England were resigned to the idea of taking out a student loan, but were much more concerned about the level of debt at the end of university and the long-term consequences. Interviewees within this group expressed anger at the level of tuition fees and the fact that they had increased so dramatically in a short space of time. They were much more likely to think about the longer-term problems they might face from having such large amounts of student debt, and consequently questioned the value of going to university. These interviewees tended to be from middle-income families and were ineligible for means-tested grants and bursaries. On the other hand, they felt unable to rely on their parents for financial help. They were highly critical of coalition reforms of A-levels which they believed would impact negatively on widening access efforts, and knew of people who had decided against going to university because of tuition fees.

These young people were well informed about fees and student loans. Reflecting the views of those who said they were 'not bothered' about debt, John (18, IDACI 2) suggested that young people were going to university without considering the consequences of such high debt. Working on the basis that he would owe a baseline figure of £40,000 (three years' fees at £27,000 plus £13,000 maintenance) he estimated the final amount he would have to repay would be around £120,000. He said, 'nobody really knows. To be honest we don't know how much debt we're going to be in. [It's hard to work out] because the interest rates go up all the time'.

Such worries encouraged some interviewees to apply for vocational subjects such as Nursing, where bursaries covered tuition fees, or to seek an apprenticeship. For example, Aalya (18, IDACI 4) had opted to study an NHS-affiliated degree, meaning she would not have to pay fees. However, her parents, neither of whom had been to university, were very worried about student debt and encouraged her to get a higher-level engineering apprenticeship instead. She shared their misgivings about repaying student debt:

> It's worrying, and I feel genuinely scared. I know they say that it won't affect your mortgage or anything like your credit notes and stuff, but for me it's just that . . . yeah if you ever fell behind with any of your payments, what's the interest that's going to come on it? How long will they be paying it for? [. . .] For us it will go on until we have retired. (Aalya, 18, IDACI 4, England)

Aalya also worried about the saturated graduate labour market, an issue raised by the majority of Scottish and English interviewees. In Aalya's case, this led her to conclude, 'So I just think sometimes, is a degree really worth it? There are always doubts in my mind about going to uni'.

CONCLUSION

Drawing on interviews with prospective students in Scotland and England, this chapter explored views of the funding of higher education, as well as individual attitudes to student debt and knowledge of the operation of the funding system both north and south of the border. Overall, Scottish interviewees were supportive of free tuition but had concerns about its sustainability, leading some to suggest that those from the most affluent backgrounds should contribute to the cost of higher education. Young people in the north of England questioned the trebling of tuition fees but on the whole accepted the principle of student contributions. In both England and Scotland, interviewees expressed concern that tuition fees might deter young people from poorer backgrounds from going to university.

The young people interviewed in England have grown up in an era of tuition fees and have clearly internalised the message that higher education delivers private benefits, and as a result individuals are expected to contribute to its cost. Little mention was made of the wider social benefits of higher education. The extent to which young people were prepared to adopt the role of critical consumers, as envisaged by the government, was a moot point. Young people from poorer backgrounds had not yet investigated the means-tested grants and bursaries which might be available, but were setting their sights on local higher education options to reduce costs. The cost of tuition appeared to be less of a concern for students from wealthier backgrounds, most of whom were aware of the greater labour market value of degrees from higher-status institutions. Overall, English students seemed to have decided that there is 'no point worrying' about recent fees increases, with many expecting that they would not have to pay back their debt in full. The future impact of emerging from university with very high financial liabilities was clearly not a cause for worry at this point in their lives. However, the 'Class of 2012' is clearly a guinea pig generation, for whom the cumulative impact of high housing costs and tuition fees, coupled with a diminishing graduate premium, is unknown (Brown et al., 2012).

Many Scottish interviewees, especially those from lower socioeconomic backgrounds, intended to avoid student debt as far as possible. Despite Scotland's policy of free higher education tuition, student finance plays a significant role in determining Scottish young people's choice of university, with students from disadvantaged backgrounds favouring local institutions on cost grounds. This presents something of a paradox, since free tuition seems to have made Scottish young people more, not less, debt averse. Some of the young people interviewed in Scotland had not yet applied to university and said that they intended to research higher education in greater depth. However, even those who had already been offered a place were still vague about student finance.

Closely linked to debt aversion among the Scottish interviewees was a poor understanding of the real costs and benefits of going to university. Although reluctant to contemplate taking out a loan, as discussed in Chapter 3, 67 per cent of Scottish students do so (rising to 87 per cent among those from families with incomes of less than £10,000). There is clearly a gap between Scottish students' aspirations of emerging from university without debt and the reality of being compelled to do so to meet living costs (NUS, 2009). Interviewees noted that little information was provided about the practicalities of going to, and paying for, university or college, and that often this information was provided after applications were made to UCAS. If pupils are to make informed decisions about their future, such information needs to be improved, provided sooner and possibly targeted at those from lower-income backgrounds.

In Chapter 3, Hunter Blackburn shows that in Scotland students from families with lower incomes take on the greatest levels of debt, although the interviews discussed in this chapter show that debt aversion was greatest among this group. This study focused on those who had decided to apply to university, but there are also important questions around which students are cooled out of higher education at an earlier stage because of the prospect of debt. While these issues are beginning to be explored in the English literature, the question of student debt has been ignored in Scotland because it is assumed that the abolition of tuition fees has obviated the need for such a discussion. The points raised by young people in this chapter suggest that, far from being settled, student debt in Scotland remains a serious issue, with fear of debt having a major impact on many young people's higher education decisions. A much wider debate on student debt in Scotland is sorely needed.

REFERENCES

Ahier, J. (2000), 'Financing higher education by loans and fees: theorizing and researching the private effects of public policy', *Journal of Education Policy*, 15: 6, 683–700.

Brennan, D., C. Little and V. Dyke (2005), *Survey of Higher Education Students' Attitudes to Debt and Term Time Working and their Impact on Attainment*, Bristol: HEFCE.

Brown, P., H. Lauder and D. Ashton (2012), *The Global Auction: The Broken Promises of Education, Jobs and Income*, Oxford: Oxford University Press.

Callender, C. (2003), *Attitudes to Debt: School Leavers' and Further Education Students' Attitudes to Debt and their Impact on Participation in Higher Education*, London: Universities UK.

Callender, C. and J. Jackson (2005), 'Does the fear of debt deter students from higher education?', DOI: 10.1017/S004727940500913X, *Journal of Social Policy*, 34: 4, 509–40.

Callender, C. and J. Jackson (2008), 'Does the fear of debt constrain choice of university and subject of study?', DOI: 10.1080/03075070802211802, *Studies in Higher Education*, 33: 4, 405–29.

Christie, H. and M. Munro (2003), 'The logic of loans: students' perceptions of the costs and benefits of the student loan', *British Journal of Sociology of Education*, 24: 5, 621–36.

Curtice, J. (2014), 'John Curtice: free tuition far from popular', *The Scotsman*, 26 August 2014, http://www.scotsman.com/news/john-curtice-tuition-fee-policy-far-from-pop ular-1-3521000 (accessed 10 March 2015).

Curtice, J. and R. Ormston (2011), 'Is Scotland more left-wing than England?', *British Social Attitudes 28, Special Edition*, No. 42, 5 December 2011.

Dearden, L., E. Fitzsimons and G. Wyness (2011), *Impact of Tuition Fees and Support on University Participation in the UK*, London: Centre for the Economics of Education, London School of Economics and Political Science (LSE).

Department for Business, Innovation and Skills (BIS) (2014), *Learning from Futuretrack: Studying and Living at Home*. BIS Research Paper No. 167, London: BIS.

Hutchings, M. (2003), 'Information, advice and cultural discourses of higher education', in L. Archer, M. Hutchings and A. Ross (eds), *Higher Education and Social Class*, London: RoutledgeFalmer.

Mangan, J., A. Hughes and K. Slack (2010), 'Student finance, information and decision-making', DOI 10.1007/s10734-010-9309-7, *Higher Education*, 60: 5, 459–72.

National Committee of Inquiry into Higher Education (1997), *Higher Education in the Learning Society: Report of the Scottish Committee*, London: Her Majesty's Stationery Office.

National Union of Students (NUS) Scotland (2009), *Mind the Gap: A Survey of First-year Students' Financial Expectations*, Edinburgh: NUS.

Panelbase (2014), *Panelbase Online Survey for Wings Over Scotland with 1,046 Respondents, 16 and Older, 8–14 May 2014: Do you think it is likely that in the next 10 years students in Scotland will have to pay towards university tuition?*, http://www.panelbase.com/media/polls/F4108WingsoverScotland210514.pdf (accessed 21 April 2015).

Purcell, K., P. Elias, R. Ellison, G. Atfield, D. Adam and I. Livanos (2008), *Applying for Higher Education – the Diversity of Career Choices, Plans and Expectations: Findings from the First Futuretrack Survey of the 'Class of 2006' Applicants for Higher Education*, Manchester: Futuretrack.

Raffe, D. and L. Croxford (2015), 'How stable is the stratification of higher education in Scotland and England?', *British Journal of Sociology of Education*, 36: 2, 313–35.

ScotCen (2013), *Scottish Social Attitudes Survey*, Edinburgh: ScotCen Social Research, http://whatscotlandthinks.org/questions/who-should-pay-towards-the-costs-of-stud ents-tuition-4#bar (accessed 10 March 2015).

Sodexo (2014), *The Sodexo University Lifestyle Survey 2014*, Sodexo and Times Higher Education, London: Sodexo.

West, A., J. Roberts, J. Lewis and P. Noden (2015), 'Paying for higher education in England: funding policy and families', *British Journal of Educational Studies*, 63: 1, 23–45.

Which? (2014), *A Degree of Value: Value for Money from the Student Perspective*, London: Which?.

Willetts, D. (2010), The Pinch: How the Baby Boomers Took their Children's Future, London: Atlantic Books.

5

Cross-border Flows of Students within the UK

Susan Whittaker, David Raffe and Linda Croxford

INTRODUCTION: WHY DO CROSS-BORDER FLOWS MATTER?

Around one in fourteen UK residents who enter full-time undergraduate courses move to a different home country of the UK to do so. In this chapter we examine the types of students who move, their reasons for doing so, and the trends and patterns of what we shall call 'cross-border flows'. We also reflect on the ways in which devolution and related changes have influenced these flows. We start by considering why cross-border flows matter.

First, they matter for students and institutions. They allow students to access a wider range of higher education courses than may be available within the home country. They may provide educational benefits, broadening the horizons of the students who move. They may also benefit the institutions which these students enter, and the other students who attend them, by increasing the diversity of the student body. However, they thereby raise questions of fairness and equality of access. Many students may lack the resources, knowledge and confidence to consider and take up opportunities in a part of the UK in which they are not normally resident. Conversely some students, especially from Northern Ireland, may have to be mobile in order to access higher education (HE) at all. And if institutions only attract a socially unrepresentative group of students from the rest of the UK (rUK students), the benefits in terms of student diversity will be lost. Even when rUK students do enhance the diversity of institutions' intakes, the benefits are not spread equally across institutions, some of which attract much higher proportions of rUK students than others.

Cross-border flows also matter to governments, and especially the devolved administrations, where they account for a much larger proportion of total student numbers than for England. They have implications for the supply of skilled manpower: students who leave the home country to study may not return when they have qualified. They have implications for the resourcing of universities and for the sustainability of the devolved administrations' diverging funding arrangements.

The devolved administrations have not increased fees for their own students to the same extent as in England, but they have charged English-level fees for rUK students and the fee income from these students has helped to alleviate funding pressures. Conversely, the devolved administrations may incur extra costs if (as in Wales at the time of writing) they wish to preserve the options for their own students by subsidising the higher costs of study elsewhere in the UK. The devolved administrations also wish to avoid large fluctuations in cross-border flows in order to protect the viability of their own institutions and to maintain sufficient places for home students. They may do this by taking rUK students out of the student number cap, and by not allowing their country to be a cheaper option for students from England, the home country of the vast majority of UK students.

Finally, cross-border flows matter in the context of devolution and constitutional change within the UK. To the extent that devolution has encouraged the development of distinct higher education systems in the four home countries, and accentuated the borders between them, cross-border flows have become more significant. Cross-border flows illustrate the continued interdependence of the four systems, and of the ways in which policy decisions in one jurisdiction may impact on the others.

Cross-border flows have been influenced by devolution, or by the divergent policies pursued by England and the devolved administrations, which have changed the opportunities and incentives to cross borders. Changes in tuition fees have sometimes created additional incentives to study in the home country. Divergent policies for the school curriculum and qualifications may have made it harder to access higher education elsewhere in the UK compared with the home country. The devolved administrations have encouraged their higher education institutions to adopt a lifelong-learning perspective which encourages greater coherence between universities and other educational sectors; this may have made pathways to higher education smoother for students who remain within the home country, but more problematic for those who cross borders. And policy decisions since devolution may have changed other factors which influence cross-border flows, such as the supply of higher education places and their distribution across institutions and subjects, the information and guidance for potential applicants, and programmes to promote access and participation led by local institutions. Finally, devolution may have influenced the national identities of students, or even the strength of ethnic and family ties, which themselves have shaped cross-border flows.

In this chapter, therefore, we address a series of questions that arise from these issues. How do students make choices about where to study? What are the patterns and trends of cross-border flows within the UK? Which types of students cross borders, and what purposes might this serve for them? Do cross-border flows contribute to inequalities in higher education? Have fee differentials, and the 2012 fee changes, had an impact? How have cross-border flows been affected by devolution, and how might they be affected by any further constitutional change? To answer these questions we draw on reviews of the literature, on interviews with potential future students in England and Scotland conducted as part of the ESRC project, and on analyses of Higher Education Statistics Agency (HESA) data on entrants to undergraduate courses in UK higher education institutions. Further details of these sources and our analyses are provided by Croxford and Raffe (2014a; 2014b) and Whittaker (2014); Minty (2014) documents the young people's interviews. The HESA analyses are restricted to young entrants (aged under 21), for whom the widest range and most complete set of data were available. We present data for selected years since 1996, but we focus on 2012 entrants, the first cohort affected by the most recent increase in tuition fees in England.

HOW DO STUDENTS MAKE CHOICES ABOUT WHERE TO STUDY?

Applicants considering what to study and where are influenced by a number of factors, including their social background, finances, family, school background and qualifications. These shape applicants' views about what they want to do, but also about which options are possible for them. Students from all backgrounds may practise 'self-exclusion' – ruling out options – but with differing effects. For example, Ball et al. (2002) found that those who prioritised choice of institution by where they would fit, culturally and/or ethnically, and who considered their family and home life important, were the least likely to apply to high-tariff institutions. Students from low-income families are more sensitive to distance (Gibbons and Vignoles, 2009) and more likely to stay in the family home as a student (Davies et al., 2008; Forsyth and Furlong, 2003; Holdsworth, 2009; Purcell et al., 2008) (as also discussed by Minty in Chapter 4). On the other hand, middle-class pupils with a family history of higher education are more likely to wish to study a long distance from home (Belfield and Morris, 1999; Gibbons and Vignoles, 2009) as are those applying to Russell Group universities (Purcell et al., 2008), those from independent schools and those with higher GCSE scores (Davies et al., 2008). Aggregate differences in institution type and location entered have also been found in relation to different ethnic groups (Connor et al., 2004; Gibbons and Vignoles, 2009; Shiner and Modood, 2002).

While there is plenty of research on student choice and participation in higher education, fewer studies have explored this in relation to cross-border movement within the UK (examples are Bond et al., 2010; Fitz et al., 2005; Hinton, 2011; Osborne, 2001, 2006; Pollak, 2012; Purcell et al., 2006). Probably the most detailed study is Osborne's (2001, 2006) research with Northern Irish students. He identified 'determined leavers' as predominantly middle-class students attending older universities in northern England and Scotland which they perceived as 'better' than the ones in Northern Ireland, providing new experiences and better graduate job opportunities. He also identified 'reluctant leavers' who would not have chosen to leave Northern Ireland but for lack of places, and who were more likely to be from intermediate- and working-class backgrounds.

The qualitative research with school pupils, which formed a strand of the ESRC project, provides additional data on the factors in choice, and specifically on views on cross-border mobility. The Scottish interviewees showed little interest in studying outside Scotland. Their main reason was to avoid tuition fees, but many felt that the quality of Scottish universities was high and did not require them to leave, unless for an experience they could not get in Scotland, such as access to Oxbridge. There was little appetite to leave Scotland even if there had not been a fee differential. Most interviewees wanted to stay close to home and retain family ties. The English interviewees lived in the north of England; they did not consider it unusual to apply to a Scottish university, particularly on the basis of its institutional reputation, but they were less likely to take up an offer than from an English university. A few students were put off by the four-year degree in Scotland, not due to the cost of an additional year of study, but because of concerns about whether they would be challenged in the first year of undergraduate study. Within the sample of interviewees there was evidence of a complexity of factors related to finances, social background, geography, psychology, policy and issues of institutional reputation and subject access (Minty, unpublished). This range and complexity of factors is supported in the wider range of available qualitative and quantitative research (summarised in Whittaker, 2014).

Somewhat different perspectives on student choice are provided by the current policy rhetoric, especially in England, which presents higher education as a market (Browne, 2010; Department for Business, Innovation and Skills, 2011), and by sociological analyses of higher education as a factor in positional competition. In the market model, students act as both consumers and investors. In their role as consumers they anticipate immediate gains from the experience of higher education, and as investors they hope for longer-term gains, if the higher education experience and credentials gained can be converted after graduation into increased future earnings and improved employability. Both roles require that students are able to make informed choices and seek to maximise their utility as consumers and their returns as investors. The applicability of market models has been questioned (Marginson, 2013), and in practice information is not evenly accessed, understood and given equal importance by all applicants (Naidoo et al., 2011).

Theories of positional competition assume that a hierarchy of institutions and programmes exists within higher education, that some students understand this hierarchy and seek to assure their place near the top through tactical decision-making which can result in conflict as students seek to gain positional advantage. Students and institutions play a 'matching game' (Brown, 2013; Marginson, 2006). One tactic uses geographical mobility to access elite higher education institutions or courses that can help to maintain or achieve positional status, and this tactic is likely to be more available for those already in a relatively privileged position. Choice of location, and a decision that requires mobility, may then serve consumption, investment or positional purposes, or a combination of these, for different groups of students.

WHAT ARE THE PATTERNS AND TRENDS OF CROSS-BORDER FLOWS WITHIN THE UK?

We build on earlier research (Raffe and Croxford, 2013) which analysed cross-border flows up until 2010. This showed that the proportion of students crossing internal borders to study had declined, albeit unevenly, since devolution.

Cross-border study was associated with the educational, social and ethnic backgrounds of students, although some of these associations varied across students from different home countries. However, the characteristics of cross-border movers did not change much in the period 1996–2010. Movers were more likely to enter higher-status institutions, but this too varied according to country of domicile and the largest flow in terms of absolute numbers was to post-1992 institutions in England. There was similar complexity relating to the subjects taken by movers and stayers, which partly reflected the varying balance of supply and demand for each subject within countries. The research concluded that UK higher education had not become a 'two-tier structure in which advantaged students and elite universities inhabit a UK-wide system and other students and institutions inhabit more narrowly bounded systems' (Raffe and Croxford, 2013: 132). In this chapter we provide overarching findings and key points regarding cross-border flows in the following years, 2011 and 2012.

Institutions and Subjects

In 2011 and 2012 about 7 per cent of full-time first-degree students domiciled in the UK moved to another home country of the UK to study. This proportion varied widely across the four home countries, as did inflows of students into each country. Cross-border mobility was far more common for young full-time entrants from Wales and Northern Ireland than from Scotland and England (Croxford and Raffe, 2014a), and this had been the case since before devolution (see Table 5.1). However the proportions of rUK students studying at institutions in each home country tell a different story: Wales had by far the highest proportion of 'movers-in', followed by Scotland, and with England and Northern Ireland far behind.

Destinations of Welsh and Northern Irish Movers-out

About 40 per cent of Welsh entrants and a third of Northern Irish entrants left their home country in 2012, mostly to go to higher education institutions in England. The Welsh movers mainly went to the south-west or north-west of England, and Northern Irish movers mainly went to cities in northern England or Scotland. More Welsh movers than stayers entered Russell Group universities, but Welsh movers together with Northern Irish movers were also more likely to enter post-1992 institutions (see Table 5.2). This is partly because most movers from these countries went to England, the home country with the highest proportion of post-1992 universities. This did not change after 2010. The fee difference and higher cost of moving for Northern Irish students in 2012 did not lead to more concentration in the universities with the highest and most selective entry levels ('higher-tariff' universities). Students did not increasingly use mobility to gain the positional status that going to a higher-tariff university could bring.

Table 5.1 Movers-out as percentage of young full-time entrants by home country of domicile, and movers-in as percentage of young full-time entrants by home country of institution, by year of entry

	1996	2004	2010	2011	2012
Movers-out, by country of domicile					
England	6	5	4	4	5
Scotland	8	7	6	6	5
Wales	48	39	34	36	42
Northern Ireland	42	29	32	35	31
Movers-in, by location of higher education institution					
England	5	4	3	3	4
Scotland	21	17	14	14	17
Wales	55	46	47	51	49
Northern Ireland	2	1	2	3	3

Source: Higher Education Statistics Agency Student Record, 2012–13. Copyright Higher Education Statistics Agency Limited, 2013

Destinations of Scottish and English Movers-out

Most Scottish- and English-domiciled students (around 95 per cent) studied in their home country. Even those who applied to institutions in another country were more likely to enter an institution in their own country; applications to other countries were often fallback or aspirational options (Raffe and Croxford, 2013; Wakeling and Jeffries, 2013; Minty, unpublished).

Scottish-domiciled movers were spread across some 120 different institutions outside of Scotland in 2012, but a relatively small number of institutions, including nine Russell Group universities, accounted for half of movers. These had a wide geographical spread around England. Scottish movers were more likely to move to higher-tariff universities than was the case for Welsh and Northern Irish movers. The most popular universities with movers also included two post-1992 universities located close to Scotland's border and one specialist university in London. Those entering lower-tariff institutions were likely to enter an institution close to Scotland.

By far the largest number of movers were English-domiciled, reflecting the vastly higher number of English-domiciled students overall. They entered around thirty different higher education institutions outside England, a much smaller number than for the movers from other countries reflecting the smaller scale of the non-English higher education sectors. Eight of these institutions, six in Wales and two in Scotland, accounted for 90 per cent of movers. Three were higher-tariff universities (Russell Group or ancient Scottish university), three were pre-1992 universities and two were post-1992 universities. A single university accounted for a fifth of all English movers.

English- and Scottish-domiciled movers were more likely than stayers to enter older, higher-status institutions (see Table 5.2). Movers were even more likely to enter higher-status institutions after the 2012 fee changes. The proportion of English movers entering Russell Group universities rose in 2012; more Scottish movers entered Oxford or Cambridge, but this was balanced by a fall in the proportion entering other Russell Group universities. This suggests that when levels of mobility are generally low and concentrated among the more advantaged, those students are more strongly inclined to use geographical mobility as a tactic to gain the most from their higher education experience as possible, in consumption, investment or positional terms, through entering high-status institutions.

Subject Destinations

More movers than stayers from all countries studied Medicine or Arts, and fewer studied Social Sciences or Law (see Table 5.3). The pattern for other subjects varied according to the supply and demand for each country. The subject patterns shown in Table 5.3 were associated with institutional patterns in Table 5.2. For example, movers to higher-status universities were relatively likely to take Medicine and traditional humanities subjects, some of which were less commonly available in other universities.

Table 5.2 Institution type of young full-time stayers and movers by country of domicile

Domicile	Stayer/mover	Russell Group	Other pre–1992	Post-1992	Other higher education institution	n=100%
England	Stayed in England	20	20	54	6	231,292
	Stayed within region	*12*	*17*	*65*	*7*	*103,437*
	Moved between regions	*27*	*22*	*46*	*6*	*127,544*
	Moved out of England	39	42	18	1	11,678
	to Wales	*32*	*46*	*22*	*0*	*8,098*
	to Scotland	*52*	*36*	*8*	*4*	*3,396*
		(see note)				
Scotland	Stayed in Scotland	19	34	40	8	21,323
	Moved out of Scotland	38	21	32	9	1,082
Wales	Stayed in Wales	17	41	42	0	8,484
	Moved out of Wales	24	22	49	6	6,099
Northern Ireland	Stayed in Northern Ireland	45	49	0	6	7,260
	Moved out of Northern Ireland	25	22	49	4	3,293
	to England	*26*	*12*	*57*	*5*	*2,392*
	to Scotland	*22*	*50*	*27*	*1*	*782*
		(see note)				

Note: The four 'ancient' (pre-1600) Scottish universities accounted for 72 per cent of English movers and 31 per cent of Northern Irish movers

Source: Higher Education Statistics Agency Student Record, 2012–13

Table 5.3 Subject area of young full-time stayers and movers by country of domicile

Domicile	Stayer/mover	Medicine and Veterinary Medicine	Subjects allied to Medicine	Sciences	Engineering and Technology	Social Science and Law	Arts	n=100%
England	Stayed in England	3	7	24	7	34	25	231,292
	Stayed within region	2	8	25	7	37	21	103,748
	Moved between regions	4	7	23	8	31	27	127,544
	Moved out of England	5	5	32	7	21	31	11,678
	to Wales	4	5	36	7	23	26	8,098
	to Scotland	7	3	24	5	18	41	3,396
Scotland	Stayed in Scotland	4	10	24	12	34	15	21,323
	Moved out of Scotland	6	6	16	12	25	35	1,082
Wales	Stayed in Wales	2	6	27	6	37	22	8,484
	Moved out of Wales	6	9	23	8	28	26	6,099
Northern Ireland	Stayed in Northern Ireland	4	12	22	13	35	14	7,260
	Moved out of Northern Ireland	8	13	20	7	33	18	3,293
	to England	7	12	19	8	36	19	2,392
	to Scotland	12	17	22	5	27	17	782

Source: Higher Education Statistics Agency Student Record, 2012–13

The supply of subjects within the home country was associated with mobility in two ways: movers from all countries were relatively likely to enter restricted or selective subject areas such as medicine, dentistry or the creative arts; and many movers, especially from Northern Ireland and Wales, entered popular subjects for which there was a greater supply outside the home country, and/or for which entry was possible with lower levels of attainment. In Northern Ireland the supply of places in most subject areas fell short of the corresponding number of Northern Irish applicants and entrants.

This suggests that movers from England and Scotland were most likely to use mobility to access high-status higher education, and thus for positional gain. Mobility appeared to serve a wider set of purposes for movers from Wales and Northern Ireland, and to be relevant to a wider range of students. Linking mobility to student characteristics sheds further light on this.

WHICH TYPES OF STUDENTS CROSS BORDERS, AND WHAT PURPOSES MIGHT THIS SERVE FOR THEM?

Compared with stayers, more movers from each country came from managerial- or professional-class backgrounds, attended independent schools, had parents with higher education qualifications and/or were high attainers (Croxford and Raffe, 2014a). Fewer movers than stayers were from working-class backgrounds or low-participation areas, although the low-participation measure used by the Higher Education Statistics Agency (HESA) is acknowledged to be less appropriate for Scotland and Northern Ireland. (At the other end of the mobility spectrum, students who continued to live in the parental home were relatively likely to have attended a state school, to come from working-class backgrounds and/or to be of Pakistani or Bangladeshi origin.)

Some patterns varied across countries. English ethnic-minority students were less likely than white students to leave their home country; Scottish-, Northern Irish- and Welsh-domiciled ethnic-minority students were more likely to do so, most frequently to enter higher education institutions in Greater London, the north-west or (if Welsh-domiciled) the south-west region. Many ethnic-minority students moved to locations with a broader ethnic mix than their home country. Previous research has found this to be a factor in student choice, but not necessarily the main one and not for all students (Ball et al., 2002; Connor et al., 2004; Purcell et al., 2008; Shiner and Noden, 2014).

High-attaining students from all home countries were relatively likely to be movers, but whereas the lowest-attaining English and Welsh students were relatively likely to be stayers, in Northern Ireland and Scotland they were more likely to be leavers – perhaps the 'reluctant leavers' discussed earlier. (The association between attainment and moving among Northern Irish and Scottish students was therefore associated with high and low levels of attainment, with medium-level attainers the least likely to move.) Among students at each level of attainment, movers were more likely than stayers to enter higher-tariff universities. There were some country differences in the patterns for males and females. Amongst English movers, high-attaining females were more likely to move than high-attaining males; males were more likely to move if they were low or medium-level attainers. English-domiciled female movers were also more likely to enter a Russell Group university than male movers. Conversely female movers from Scotland, Wales and Northern Ireland were less likely to enter a Russell Group university than male movers.

Our analysis could not directly explore student motivation, but it is consistent with the evidence reviewed earlier that decisions about where to study are influenced by a wide range of factors. For many students the outcome was that they followed the established pathways of those from similar geographical, class, ethnic and school backgrounds. There were broad groups of applicants for whom applying to higher education was unproblematic; their decisions focused on attending the right type of institution or the right course, and considering options throughout the UK could help them to do this. Other applicants needed to overcome a number of real or perceived barriers to enter higher education at all, which could limit their options, including the possibility of moving to an unfamiliar location. Even in a scenario where crossing borders might help financially constrained students to reduce debt, these students would have been least likely to have the capacity to be mobile to take advantage of this (Wakeling and Jeffries, 2013). Conversely, our evidence confirms that many mobile students were those least likely to be concerned about fee differences.

Cross-border movement, therefore, was more common to high-tariff institutions, and amongst students from independent schools and the higher middle classes. It could meet the consumption and investment purposes of relatively advantaged students, and for many students, especially those from England and Scotland, it was a means of obtaining positional advantage. However, the destinations and characteristics of many movers out of Northern Ireland and Wales, and a minority of movers out of Scotland and England, suggest a more complicated picture: these students sought access to a desired subject at an appropriate entry level in a relatively accessible location in terms of geographical and/or social distance.

WHAT PREVENTS POLICIES FROM ADDRESSING INEQUALITIES IN CROSS-BORDER FLOWS?

We have documented inequalities in the propensity to cross borders associated with social class, independent schooling, prior attainment, ethnicity and local area. We have also suggested that many students crossed borders in order to maximise their consumption or investment benefits from higher education and/or to obtain positional advantage. Cross-border study provides, at least for some students, a channel for the reproduction of inequalities and for transmitting them between generations. This does not necessarily mean that it is a cause of these inequalities. Nevertheless, it is surprising that, at a time when inequalities of access to higher education are high on the policy agenda in all the home countries, so little attention is paid to their association with cross-border study. There are at least three reasons for this.

An Invisible Problem

In each home country, data used to monitor higher education participation and set policy targets only include students who were resident in that country before entering higher education. For example, the Scottish Government and Scottish Funding Council use the Scottish Index of Multiple Deprivation (SIMD) to measure socioeconomic background and to set targets for widening participation, but this only covers Scottish residents. Inequalities associated with cross-border study are not covered by these data, and lack visibility in policy debates. For example, the high proportion of Scottish independent school pupils who leave for elite universities in England is almost invisible on the Scottish policy radar. Measures based only on home-domiciled students also tend to underestimate the true extent of inequality in overall access to higher education. RUK students tend to come from relatively advantaged backgrounds, so measures which exclude them typically underestimate the participation of these students and overestimate the participation of less advantaged students. This effect, of minimising the extent of inequality, is greater where the proportion of rUK students is large, as in Wales (Croxford and Raffe, 2014a) or in the ancient universities of Scotland.

Association with Advantage rather than Disadvantage

The widening participation agenda tends to focus on the most disadvantaged students. In practice, however, inequalities in access to higher education cover the whole spectrum of advantage and tend to be greatest at the most advantaged end of the range – for example, between children of higher managerial and professional parents and children of lower managerial and professional parents. If governments were concerned with inequality and social mobility – both 'relative' concepts – they would pay as much attention to these inequalities as to those affecting the most disadvantaged. Cross-border study tends to be associated with the most advantaged end of the spectrum – for example, in the contrast between independent and state school pupils, or between those in the highest attainment quintile and those in other quintiles – and consequently receives less policy attention.

Outside the Scope of Country-specific Policies

The most effective widening participation measures tend to operate within specific countries of the UK, and are based on some element of collaboration or synergy between higher education institutions and schools or other stakeholders in that country. For example, in Scotland the Schools and Higher Education Programme, which involves regional partnerships of universities and schools with a weak tradition of progression to higher education, is recognised to be one of the more effective measures currently in force (Scottish Funding Council, 2013). In England, the Aimhigher programme of outreach activity in primary and secondary schools was similarly judged to have enjoyed some success (Doyle and Griffin, 2012). Conversely, measures not specific to one country, such as the provision of bursaries, have been less effective means of widening participation overall (Harrison and Hatt, 2010; Milburn, 2012). Study in another jurisdiction of the UK is therefore outside the scope of many of the more effective widening participation measures.

HAVE FEE DIFFERENTIALS, AND THE 2012 FEE CHANGES, HAD AN IMPACT?

Since 1999 the devolved administrations have pursued divergent policies for student tuition fees. Tuition has been free for Scottish-domiciled students study-ing in Scotland since 2000, subject to a deferred payment of £2,000 which was abolished in 2007; at the other extreme tuition fees for English students have risen in stages to an annual maximum of £9,000 in 2012. Welsh and Northern Irish students pay a smaller annual fee of less than £4,000. However, for many students tuition fees have been higher if they attend institutions outside their home country. This has been the case for Scottish students since 2000, for Welsh students from studying between 2007 and 2009, and for Northern Irish students since 2012. Have these fee differentials discouraged cross-border flows, and have they tended to restrict such flows to more affluent students whose higher education choices are less constrained by the costs of study?

The proportion of Scottish-domiciled students studying elsewhere in the UK has declined since 1996, albeit from a relatively low base (see Table 5.1), and this may partly reflect the rising fee differentials after 2000. However, there were no appreciable effects on the types of students who moved out of Scotland (Raffe and Croxford, 2013; Croxford and Raffe, 2014a). During the period when Welsh students faced higher fees if they studied outside Wales the proportion of movers-out dipped slightly, but again there was no significant change in the social and educational characteristics of movers. Other research (for example Wakeling and Jefferies, 2013) similarly suggests that the impact of fee differentials on cross-border flows has been modest and variable. This is perhaps not surprising: tuition fees may not be the most salient aspects of costs, especially when their payment is deferred and supported by relatively generous and progressive loan arrangements. And financial considerations may be outweighed by other influences on student choices, as discussed above.

However, the existing research largely concerns the period before 2012, when fees, and fee differentials, were relatively modest. Have the much larger changes in 2012 had more impact? We might expect them to have discouraged cross-border study, if more students chose nearer and cheaper places to study in order to com-pensate for the increased costs of tuition. We might expect them to have had most impact on students domiciled in Northern Ireland (facing fee differentials for the first time) or in Scotland (facing much larger fee differentials than before). And we might expect them to have had least impact on the most affluent students, whose choices are least influenced by the costs of study. To explore this, we compare cross-border mobility in 2012 with 2010 and 2011, before the new fee levels were introduced (for further details see Croxford and Raffe, 2014b).

Our analysis suggests that the 2012 changes had only a modest, if uncertain, impact on cross-border flows. Although the proportion of movers-out of Northern Ireland and Scotland declined (see Table 5.1), in Northern Ireland this could be wholly attributed, and in Scotland partly attributed, to the large reduction in the number of successful applicants in 2011 who deferred entry to 2012, compared with applicants in previous years. In Scotland it may also have reflected a longer-term trend. The proportion of movers-out of both England and Wales increased in 2012. Except among Welsh students, cross-border study was more strongly associated with an independent school background, suggesting that more affluent students were less influenced by fee differentials. However, controlling for the independent-school effect there was no change in the social-class background of movers from Scotland and Northern Ireland, and only small (and not easily inter-preted) changes in England and Wales. In most other respects the backgrounds of movers changed little, although in Scotland and Northern Ireland students with low levels of attainment increased as a proportion of students who left the home country, possibly due to displacement effects as more of the better-qualified stu-dents filled places at home.

The 2012 fee changes, therefore, appear to have had only a modest impact on the level and composition of cross-border flows, but we would need to observe flows over several cohorts of entrants to be more certain about the longer-term impacts. On the one hand, higher education in the UK has not been static; any impacts of fee changes have been superimposed on the impacts of other changes and of longer-term if fluctuating trends. On the other hand, the most evident impact of fee changes was that fewer students who were offered places in 2011 deferred entry until 2012, making year-on-year changes much harder to interpret.

WHAT IS THE IMPACT OF DEVOLUTION, AND OTHER POSSIBLE CONSTITUTIONAL CHANGE?

Cross-border flows have declined in the years since devolution (see Table 5.1), but only among Scottish-domiciled students have they followed a continuous down-ward trend. An earlier analysis concluded that devolution, or the policy changes consequent on devolution, had contributed to this decline (Raffe and Croxford, 2013), but drew attention to the complexity of the processes involved. The policy changes most likely to have influenced cross-border flows are the increases in tuition fees, but as we have seen their impact has been small; our analyses appear to confirm the conclusions of other research, that financial factors in general and the prospect of tuition fee debt in particular are relatively minor influences on students' choices of where to study in higher education. Moreover, the devolved administrations have sought to limit the impact of the fee differentials and to maintain existing cross-border flows. However, the Welsh government may decide that its subsidy to Welsh students who study elsewhere in England is unaf-fordable in the longer term, and withdraw it; on the basis of recent evidence this would result in a modest but significant reduction in the number of movers-out from Wales.

It is possible that devolution may have more effect over the longer term. It may encourage a stronger sense of national identity, and a greater awareness of higher education opportunities in the home country, discouraging mobility. On the other hand, if rUK countries are increasingly perceived as 'foreign' they might benefit from the rising demand for international study. As we discussed earlier, policies which encourage stronger links between schools and higher education in the devolved countries may encourage students to remain in the home country. Student choices of higher education tend to follow the pathways established by earlier cohorts of students from similar backgrounds; they are slow to change, but may if there are clear pressures to do so. Policies which affect the supply of places may have a quicker impact, because even if applicants make the same choices as before applications which would formerly have been unsuccessful could now result in admission. The plan to remove the cap on student numbers in English higher education institutions from 2015 could affect cross-border flows. For example, the English students who would currently enter Scottish universities because they failed to access high-tariff English universities might now be able to find desirable places in England instead. This would be a concern for the institutions in relation to both their finances and their wider mission, as well as to government in terms of loss of funding. However this would depend on higher-tariff universities in England increasing the number of student places, and as a notable increase in student numbers could affect their highly selective, elite status it is not an inevitable outcome. The impact of the removal of the student cap may however be felt more immediately and strongly by higher education institutions in Wales if much of the inward movement is accounted for by students unable to access suitable places in England.

Future trends may also be shaped by factors other than policy changes. The balance of supply and demand is also affected by demographic changes, such as the anticipated reduction of the size of the young cohort; this too might reduce the number of students who cross borders in order to find courses in desired subjects with entry requirements they can satisfy. On the other hand, a decline in domestic demand might lead institutions to recruit rUK students more actively. Tindal, Findlay and Wright (2014) estimate, based on population projections, that there could be a total loss of 5,400 Scottish students at Scottish universities by 2023. This could lead institutions to intensify their efforts to recruit rUK students, although it might also encourage them to attract more EU and international students.

Paradoxically, an independent Scotland might experience an increased flow of students across the border with the residual UK. Currently Scotland discriminates between rUK students, who are charged maximum fees of £9,000 per annum, and other EU and Scottish students who receive free tuition. This is permitted under EU law while Scotland remains part of the UK, but would contravene it if Scotland were independent. In the referendum campaign the Scottish Government (2013) argued that it could make a strong case to the EU to continue the current arrangement, but most expert legal opinion suggested that this would be unlikely to succeed. The likely consequence would be an increased flow of 'fee refugees' from

England, slow at first but eventually large enough to displace a large number of Scottish-domiciled students.

The effect of independence on cross-border flows would also depend on the extent to which the institutions of the UK's higher education area were preserved. For example, UCAS currently provides an integrated UK-wide admissions service which makes it as easy to apply to institutions spread across the UK as to institutions in the home country only. If this were discontinued, cross-border flows might fall sharply, as the relatively limited flows with the Republic of Ireland might indicate. More broadly, the UK-wide scope of infrastructural support, quality assurance, assessment arrangements and of most disciplinary and professional bodies may sustain confidence in the consistency of provision and standards across the UK and therefore encourage cross-border study. The Scottish Government (2013) claimed that an independent Scotland would be able to negotiate the continuation of these UK-wide institutions and arrangements, but this claim has not, of course, been put to the test.

CONCLUSION

Cross-border flows are an important aspect of the continued interdependence of the UK's four higher education systems, and of the ways in which policy decisions in one jurisdiction may impact on the others. This interdependence presents challenges for policy-makers, especially in the devolved administrations which, because of differences in scale, are much more affected than England. Decisions about fees are constrained by the need to avoid damaging fluctuations in the flow in and out of each system. Decisions about funding must avoid creating funding gaps with the other systems. Measures to promote greater equality of access are constrained by the need to focus on home students studying in the home country. And the four higher education systems continue to be linked in the UK's higher education area described above.

Constitutional debate before and since the Scottish independence referendum has largely focused on the nature and extent of powers to be held by the Scottish Parliament, and reflects wide agreement that they should be strengthened. There has been remarkably little discussion of another limitation of the current devolution settlement: its failure to provide effective mechanisms for policy coordination across the four administrations (Raffe, 2013; Trench, 2008). But the issues involved in cross-border flows could only be addressed through collaboration between the respective UK Governments. Such collaboration would not be easy to secure. On the one hand, it would depend critically on the full participation of England, which is either the origin or destination country for most students crossing borders within the UK, but is itself only marginally touched by the issue. On the other hand, the devolved administrations would be reluctant to establish an arrangement which would almost certainly lead them to cede power to the dominant partner, England (Keating, 2009). However, with higher education systems increasingly interlinked, not only within the UK but internationally, policy approaches based on the permanence and inviolability of national boundaries are no longer tenable.

REFERENCES

Ball, S. J., J. Davies, M. David and D. Reay (2002), '"Classification" and "Judgement": social class and the "cognitive structures" of choice of higher education', *British Journal of Sociology of Education*, 23: 1, 51–72.

Belfield, C. and Z. Morris (1999), 'Regional migration to and from higher education institutions: scale, determinants and outcomes', *Higher Education Quarterly*, 53: 3, 240–63.

Bond, R., K. Charsley and S. Grundy (2010), 'An audible minority: migration, settlement and identity among English graduates in Scotland', *Journal of Ethnic and Migration Studies*, 36: 3, 483–99.

Brown, P. (2013), 'Education, opportunity and the prospects for social mobility', DOI: 10.1080/01425692.2013.816036, *British Journal of Sociology*, 34: 5–06, 678–700.

Browne, J. (2010), *Securing a Sustainable Future for Higher Education: An Independent Review of Higher Education Funding and Student Finance in England*, London: Department for Business, Innovation and Skills (BIS).

Connor, H., C. Tyers, T. Modood and J. Hillage (2004), *Why the Difference? A Closer Look at Higher Education Minority Ethnic Students and Graduates*, London: Department for Education and Skills (DfES).

Croxford, L. and D. Raffe (2014a), *Working Paper 4 – Student Flows Across the UK's Internal Boundaries: Entrants to Full-time Degree Courses in 2011*, Edinburgh: University of Edinburgh, Centre for Research in Education Inclusion and Diversity (CREID).

Croxford, L. and D. Raffe (2014b), *Working Paper 8 – The Impact of the 2012 Tuition Fee Changes on Student Flows Across the UK's Internal Borders*, Edinburgh: University of Edinburgh, Centre for Research in Education Inclusion and Diversity (CREID).

Davies, P., K. Slack, A. Hughes, J. Mangan and K. Vigurs (2008), *Knowing Where to Study? Fees, Bursaries and Fair Access*, London: The Sutton Trust.

Department for Business, Innovation and Skills (BIS) (2011), *Higher Education: Students at the Heart of the System*, London: BIS.

Doyle, M. and M. Griffin (2012), 'Raised aspirations and attainment? A review of the impact of AimHigher (2004–2011) on widening participation in higher education in England', *London Review of Education*, 10: 1, 75–88.

Fitz, J., C. Taylor and L. Pugsley (2005), *Attitudes Towards Participation in Higher Education in Wales 2005: A Report for the Independent Study into the Devolution of the Student Support System and Tuition Fee Regime in Wales*, Cardiff: Cardiff University.

Forsyth, A. and A. Furlong (2003), *Losing Out? Socioeconomic Disadvantage and Experience in Further and Higher Education*, Bristol: Policy Press.

Gibbons, S. and A. Vignoles (2009), *Access, Choice and Participation in Higher Education*, London: Centre for the Economics of Education, London School of Economics and Political Science (LSE).

Harrison, N. and S. Hatt (2012), 'Expensive and failing? The role of student bursaries in widening participation and fair access in England', *Studies in Higher Education*, 37: 6, 695–712.

Hinton, D. (2011), '"Wales is my home": higher education aspirations and student mobilities in Wales', *Children's Geographies*, 9: 1, 23–34.

Holdsworth, C. (2009), '"Going away to uni": mobility, modernity and independence of English higher education students', *Environment and Planning A*, 41: 8, 1849–64.

Keating, M. (2009), 'Social citizenship, devolution and policy divergence', in S. Greer (ed.), *Devolution and Social Citizenship in the UK*, Bristol: Policy Press, pp. 97–116.

Marginson, S. (2006), 'Dynamics of national and global competition in higher education', *Higher Education*, 52: 1, 1–39.

Marginson, S. (2013), 'The impossibility of capitalist markets in higher education', *Journal of Education Policy*, 28: 3, 353–70.

Milburn, A. (2012), *University Challenge: How Higher Education Can Advance Social Mobility: A Progress Report by the Independent Reviewer on Social Mobility and Child Poverty*, London: Cabinet Office.

Minty, S. (2014), *Working Paper 7 – Young People's Views of Tuition Fees and Their Attitudes Towards Debt*, Edinburgh: University of Edinburgh, Centre for Research in Education Inclusion and Diversity (CREID).

Minty, S. (unpublished), *Deciding Where to Study*, Edinburgh: University of Edinburgh, Centre for Research in Education Inclusion and Diversity (CREID).

Naidoo, R., A. Shankar and E. Veer (2011), 'The consumerist turn in higher education: policy aspirations and outcomes', *Journal of Marketing Management*, 27: 11–12, 1142–62.

Osborne, R. D. (2001), 'Higher education, participation and devolution: the case of Northern Ireland', *Higher Education Policy*, 14: 1, 45–60.

Osborne, R. D. (2006), 'Access to and participation in higher education in Northern Ireland', *Higher Education Quarterly*, 60: 4, 333–48.

Pollak, A. (2012), 'Cross border undergraduate mobility: an obstacle race that the students are losing?' *The Journal of Cross Border Studies in Ireland*, 7, 99–116.

Purcell, K., P. Elias, R. Ellison, G. Atfield, D. Adam and I. Livanos (2008), *Applying for Higher Education – the Diversity of Career Choices, Plans and Expectations: Findings from the First Futuretrack Survey of the 'Class of 2006' Applicants for Higher Education*, Manchester: Higher Education Career Services Unit (HECSU) and Warwick Institute for Employment Research (IER).

Purcell, K., N. Wilton and P. Elias (2006), *Scotland's Class of 99: the Early Career Paths of Graduates Who Studied in Scottish Higher Education Institutions – A Report to the Scottish Further and Higher Education Funding Council*, Edinburgh: Scottish Further and Higher Education Council and Warwick Institute for Employment Research (IER).

Raffe, D. (2013), 'Was devolution the beginning of the end of the UK higher education system?', *Perspectives: Policy and Practice in Higher Education*, 17: 1, 11–16.

Raffe, D. and L. Croxford (2013), 'One system or four? Cross-border applications and entries to full-time undergraduate courses in the UK since devolution', *Higher Education Quarterly*, 67: 2, 111–34.

Scottish Funding Council (SFC) (2013), *Learning for All: Seventh Update Report on Measures of Success 2013*, Edinburgh: SFC.

Scottish Government (2013), *Scotland's Future: Your Guide to an Independent Scotland*, Edinburgh: Scottish Government.

Shiner, M. and P. Noden (2014), '"Why are you applying there?": "race", class and the construction of higher education "choice" in the United Kingdom', DOI: 10.1080/01425692.2014.902299, *British Journal of Sociology of Education*, 1–22.

Shiner, M. and T. Modood (2002), 'Help or hindrance? Higher education and the route to ethnic equality', *British Journal of Sociology of Education*, 23: 2, 209–32.

Tindal, S., A. Findlay and R. Wright (2014), *The Changing Significance of EU and International Students' Participation in Scottish Higher Education – Working Paper 49*, St. Andrews: Economic and Social Research Council, Centre for Population Change.

Trench, A. (2008), *Devolution and Higher Education: Impact and Trends*, London: Universities UK.

Wakeling, P. and K. Jefferies (2013), 'The effect of tuition fees on student mobility: the UK and Ireland as a natural experiment', *British Educational Research Journal*, 39: 3, 491–513.

Whittaker, S. (2014), *Working Paper 2 – Student Cross-border Mobility Within the UK: A Summary of Research Findings*, Edinburgh: University of Edinburgh, Centre for Research in Education Inclusion and Diversity (CREID).

6

Widening Access to Higher Education in Scotland, the UK and Europe

Elisabet Weedon

INTRODUCTION

Despite the massification of higher education from the 1980s onwards, the Dearing and Garrick Reports published in 1997 expressed concerns over the under-representation in higher education of certain social groups (National Committee of Inquiry into Higher Education, 1997a, 1997b). This prompted the development of a range of measures to encourage wider participation, including work with school pupils from non-traditional backgrounds. In Scotland, better use of articulation between further and higher education was advocated in the Garrick Report as one way of promoting higher levels of university participation (National Committee of Inquiry into Higher Education, 1997b). Although widening participation emerged as an issue somewhat later across Europe it is now promoted by the social dimension in the Bologna Process (see, for example, Eurydice, 2014).

This chapter examines strategies to promote widening access across the four nations of the UK, with the main focus on Scotland and England. A central question is whether, in the light of devolution, widening access is an area characterised by a greater degree of convergence or divergence (Gallacher and Raffe, 2012). In line with the goals of the Bologna Process, it is also interesting to consider whether within the EU there is evidence of higher education convergence across EU member states and other countries within the European Higher Education Area. These issues are explored using administrative data from the Scottish Funding Council (SFC), the Higher Education Statistics Agency (HESA), Eurostat and the Eurostudent survey. In addition, we also draw on data from interviews with key informants which were conducted as part of the ESRC project. The following questions are addressed:

- What are the main strategies for promoting widening access to higher education by non-traditional students and what monitoring is in place in different parts of the UK? Has devolution led to greater convergence or divergence across the UK in the field of widening access?

- What measures are in place in Europe to promote widening access and how is progress monitored?
- What evidence is there of an increase in students from non-traditional backgrounds in the UK, Sweden and Germany and what similarities and differences are evident across these three member states?

STRATEGIES FOR WIDENING ACCESS AND MAIN TARGET GROUPS: UNITED KINGDOM

This section examines similarities and differences across the UK in policy and strategies developed to encourage widening access, the use of performance indicators to monitor progress, recent initiatives and the extent to which there is evidence of greater social stratification across institutions.

Background

Since the 1990s, across the UK there has been a major policy focus on widening access, partly driven by concerns that the cost of tuition would deter those from less affluent backgrounds. Debates on funding and widening access of the late 1990s coincided with the establishment of the Scottish Parliament and the devolution of powers from Westminster to administrations in Scotland, Wales and Northern Ireland. As discussed in Chapters 1 and 3, one of the main areas of policy divergence has been in approaches to the funding of higher education. Free higher education was described as a 'core part of Scotland's educational tradition' in the White Paper on Scottish independence (Scottish Government, 2013: 198), although, as noted in Chapter 3, the abolition of tuition fees is a recent policy development, and the tradition in Scotland has been to charge students to study at university. The rationale underpinning the decision to abolish tuition fees in 2000 and the graduate endowment in 2007 was to attract a greater number of students from poorer backgrounds into higher education in Scotland. One of the issues explored in this chapter is whether Scotland has been more successful in this regard than other parts of the UK, particularly England, where tuition fees trebled in 2012.

In the UK the main target group of widening access initiatives have been students from lower socioeconomic backgrounds, with progress measured by a range of performance indicators published annually by the Higher Education Statistics Agency (HESA). Data on the recruitment of disabled students have also been published, but there have been very few outreach initiatives aimed at this group. In addition, there have been targets relating to specific groups and subject areas such as increasing the proportion of women in science and engineering and men in areas such as education. In relation to students from lower socioeconomic backgrounds, there has been a particular focus on access to more selective institutions and professional areas such as Medicine which have traditionally recruited disproportionately from higher socioeconomic backgrounds.

Widening Access – Policy and Strategies

The regulation of widening access in Scotland and England

Widening access was strongly promoted by the Dearing Report which also advocated a student contribution to tuition costs. The increase in fees to £3,000 in 2006 was linked to an income-contingent loan and this sparked concern about the impact on students from lower socioeconomic backgrounds. To garner parliamentary support for an increase in fees, the Labour government established the Office for Fair Access (OFFA) in England. Its remit was to ensure that universities put in place financial support for students from lower socioeconomic backgrounds to ensure that these students were not deterred by higher fees. In 2006–7, any institution charging fees above £2,700 was obliged to offer a bursary of a minimum of £300 to students on maximum maintenance loan. Institutions in England were required to submit an access agreement and an annual monitoring return demonstrating the type of outreach activities that they were engaged in as well as support provided for students from low-income families. In Wales there was a similar arrangement whilst in Northern Ireland a national, rather than institutional, scheme provided similar levels of support. When further fee increases were introduced in 2012, English institutions charging above £6,000 were required to complete an access agreement to demonstrate how the additional fee income would be used to support students from lower socioeconomic backgrounds.

Scotland has been slower than the rest of the UK to develop systems to regulate access to university, possibly because of the belief that the lack of tuition fees would automatically lead to improved participation rates by students from poorer backgrounds. Key informants from Scottish universities were aware that England had led the way in this regard:

> if you compare [Scotland] with England, the English funding system is putting a real responsibility on the universities to provide financial support for students from less advantaged backgrounds. That hasn't emerged as an issue in Scotland because of the different systems we've got. (Senior academic, post-92 university, Scotland)

However, over recent years bodies such as the Scottish National Union of Students (NUS) drew attention to Scotland's relatively poor record on widening access, reflected in significantly lower levels of expenditure by the Scottish Government (Gallacher and Raffe, 2012). Responding to these criticisms, the Scottish Government passed the Post-16 Education (Scotland) Act which came into effect in June 2013. Under the terms of the Act, the outcome agreements submitted to the Scottish Funding Council (SFC) as a condition of grant have to include detailed targets and action plans relating to widening access. Whilst the SFC, like OFFA, is able to enforce financial penalties on institutions failing to make adequate progress on widening access, it is likely that this power will be used as the basis for negotiation rather than enforcement.

University autonomy, performance indicators and widening access

There has been ongoing controversy north and south of the border over the regulation of access because of managers' fears that government interference undermines university autonomy which is perceived to be one of the strengths of the UK system. Ambivalence about the efficacy of OFFA is reflected in the views of one of our English key informants:

> Does [OFFA] work? A really good question and I'm not sure what the answer to that is. It's a lot of bureaucracy and a lot of compliance. But compliance processes and bureaucratic process can achieve certain things, minimum standards and so on and no doubt it has achieved that, but I think the sector was probably there anyway, most of them. I think you need something else in order to get true transformative change. So I think OFFA, as a regulatory tool, has limited ability to do things. It may be that it's still worth doing but you shouldn't put all your hope in that cause, that's not going to do it. (Spokesperson, higher education-related organisation, England)

There have also been ongoing arguments about which groups of students should be regarded as under-represented and, following from this, which metrics should be used to measure progress (Riddell et al., 2013; Weedon, 2014). Universities in England, Wales and Northern Ireland use a range of measures to capture students' social background, including a measure of neighbourhood participation (POLAR). This identifies geographical differences in rates of university participation, enabling resources to be targeted on schools and students within low-participation areas. The POLAR metric is deemed an inappropriate measure for Scotland, because it is based on UCAS data and therefore does not include colleges which account for almost 30 per cent of higher education participation in Scotland. The SFC specifies that all universities must use the Scottish Index of Multiple Deprivation (SIMD) in order to report on participation by different social groups. This is a neighbourhood measure of deprivation, and university managers point out that not all individuals living in areas of deprivation are themselves poor. Similarly, deprivation is unevenly distributed across Scotland, with concentrations in the Glasgow conurbation. Universities with rural hinterlands find it much harder to recruit students from the bottom two SIMD quintiles, as noted by the key informant quoted below:

> I do have a problem with the definition of widening participation . . . The definition of widening participation is completely based on the Scottish Index of Multiple Deprivation. That is an index which by its very nature is heavily biased towards urban areas. There are almost no postcodes of a deprived nature in rural areas. Therefore [certain] universities are heavily disadvantaged despite the fact that a lot of effort is put into low progression schools to support people being the first generation to go to university from their family and to those who have low household incomes. All those are important issues which are not taken into account by the current definitions. And therefore for some universities it is almost impossible to get high numbers [and] in areas like ours, rural areas, there are many poor people who are not discussed as such. (Senior manager, pre-92 university, Scotland)

Recognising this problem, as shown in Table 6.1, the SFC permits institutions to use 'any other measure, or set of measures, for deprivation . . . to demonstrate their success in improving access' (Scottish Funding Council 2012: 4).

Clearly, all social metrics have upsides and downsides and it is important to have a consistent measure to enable progress to be tracked over time. Other proxy measures of social class which are employed across the UK include parents' occupational status. However, this information is missing from a fifth of students when they complete their UCAS forms and may be inaccurate. The use of different geographical indicators across the UK is one of the factors complicating cross-border comparisons.

Widening access initiatives

Prior to 2011 the Higher Education Funding Council for England (HEFCE) funded Aimhigher, a programme aimed at schools in low-participation areas to raise aspirations and attainment and to strengthen progression routes from vocational programmes. The programmes also provided advice and guidance to parents and teachers (Riddell et al., 2013).This was replaced by the National Scholarship programme focusing on supporting students from low income backgrounds as they entered university. The outreach work previously provided by Aimhigher has increasingly become the responsibility of English universities, which are expected to use part of the tuition fee income to fund work with local schools and provide financial support through bursaries and fee waivers. Funding for the National Scholarship programme has been reduced and from 2015 onwards focused on low-income postgraduate students (http://www.hefce.ac.uk/whatwedo/wp/current/nsp/). HEFCE also allocates funding to institutions to support retention work, with a focus on students from disadvantaged backgrounds and disabled students (http://www.hefce.ac.uk/whatwedo/wp/current/howfund/).

In Scotland, the SFC funds the Schools for Higher Education Programme (SHEP). This enables universities to support pupils in schools with low higher education participation rates and is broadly similar to the Aimhigher programme, with the aim of encouraging prospective students into university. Despite the fact that such programmes have been funded relatively generously, particularly in England, since the late 1990s, there is little robust evidence on their effectiveness for specific groups (Riddell et al., 2013). It has also been noted that, even when working well, such programmes are only likely to achieve marginal improvements in access to university by socially disadvantaged groups because of the strong association between social class and school attainment.

To summarise, whilst England traditionally placed greater emphasis on widening access compared with Scotland, there are now strong similarities across the UK in the types of initiatives used (see Table 6.2). These include outreach work with primary and secondary school pupils, summer schools, buddying systems and contextualised admissions procedures which are discussed further below.

Table 6.1 Aims and measures of widening access identified in the current Scottish Funding Council outcome agreements

Outcome	National measure
More even patterns of participation of different groups of learners, including those from areas of deprivation, from protected characteristics groups and care backgrounds. An increase in the number of students articulating with advanced standing from HNC/HND to degree level study. More institutions applying best practice in contextualised admissions.	1 The number and proportion of Scottish-domiciled learners articulating from college- to degree-level courses with advanced standing. 2 The number and proportion of Scottish-domiciled undergraduate entrants from the 20 per cent and 40 per cent most deprived postcodes. 3 The number and proportion of Scottish-domiciled undergraduate entrants from the Schools for Higher Education Programme (SHEP) (that is, schools with consistently low rates of progression to higher education). 4 (where under-represented) The number and proportion of Scottish-domiciled undergraduate entrants by different protected characteristics and care leavers.

Source: Scottish Funding Council, 2014

Table 6.2 Successful types of widening access initiatives across the UK

Type of intervention	Target group
Talks in low-progression schools to raise awareness and aspirations	Pupils in early years of secondary school, or even primary schools
Involvement of students as mentors and role models in community activities	
Talks about subject choices, in school or on campus	Pupils in S3 and S4
Campus visits involving current students	
Campus visits	Pupils in S5 and S6 about to make progression decisions
Discussions of options; taught subject sessions and lectures	
Talks on budgeting and availability of bursaries	
Guidance on applications and interviews	
Mentoring from current students	
Summer schools	
Talks and discussion groups with parents/carers	Parents/carers, especially those with no prior higher education experience
Talks in colleges and on university campus	Students moving from college to higher education
Summer schools	
Opportunities for articulating students to form networks and use the university facilities before formal entry	
Pre-entry summer schools	Mature entrants from access courses; pupils from under-represented groups about to start university courses

Source: Riddell et al., 2013: 55–6

Contextualised admissions policies

Contextual admission policies recognise that students from low-participation schools and neighbourhoods face greater barriers in terms of acquiring school qualifications compared with those from more advantaged backgrounds and private schools. However, once they reach university, students with lower grades from socially disadvantaged backgrounds may perform better than their counterparts from high-participation schools (Lasselle et al., 2014). Institutions may therefore tailor admissions criteria in relation to student background, setting a minimum qualifications level for a particular course which all students must fulfil, but requiring students from socially advantaged schools to achieve higher qualifications. Whilst many institutions support the broad principles of contextualised admissions, there is little evidence that such practices are being widely used (Lasselle et al., 2014), partly because of resistance from middle-class parents who may feel that advantage is being eroded. Indeed, there is evidence that young people from lower-income backgrounds are less likely to gain a place in a Russell Group university compared with those from more advantaged backgrounds with similar qualifications (Boliver, 2013).

The role of colleges in Scotland

Whilst there are many similarities in approaches to widening access across the UK, a central difference in Scotland and Northern Ireland is the greater role assigned to colleges in widening access. In 2009–10, just over 18 per cent of higher education students in Scotland and Northern Ireland were studying sub-degree programmes at a college, compared with 5 per cent in England and 1 per cent in Wales (Bruce, 2012). It is worth noting that the Welsh Government is attempting to promote the role of colleges in widening access (Higher Education Funding Council Wales, 2014). Colleges have traditionally been effective in recruiting students from lower socioeconomic backgrounds and offering more flexible routes, including articulation into the last two years of a university degree programme (Gallacher, 2009). Following the allocation of additional funds by the Scottish Government, there has been an increase in the number of students moving from college into the last two years of a university programme, increasing from 3,019 in 2011–12 to 3,469 in 2012–13 (Universities Scotland, 2014).

Although colleges have succeeded in recruiting young people from low-income backgrounds, Gallacher (2014) has drawn attention to the downsides of such provision. As is the case in the US community college system, there is a danger that young people from lower socioeconomic backgrounds are diverted into low-status programmes which disadvantage them in the labour market. Articulation routes are typically from college to post-92 institutions, limiting access to high-status courses and routes into certain professions such as law and medicine. In addition, the type of teaching and learning which takes place in some college sub-degree programmes is based on demonstrating practical skills, and students may be ill-equipped to complete the last two years of a university degree. Since Scottish Government higher education statistics often include students on degree and sub-degree programmes in colleges and universities, there is a hidden assumption of parity between such programmes. Whilst different types of higher education may be of value to participants, programmes do not provide equal labour market returns and there is a danger that these differences are glossed over.

The Impact of Widening Access Initiatives on Social Inequality

As noted in Chapter 3, public discourse on higher education in Scotland has been informed by the idea that, in comparison with England, the Scottish system is intrinsically fairer, providing 'open access' to students from socially disadvantaged backgrounds through the absence of tuition fees. This positive view of Scottish egalitarianism was reflected not just by Scottish key informants, but also by English interviewees:

> I still have more of a sense that Scottish higher education is [regarded as] a social good, where I think in England that sense has been lost a bit, certainly officially. (Spokesperson, higher education-related organisation, England)

It is important to assess whether this perception of greater social justice within the Scottish higher education systems is supported by data on patterns of participation. Direct comparisons between the two countries' higher education systems are difficult to make because of institutional differences. Nonetheless, as illustrated by Figures 6.1 and 6.2, higher education participation in both countries is characterised by marked levels of social inequality. There is a particularly

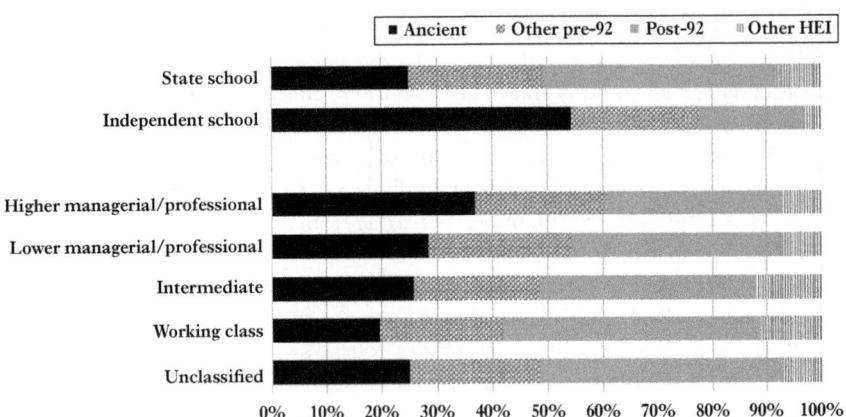

Figure 6.1   Higher education institution attended by background: young Scottish-domiciled students entering Scottish institutions in 2012–13

Source: Higher Education Statistics Agency Student Record, 2012–13. Copyright Higher Education Statistics Agency Limited, 2013

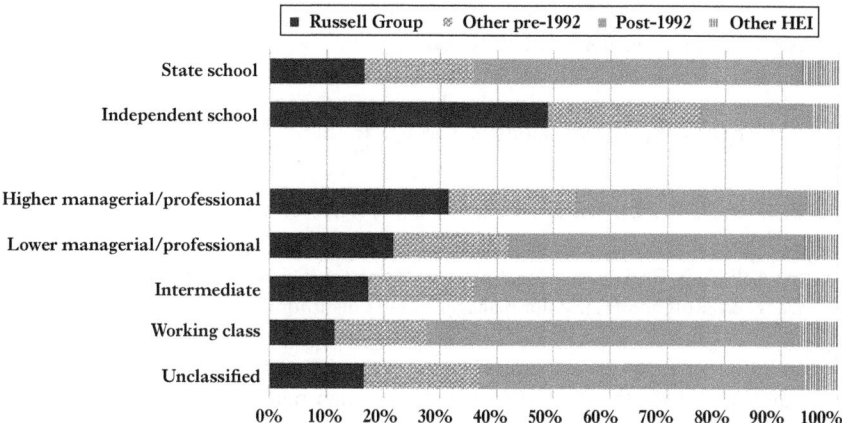

Figure 6.2   Higher education institution attended by background: young English-domiciled students entering English institutions in 2012–13

Source: Higher Education Statistics Agency Student Record, 2012–13. Copyright Higher Education Statistics Agency Limited, 2013

noticeable divide between the institutions attended by pupils educated in state schools and private fee-paying schools, which cater for 5 per cent of pupils in Scotland and 7 per cent of pupils in England. In 2012–13, 55 per cent of pupils educated in Scottish private schools, as opposed to 25 per cent of state school pupils, attended one of Scotland's ancient universities. In Scotland, the proportion of pupils from the 20 per cent most deprived areas attending an ancient university has increased only marginally over the course of a decade (from 7.9 per cent in 2004–5 to 8.2 per cent in 2012–13 – see Table 1.3). In England, just under 50 per cent of pupils educated in the private school sector attended a Russell Group university, compared with about 18 per cent of state school pupils, and again there has been virtually no change in this disparity over the course of a decade.

The crucial question arises as to whether the abolition of tuition fees and the graduate endowment in Scotland led to a reduction in social class stratification and, conversely, whether the increase in student fees in England over this period led to an intensification of social class differences between institutions. Analysis of Universities and Colleges Admissions Service (UCAS) data from 1996 to 2010 shows that in both England and Scotland the institutional hierarchy remained stable, with a slight increase in social class differences between institutions towards the end of this period (Raffe and Croxford, 2015). These findings suggest that the presence or absence of tuition fees is not the crucial factor in producing a more egalitarian higher education system. As suggested by a number of our key informants, the most powerful way of tackling social inequality in universities may lie in addressing inequalities in educational outcomes at school level:

> We are committed to doing things that we think are sensible to do. At the same time, part of the problem arises with the school system . . . we don't think that it's appropriate that you leave the school system as it is if it's creating difficulties and look to higher education to solve those problems . . . There needs to be a focus on the pipeline as well. (Senior manager, pre-92 institution, Northern Ireland)

And

> The difficulty is that universities can only do a limited amount to correct the deep inequalities in British life which throw up disproportionately more candidates coming from better off homes. (Senior manager, pre-92 institution, England)

Whilst progress in widening access was seen by many respondents to be slow and inadequate, it is worth noting that it is better than many of its European neighbours. The section below examines the development of widening participating in Europe in order to place Scotland in a broader context.

STRATEGIES FOR WIDENING ACCESS IN EUROPE

The Bologna Process, initiated by four European education ministers in 1998, has been instrumental in developing a European Higher Education Area (EHEA) within which there is a commitment to modernising and harmonising higher education systems. This has included creating common degree structures, quality assurance systems, a European qualifications framework, and student and staff mobility programmes. Whilst the EU does not have legally enforceable powers over education policies, it exerts soft power via the Open Method of Coordination (OMC). Member countries of the EHEA are encouraged to harmonise approaches through the use of a common set of performance indicators, including some relating to increasing participation. For example, the EU 2020 Education and Training strategy specifies that by 2020 at least 40 per cent of 30- to 34-year-olds should have completed third-level education; however there is no indicator encouraging widening participation for under-represented groups. Data from Eurostat (Figure 6.3) indicate considerable diversity across Europe, so that some countries such as the UK have already reached this target but others, such as Italy and Romania, are well below it.

Whilst there is a strong emphasis on education as a driver of economic prosperity (Holford, 2014), there is also a recognition of the potential of education to promote social cohesion and mobility. The social dimension of the Bologna Process reflects the ambition that 'the student body entering, participating in and completing higher education at all levels should reflect the diversity of our populations' (Education, Audiovisual and Culture Executive Agency, 2012). Bologna signatory countries are therefore expected to promote social equality in rates of participation, although considerable variation remains. All countries show an increase in participation rates as can be seen in Figure 6.3.

As a result, graduation rates have increased from 18 per cent in 1995 to 36 per cent in 2007, however, this has not necessarily led to a more socially diverse student

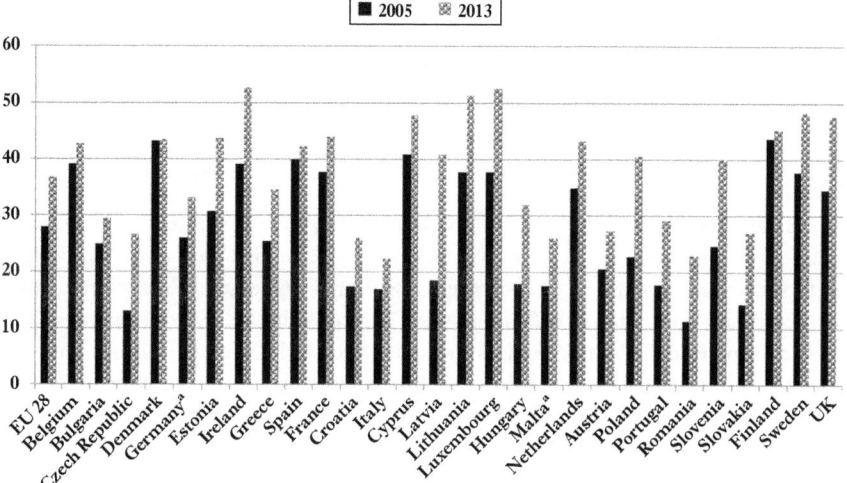

Figure 6.3   Changes in the proportion of 30–34-year-olds with tertiary education in EU28 countries between 2005 and 2013, percentages

a   break in data series in 2005

Source: Eurostat 2014

Note that Eurostat uses the term 'tertiary education' rather than 'higher education' to refer to all advanced post-school education.

population (Sursock and Smidt, 2010: 69). Countries with highly selective school systems and inflexible higher education admissions procedures tend to do less well in including non-traditional students. There is also wide variation in which groups of students are identified as under-represented throughout Europe. According to a Eurydice Report published in 2014, data are gathered in relation to the following categories of students in different jurisdictions:

- qualification prior to entry (twenty-seven jurisdictions)
- socioeconomic status (nineteen jurisdictions)
- disability (seventeen jurisdictions)
- labour market status prior to entry (thirteen jurisdictions)
- labour market status during studies (twelve jurisdictions)
- ethnic/cultural/linguistic minority status (eight jurisdictions)
- migrant status (thirteen jurisdictions)

Data gathering is only a first step in monitoring, and the report noted that only a small number of countries were able to comment on the composition of the student body in their country. A minority of countries reported that the student body had become more diverse over the previous decade. The report reflected somewhat pessimistically that:

it is unclear why there is such a lack of information at national level when the systems are in place to collect data [and] it appears likely that, in some national contexts, issues related to diversity are of marginal national and public interest, and that the data collected is not being analysed or not being publicised. (Eurydice, 2014: 19)

Case Studies of Widening Access in Two European Countries

At the European level, attempts have been made to promote greater social equality in access to higher education, however at a country level this does not seem to be a high priority and a number of contentious issues have emerged. To explore this in further detail, we examine widening access measures in two European countries, Sweden and Germany, and compare these with Scotland. Using Esping-Andersen's typology (Esping-Andersen, 1990), Germany and Sweden represent different types of welfare regime. Germany is characterised as lying within a conservative-corporatist tradition, whilst Sweden reflects the social democratic Nordic model. In contrast, England and Scotland are examples of liberal welfare regimes found across the English-speaking world. In addition to differences in fiscal and labour market regimes, there are important differences in the school systems. Germany has a highly selective system whilst Scotland and Sweden have comprehensive school systems. The English school system has both selective and comprehensive elements. Countries with a more selective school system generally have higher education systems stratified along social class lines. Among these countries, Sweden, with its social democratic welfare regime and comprehensive school system, has the longest tradition of widening access. As might be predicted, Germany has offered far fewer opportunities for non-traditional students. This can be seen below in Figure 6.4 which uses data from two Eurostudent surveys showing students entering higher education via non-traditional routes. A different range of countries chose to participate in the first and second surveys, and Scotland did not participate in the second. In relation to the use of non-traditional routes, it can be seen that Scotland falls in between Sweden and Germany in the first survey, as does England and Wales. Both Sweden and Germany show a decrease in opportunity in the later survey, although this may be explained by changes in wording.

The section below explores each country in more detail and looks at some of the measures used to increase participation of non-traditional students and to consider the extent to which they are reflective of the aims of the social dimension of the Bologna Process.

Germany

The school system in Germany is highly stratified and selection occurs at an early age, with pupils channelled into a vocational or academic track at the end of primary school with limited opportunity to change track (Orr and Hovdhaugen, 2014). In theory, students who have completed the academic track of upper secondary have a guaranteed right of entry to higher education, although this is subject to a place being available (Eurydice, 2014). In the ESRC study, our German key informant

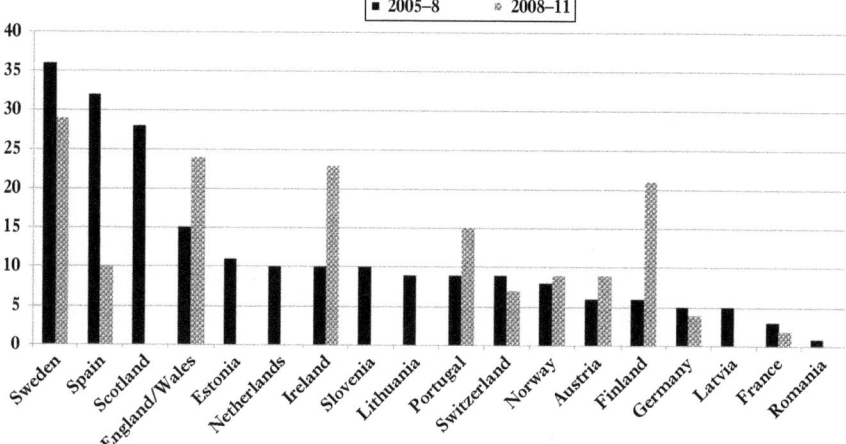

Figure 6.4   Share of students in European countries entering university through non-traditional routes, percentages

Note: There was a change in the wording of the question in the second survey

Sources: Eurostudent 2008, 2011

spoke of the strong influence of parental background on the probability of a pupil attending higher education:

> The major problem for Germany is that it's very socially selective at the door . . . One . . . poster which was used in a student protest in Germany was . . . 'I want different parents'. And it was to do with the fact that your parents actually pretty much determine a lot of your chances within the education system. (Key informant, Germany)

There have been some recent changes aimed at opening up opportunities for those with vocational upper secondary certificates. Students from these courses can now gain entry to applied science institutions but not to the older, more selective universities. There are also subject restrictions and access is most common in areas such as engineering. These institutions are viewed by some as of lower status than traditional universities (Leichsenring, 2011). A further route has opened up based on accreditation through prior learning, work experience or special examination.

It can be seen from Table 6.3 that the most common route into university is the traditional one, which is used by more than 80 per cent of students. It is also evident that there is a close link between the level of parental education background (used as a proxy for low socioeconomic background in the Eurostudent survey) and route into higher education. Students whose parents have lower educational qualifications are less likely to use the traditional route and more likely to access university via alternative vocational routes. A very small proportion of students gain entry based on prior learning/experience or special examination but

Table 6.3 Entry routes to higher education in Germany by all students and those from low parental education background, 2010

	All students	Students from low education background[a]
General academic track upper secondary certificate (*allgemeine Hochschulreife*)	82.7%	72.2%
Upper secondary certificate with limited entry to higher education based on subject (*fachgebundene Hochschulreife*)	3.4%	5.8%
Upper secondary certificate with limited entry to higher education based on subject (*Fachhochschulreife*)	13.1%	18.9%
Entry to higher education based on accreditation of prior learning, work experience and/or special examination	0.8%	3.1%
	100%	100%

[a] Low education background is used as a proxy for low socioeconomic background

Source: Orr and Hovdhaugen, 2014 (based on Eurostudent IV data)

of those that use this route more come from a non-traditional background (Orr and Hovdhaugen, 2014).

This relatively rigid and conservative system has been slow to embrace the social dimension of the Bologna process, with strong links between university attendance and family background. However, the changes to access arrangements are recent and appear to offer some opportunities that did not exist in the past.

Sweden

Sweden presents a different picture, with long-standing comprehensive school system and upper secondary routes offering both general/academic and vocational programmes (Eurydice country notes, 2014). Since the 1970s there has been a strong desire to ensure parity between these two systems in order to break the link between educational outcomes and social class. Both types of upper secondary school offered a broad curriculum and access to university (Nylund, 2012). There was also a growth in adult education and the development of the 25:4 entry route to higher education. Individuals over the age of 25 who had been in the labour market for four years could apply to sit *Högskoleprovet* (the Swedish Scholastic Aptitude Test), which allowed university entrance without formal entry qualifications. As can be seen in Table 6.4, students from families with high educational qualifications are more likely to use the traditional upper secondary route, although this is less commonly used in Sweden than in Germany.

Sweden offers greater opportunities for alternative entry which benefit students from non-traditional backgrounds. However, since 2008 it is no longer possible to use the work experience route. *Högskoleprovet* is still available but it was opened up to all students in 1991 and, according to Orr and Hovdhaugen, it is now being used by students of all backgrounds to improve their chances of gaining a place in high-demand subject areas such as Medicine. The selection process now awards additional credit for completion of advanced courses in foreign languages and/or mathematics, changes which are likely to advantage middle-class students. In Sweden, as in many other countries, there has been an increase in the number of higher education institutions and a similar stratification is emerging here as in Germany and the UK. Research evidence suggests a concentration of students from higher social class in elite institutions (Beach and Puaca, 2014). In the views of our Swedish key informant, there was a sense that Sweden was converging with the rest of Europe and that this was leading to an increase in social inequality:

> I think the Nordic countries were at the forefront of the social dimension of higher education . . . long before the Bologna Process . . . [now] I think the differences here are increasing along lines similar to the ones in other countries. (Key informant, Sweden)

Germany and Sweden have both taken steps to widen access to university for non-traditional students. However, in Germany progress has been limited and the proportion of non-traditional students is considerably lower than in Sweden, Scotland and England. In addition, as the number and type of universities increase,

Table 6.4 Entry routes to higher education in Sweden by all students and those from low parental education background, 2010

	All students	Students from low education background
Upper secondary school diploma (*Gymnasieskolan*)	71.5%	58.8%
Adult education at upper secondary level (*Kommunal vuxenutbildning*)	17%	27%
Other education (*Annan utbildningsform*)	3.8%	2.9%
Work experience (25:4) (*Arbetslivserfarenhet*)	5.2%	8.6%
Recognition of competences (*Validering av reell kompetens*)	2.5%	2.7%
	100%	100%

Source: Orr and Hovdhaugen, 2014

the higher education sector becomes increasingly stratified with students from lower socioeconomic backgrounds concentrated in less prestigious institutions. Widening access is also a contested area, with debates in Germany on tensions between widening access and academic excellence (Wolter, 2014). Policy changes in Sweden stem from a concern among the middle classes that their children's privileged access has been challenged. Nylund notes that educational reforms in 2011 reduced the general education content in upper secondary vocational education and increased the 'more specific, specialised labour market contexts' (2012: 559). As entry to higher education from this route depended on students having completed the general education component of the qualification, this is likely to reduce opportunities for access via this route. In addition to this, Nylund also notes that reduced funding for adult education will further limit access to higher education through alternative routes.

Overall, these case studies illustrate the common challenges facing European countries in attempting to equalise university access for under-represented groups. They suggest that England and Scotland are in many ways trailblazers in promoting widening access. At the same time, they illustrate the dangers of a middle-class backlash during times of austerity, as traditional beneficiaries of higher education fear that their historical advantage may be undermined by growing numbers of university students from more diverse backgrounds.

CONCLUSION

We began this chapter by discussing the extent to which devolution has produced growing diversity in approaches to widening access across the UK, with a particular focus on England and Scotland. Whilst there are differences in terms of timing and promotion of specific programmes, there are broad similarities in the language adopted and overall policy objectives. In both countries, controversy has surrounded the emergence of access regulatory regimes using outcome agreements and standardised metrics. Importantly, differences in tuition fees and student support regimes have been accompanied by stability in institutional hierarchies in both England and Scotland. In Scotland, the assumption that the absence of tuition fees would automatically produce an egalitarian higher education system has been undermined by systematic data analysis over time conducted by Raffe and Croxford (2015). However, all four countries of the UK are concerned that progress on widening access is slow, with commissions appointed to examine the issue and report after the 2015 elections.

Placing Scotland in a broader context, it is evident that concerns about social inequality in university access are common across the European Higher Education Area. There has clearly been a drive to modernise and harmonise higher education systems via the Bologna Process, but here too it is noted that progress is slow with wide country variation (EACEA, 2012):

> Available data on higher education participation shows that the goal of providing equal chances for all has not yet been achieved. This does not mean that no progress has been

made, but it is rather that there are still areas where supplementary effort is needed. In particular, the parental educational background still strongly influences chances to achieve a higher education degree. (EACEA, 2012: 100)

For many countries, in the wake of the 2008 economic crash, widening access to higher education does not appear to be a high political priority, with limited resources devoted to monitoring diversity in the student body. There is also the possibility that the drive for convergence may work in the wrong direction, with some countries reducing their efforts. For example, Sweden, which has been at the forefront of pursing egalitarian social policies, has over recent years reduced opportunities for non-traditional students to attend university. Across Europe, it appears that the expansion of the higher education system has been accompanied by growing social stratification between higher education institutions, with students from low socioeconomic backgrounds concentrated in less prestigious institutions (Weedon and Riddell, 2012). In Scotland, reflecting this trend, students from lower socioeconomic backgrounds are more likely to attend colleges, which have experienced a significant reduction in funding over recent years. Overall, the gains which have been made in widening access Europe may be fragile and are certainly in need of consolidation at a time of economic insecurity.

REFERENCES

Beach, D. and G. Puaca (2014), 'Changing higher education by converging policy-packages: education choices and student identities', *European Journal of Higher Education*, 4: 1, 67–79.

Boliver, V. (2013), 'How fair is access to more prestigious UK universities?' *British Journal of Sociology*, 64: 2, 344–64.

Bruce, T. (2012), *Universities and Constitutional Change in the UK: the Impact of Devolution on the Higher Education Sector*, Oxford: Higher Education Policy Institute (HEPI).

Education, Audiovisual and Culture Executive Agency (EACEA) (2012), *The European Higher Education Area in 2012: Bologna Process Implementation Report*, Brussels: EACEA.

Esping-Andersen, G. (1990), *The Three Worlds of Welfare Capitalism*, Cambridge: Polity.

Eurostudent (2008), *Social and Economic Conditions of Student Life in Europe: Synopsis of Indicators*, final report, Eurostudent III 2005–2008, Bielefeld: W. Bertelsmann Verlag GmbH and Co.

Eurostudent (2011), *Social and Economic Conditions of Student Life in Europe: Synopsis of Indicators*, final report, Eurostudent III 2008–2011, Bielefeld: W. Bertelsmann Verlag GmbH and Co.

Eurydice (2014), *Modernisation of Higher Education in Europe: Access, Retention and Employability*, Brussels: Education, Audiovisual and Culture Executive Agency.

Eurydice country notes (2014), https://webgate.ec.europa.eu/fpfis/mwikis/eurydice/index.php/Sweden:Assessment_in_Upper_General_and_Vocational_Secondary_Education (accessed 20 April 2015).

Gallacher, J. (2009), 'Higher education in Scotland's colleges: a distinctive tradition?', *Higher Education*, 63: 4, 384–401.

Gallacher, J. (2014), 'Higher education in Scotland: differentiation and diversion? The impact of college-university progression links', *International Journal of Lifelong Education*, 33: 1, 96–107.

Gallacher, J. and D. Raffe (2012), 'Higher education policy in post-devolution UK: more convergence than divergence?', *Journal of Education Policy*, 27: 4, 467–90.

Holford, J. (2014), 'The lost honour of the social dimension: Bologna, exports and the idea of the university', *International Journal of Lifelong Education*, 33: 1, 7–25.

Lasselle, L., J. McDougall-Bagnall and I. Smith (2014), 'School grades, school context and university degree performance: evidence from an elite Scottish institution', *Oxford Review of Education*, 40: 3, 293–314.

National Committee of Inquiry into Higher Education (1997a), *Higher Education in the Learning Society, Report of the Committee under the Chairmanship of Sir Ron Dearing*, London: Her Majesty's Stationery Office.

National Committee of Inquiry into Higher Education (1997b), *Higher Education in the Learning Society, Report of the Scottish Committee*, London: Her Majesty's Stationery Office.

Nylund, M. (2012), 'The relevance of class in education policy and research: the case of Sweden's vocational education', *Education Inquiry*, 3: 4, 591–613.

Orr, D. and E. Hovdhaugen (2014), '"Second chance" routes into higher education: Sweden, Norway and Germany compared', *International Journal of Lifelong Education*, 33: 1, 45–61.

Raffe, D. and L. Croxford (2015), 'How stable is the stratification of higher education in England and Scotland?' *British Journal of Sociology of Education*, 36: 2, 313–35.

Riddell, S., S. Edward, E. Boeren and E. Weedon (2013), *Widening Access to Higher Education: Does Anyone Know What Works?* A report to Universities Scotland, Edinburgh: University of Edinburgh, Centre for Research in Education Inclusion and Diversity (CREID).

Scottish Funding Council (2012), *Overview of University Sector Outcome Agreements, 2012–13*, Edinburgh: Scottish Funding Council.

Scottish Funding Council (2014), *University Outcome Agreement Guidance for AY 2015–16*, Edinburgh: Scottish Funding Council.

Scottish Government (2013), *Scotland's Future: Your Guide to an Independent Scotland*, Edinburgh: Scottish Government.

Sursock, A. and H. Smidt (2010), *Trends 2010: a Decade of Change in European Higher Education*, Brussels: European University Association.

Universities Scotland (2014), *Delivering for Scotland: the Third Round of Outcome Agreements for Higher Education*, Edinburgh: Universities Scotland.

Weedon, E. (2014), *Working Paper 1 – Widening Participation to Higher Education of Under-represented Groups in Scotland: The Challenges of using Performance Indicators*, Edinburgh: University of Edinburgh, Centre for Research in Education Inclusion and Diversity (CREID).

Weedon, E. and S. Riddell (2012), 'Reducing or reinforcing inequality: assessing the impact of European policy on widening access to higher education', in S. Riddell, J. Markowitsch and E. Weedon (eds), *Lifelong Learning in Europe: Equity and Efficiency in the Balance*, Bristol: Policy Press, pp. 125–50.

Wolter, A. (2014), 'Opening up higher education for new target groups: the situation of university lifelong learning in Germany in a comparative European perspective', Paper presented at the Society for Research into Higher Education seminar: *Pushing at the Academy Doors: International Developments in Higher Education-based Lifelong Learning*, London: Society for Research into Higher Education.

7

The Internationalisation of Higher Education in Scotland and the UK

Elisabet Weedon and Chung-yan (Grace) Kong

INTRODUCTION

Globally over the last forty years the number of students who leave their home country to study abroad has grown considerably. According to the Organisation for Economic Co-operation and Development (OECD), in 1975, 0.8 million students moved abroad to study; by 2012, this number had grown to 4.5 million (OECD, 2014). The reasons for migrating to study are often described in terms of 'push' factors relating to poorer higher education opportunities in the student's home country, and 'pull' factors, relating to attractive features of provision in the host country (Altbach, 2004). Traditionally, countries in the English-speaking world, such as the UK, USA and Australia, have been major recipients of international students, but these countries are now facing increasing competition, as universities vie for advantage in a global higher education market (Marginson, 2008; de Wit et al., 2013). International students are considered valuable not only to the host country, but also to individual universities since they boost institutional finance as well as generating jobs in the local economy and creating a more diverse local culture.

Using data from the Higher Education Statistics Agency (HESA) as well as key informant interviews, this chapter examines the relative importance of international students in the four countries of the UK. The issue of migrant students has become intertwined with the hot political topic of immigration more generally, and we examine how this has played out in different contexts. Finally, we present a case study of Chinese students studying mainly at an ancient Scottish university to shed light on their reasons for enrolling at this institution and their experiences of living and studying in Scotland. Gallacher and Raffe (2012) suggested that the internationalisation of higher education was an area of policy convergence across the UK, and in the conclusion we explore the extent to which this is still the case. It should be noted that throughout this chapter the term 'international student' or 'overseas student' is used to refer to a non-EU student, since those from the EU study under the same terms and conditions as home students.

INTERNATIONAL STUDENTS AND FEES REGIMES

The UK has for many years prioritised the recruitment of international students, unlike most other countries in continental Europe. Since 1979, the UK has charged unregulated full economic cost fees, with each university free to determine the cost of individual courses according to managers' judgements of what the market will bear. According to de Wit et al., this signalled the use of higher education as 'an export commodity' (p. 20), with similar markets developing more slowly in continental Europe. In this respect, the UK resembles the US, where variable fees for different categories of students have always been part of the higher education landscape. The US has traditionally dominated the international student market but according to recent OECD figures its share has decreased from 23 per cent to 18 per cent over a ten-year period (de Wit et al., 2013). These changes signal increasing competition from countries such as Russia, China, Singapore and Malaysia. Changes are also occurring in the delivery of international higher education, with some universities establishing branch campuses abroad. In addition, developments in online learning are reducing the need for students to leave their home country in order to gain a degree from an overseas institution.

In the UK, international student fees have become increasingly important to the higher education economy over recent years, especially to elite institutions which are highly attractive to international students. In 2013 Universities Scotland estimated that international students contributed £337 million to the Scottish economy through fee payments, as well as £441 million in off-campus spending (Universities Scotland, 2013). For the UK as a whole, international students generate a fee income of £3.2 billion and spend around £3.4 billion off campus (Universities UK, 2014).

THE NUMBER AND PROPORTION OF INTERNATIONAL STUDENTS STUDYING IN THE UK

As noted above, there has been a considerable increase in student mobility worldwide. According to the OECD, international students now make up 10 per cent or more of the student population in the UK, Australia, Austria, Luxembourg, New Zealand and Switzerland, and this proportion increases to nearly one-third of all students studying for advanced research degrees (OECD, 2014). In the UK, the international student population has increased steadily and, as shown in Figure 7.1, the proportion of international students is greatest in Wales at 15 per cent followed by England (14 per cent), Scotland (12 per cent) and Northern Ireland (6 per cent). Scotland has the highest proportion of EU students (9 per cent of the total) which is attributable to the fact that tuition fees for this group are paid by the Scottish Government, whereas in the rest of the UK the cost of tuition is borne by the individual student. The Scottish Government has explored the possibility of charging a registration fee to EU students, but under EU regulations this would also have to be charged to home students and is therefore deemed politically unacceptable. It should be noted that the percentages of EU and non-EU students are likely to

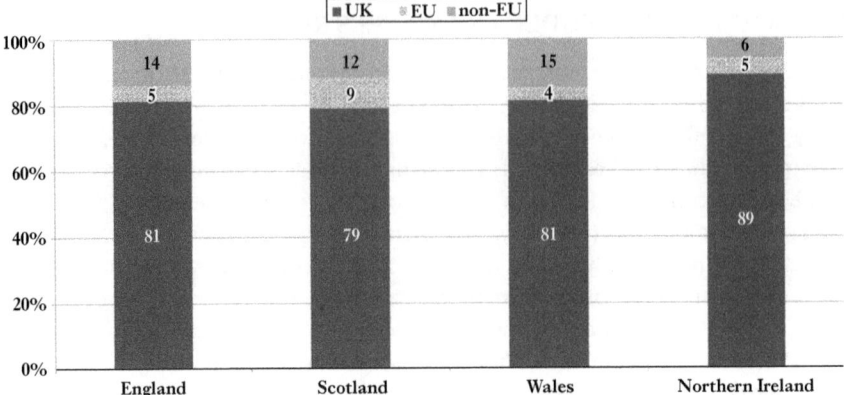

Figure 7.1   Proportion of UK, EU and non-EU students at UK higher education institutions by jurisdiction, 2013–14

Source: Higher Education Statistics Agency, 2015

fluctuate particularly in the smaller jurisdictions, and the number of international students in English institutions is much greater than in the smaller jurisdictions. In 2013 the number per jurisdiction was as follows: England: 43,868; Scotland: 3,786; Wales: 3,425; Northern Ireland: 852.

Figure 7.2 shows the country of residence of international students studying in the UK and Figures 7.3 and 7.4 provide the same data for Scotland and England. The largest group comes from China, and numbers have risen from 56,990 in 2009 to 87,895 in 2013. The second largest group comes from India but numbers have fallen considerably from nearly 40,000 in 2009 to just below 20,000 in 2013. The number of Pakistani students has also decreased (see also Table 7.1). Possible explanations for the decrease in the number of students from these countries are discussed further below.

Chinese students form the largest and most rapidly growing group of international students in all UK jurisdictions. US students represent the second largest group in Scotland and their number has increased since 2009. By way of contrast, in England the second largest group comes from India, with a decrease since 2009 in students from this country in both England and Scotland. In both jurisdictions there has also been a decrease in students from Pakistan.

Table 7.1 shows overall international student enrolments for each of the four UK jurisdictions, numbers in each group and percentage change in 2013–14. Overall enrolments have increased by about 3 per cent across the UK, with slightly larger increases in Wales and England (5 per cent and 4 per cent respectively), whilst in Scotland and Northern Ireland there has been a lower increase of 1 per cent. Table 7.2, which shows first-year enrolments, suggests a slightly different picture. Across the UK, there is a 4 per cent increase in first-year international students. England has the highest increase at 5 per cent, whilst first-year recruitment has

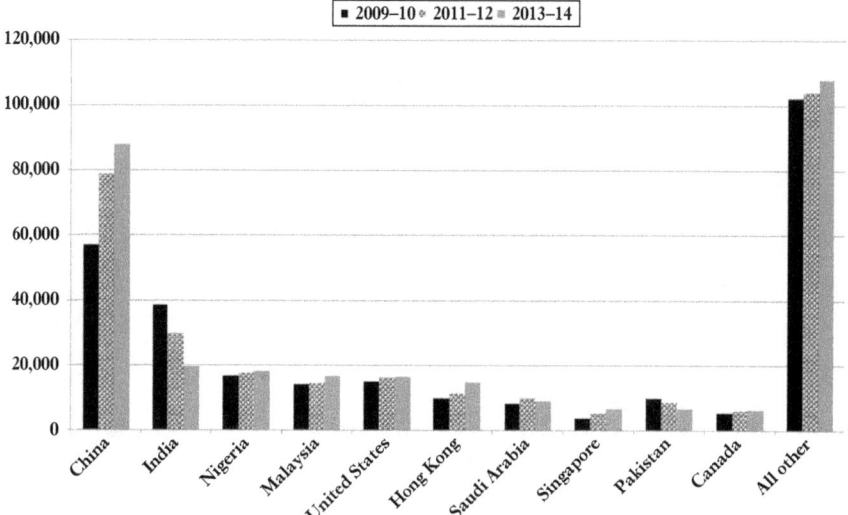

Figure 7.2 Number of international student enrolments from different countries in UK higher education institutions, 2009–14

Source: Higher Education Statistics Agency, 2015

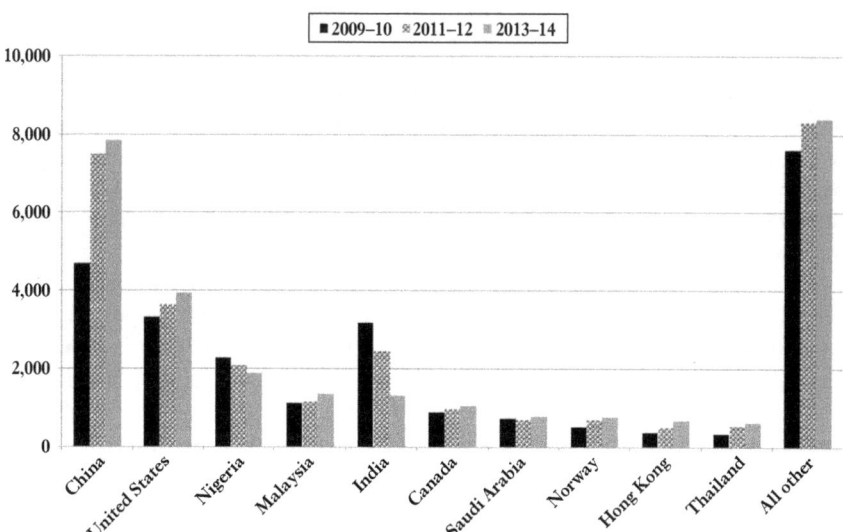

Figure 7.3 Number of international student enrolments from different countries in Scottish higher education institutions, 2009–14

Source: Higher Education Statistics Agency, 2015

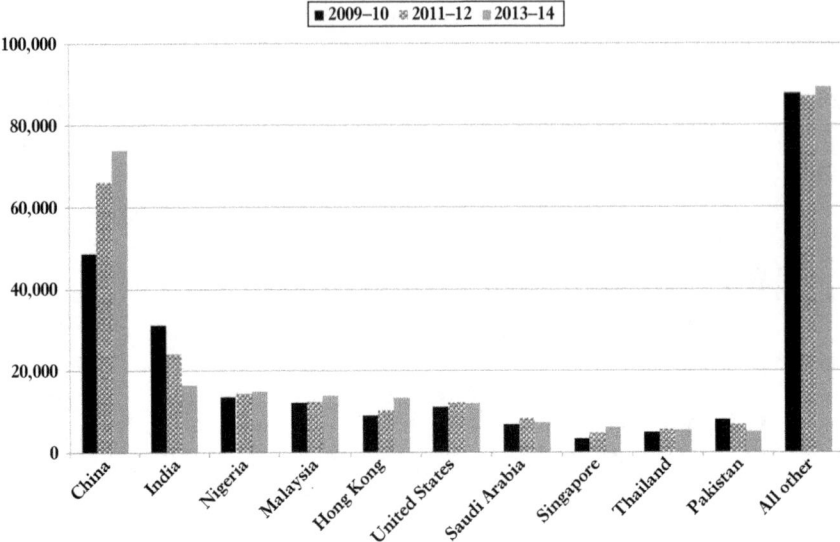

Figure 7.4   **Number of higher education international student enrolments from different countries in English higher education institutions, 2009–13**

Source: Higher Education Statistics Agency, 2015

risen by 4 per cent in Wales and 1 per cent in Scotland. The picture for Northern Ireland is completely different as it has experienced a 20 per cent fall in recruitment. Differences in relation to enrolment in Chinese students are also evident with an increase in England (leading to an overall increase across the UK) but decreases in the other three jurisdictions. Table 7.2 shows that the smaller jurisdictions are beginning to recruit from some new areas. For example, Scotland is beginning to recruit more students from Singapore, whilst more Bangladeshi students are entering university in Wales.

HESA statistics for 2012–13 show that international students represent a growing proportion of postgraduate students, making up 30 per cent of the postgraduate student population in England, Wales and Scotland and 12 per cent in Northern Ireland. By way of contrast, international students represent about 8 per cent of the undergraduate student population on average, with only a small number of universities such as the London School of Economics and the University of St Andrews having a much larger proportion at 36 per cent and 33 per cent respectively. In Scotland, international postgraduate students play an important role in sustaining the sector, making up more than a third of the postgraduate student population at a number of pre-92 universities (Edinburgh, St Andrews, Glasgow, Heriot-Watt, Stirling) and post-92 universities (Abertay, Robert Gordon, Glasgow Caledonian). Any sizeable reduction in numbers would have a major impact on the provision of courses, particularly in the older universities where postgraduate education is central to the universities' mission (see Figure 7.5). Across the

Table 7.1 Top ten countries of origin of international student enrolments in each of the jurisdictions in the UK, 2013–14

UK		Scotland		England		Wales		Northern Ireland	
Country (Number)	change 2012–13 to 2013–14	Country (Number)	change 2012–13 to 2013–14	Country (Number)	change 2012–13 to 2013–14	Country (Number)	change 2012–13 to 2013–14	Country (Number)	change 2012–13 to 2013–14
China (87,895)	5%	China (7,855)	1%	China (74,020)	6%	China (4,810)	–2%	China (1,210)	9%
India (19,750)	–12%	USA (3,940)	4%	India (16,480)	–11%	India (1,780)	–10%	Malaysia (295)	18%
Nigeria (18,020)	4%	Nigeria (1,875)	–6%	Nigeria (14,850)	4%	Bangladesh (1,340)	55%	Bangladesh (175)	–23%
Malaysia (16,635)	11%	Malaysia (1,335)	3%	Malaysia (14,005)	11%	Nigeria (1,235)	18%	India (170)	–18%
USA (16,485)	2%	India (1,315)	–21%	Hong Kong (13,415)	13%	Malaysia (1,005)	17%	USA (145)	–19%
Hong Kong (14,725)	13%	Canada (1,040)	6%	USA (11,985)	1%	Pakistan (870)	4%	Sri Lanka (115)	–34%
Saudi Arabia (9,060)	4%	Saudi Arabia (790)	10%	Saudi Arabia (7,485)	–6%	Saudi Arabia (735)	–2%	Hong Kong (85)	7%
Singapore (6,790)	13%	Norway (765)	4%	Singapore (6,075)	13%	Hong Kong (555)	5%	Pakistan (85)	–35%
Pakistan (6,665)	–7%	Hong Kong (670)	11%	Thailand (5,555)	1%	Nepal (550)	27%	Nepal (85)	–14%
Canada (6,350)	3%	Thailand (620)	13%	Pakistan (5,230)	–8%	Sri Lanka (435)	–2%	Nigeria (65)	26%
All other (107,820)	4%	All other (8,405)	3%	All other (89,330)	4%	All other (6,645)	7%	All other (775)	18%
310,195	3%	28,610	1%	258,430	4%	19,960	6%	3,200	1%

Source: Higher Education Statistics Agency, 2015

Table 7.2 Per cent change in first-year enrolments 2012–13 to 2013–14 by top ten non-EU countries in each jurisdiction

Country	UK	Scotland	England	Wales	Northern Ireland
	% change	% change	% change	% change	% change
China	4	-2	6	-7	-17
India	-8	-12	-8	-1	-45
Nigeria	7	-9	8	20	-8
USA	0	5	-1	-6	-22
Malaysia	13	7	14	9	-2
Hong Kong	7	7	8	-8	-9
Saudi Arabia	7	6	7	10	–
Thailand	5	15	4	–	–
Pakistan	-5	–	-4	1	–
Canada	5	10	–	–	–
All other	7	5	6	7	-40

Countries that feature among top ten in only one jurisdiction

Country	UK	Scotland	England	Wales	Northern Ireland
Norway	–	-3	–	–	–
Singapore	–	–	14	–	–
Bangladesh	–	–	–	52	–
Nepal	–	–	–	0	–
Brazil	–	–	–	–	a
Brunei	–	–	–	–	45
Colombia	–	–	–	–	a
Vietnam	–	–	–	–	-3
Total % change	4	1	5	4	-20

a Percentages are not calculated on fewer than 22.5 people.

– indicates that this country did not feature in top ten in the jurisdiction.

Source: Higher Education Statistics Agency, 2015

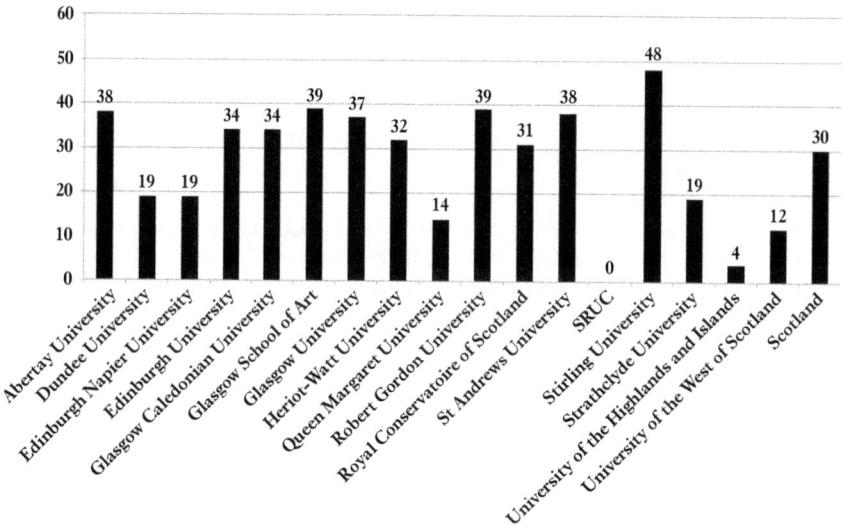

Figure 7.5 Proportion of non-EU students in postgraduate population by institution, Scotland, 2012–13, percentages

Source: Higher Education Statistics Agency, 2014

UK, international postgraduate students are concentrated in some institutions, making up around 38 per cent of the postgraduate population at the universities of Oxford and Cambridge and 55 per cent at the London School of Economics (HESA, 2014). Universities UK has highlighted a particular concern in relation to Science, Technology, Engineering and Maths (STEM) subjects as there has been a 10 per cent drop in enrolments by overseas students in these subject areas at postgraduate level. This is mainly due to the drop in Indian, Pakistani and Nigerian students (Universities UK, 2014).

This overview demonstrates that UK universities have expanded their recruitment of overseas students over recent years, particularly at postgraduate level, but that growth is uneven across the four jurisdictions, with Northern Ireland and Scotland having a lower rate of increase. A report by Universities UK voiced concern about the fall in overseas student numbers in 2012–13 and noted that this was happening at a time when student numbers globally were increasing (Universities UK, 2014).

KEY INFORMANTS' VIEWS OF OVERSEAS STUDENTS

Key informants across the UK recognised the economic and cultural importance of international students for the sector. According to a senior manager from an ancient Scottish university, international students were vital for Scotland's higher education system and wider economy:

I think for a small country that represents one tenth of one percent of the world, we need to be maximally internationally engaged. Our cultural and our economic future depend on it. (Senior university manager, Scotland)

The positive aspects of international student recruitment were also stressed by a Welsh key informant:

in general terms [universities] benefit from an international mix of students. I think that the notion of interacting with people from different countries, from different cultures is consistent with my ideas of what universities ought to be . . . In some instances . . . it is a way of supporting development in less developed parts of the world although there are all sorts of complications about that as well. So I think that there are certainly those rather high-minded arguments that are on the pro side . . . So I think that the growth in numbers of international students in all of those respects is highly desirable. (Senior academic, Wales)

However, he expressed some concern over the way that international students were sometimes treated and the high level of fees charged:

I think it is much less desirable . . . that international students are charged fees at the level that they are and that those fees would appear to be used to cross-subsidise other aspects of universities' activities. I worry about the extent to which international students are properly supported in universities . . . That is something that could be seen as highly problematic. (Senior academic, Wales)

The positive and negative aspects were also noted by a senior manager at an English Russell Group institution:

Obviously bits of [international student recruitment] are very positive. It's allowed us to maintain academic capacity which would otherwise be lost . . . The UK like the US, the vitality of our whole university and research system depends to some extent on imported talent from elsewhere . . . More negative things, obviously they are bunched in particular subjects. And that can produce distortions in the curriculum . . . I think it can produce, in certain institutions, an overdependence on income from international students . . . And then the big question is, how sustainable is this? (Senior university manager, England)

A senior Scottish academic echoed this by suggesting that there was a need to ensure that local as well as international students were catered for:

It is undoubtedly a huge source of income for the Scottish universities . . . it can only enrich the higher education community in Scotland [and] the wider Scottish community . . . So in all those respects I think it's fantastically good. I suppose the downside of it is there can be a slight danger that you then end up with universities . . . placing an undue emphasis on this. So you get places like Edinburgh and St Andrews [with] Masters programmes . . . almost entirely run for Chinese students or somebody else who are just paying them lots and lots of money. So whether we want to go too far down this road where increasingly [some courses] are mainly being provided for foreign students who will pay lots and lots of money. It seems to me there has got to be a bit of a balance maintained there. (Senior academic, Scotland)

Overall, key informants recognised the benefits of international students but also the potential problems such as viewing them purely as an economic commodity and not supporting them sufficiently. In addition the sustainability of recruitment was questioned especially at postgraduate level.

INTERNATIONAL STUDENTS, IMMIGRATION AND DEMOGRAPHY

Concerns about the recruitment of international students are linked with the issue of immigration, which is a highly contested area in the UK and across Europe, featuring prominently in national and European elections. Since 2010, higher education institutions have criticised the coalition government's immigration policy, which has attempted to reduce net migration. Statistics are based on all non-EU immigrants resident in the UK for a period of twelve months or more, with overseas students forming the largest single group of non-EU immigrants (Better Futures/ Universities UK, 2014). In 2013 more stringent rules for Tier 4 visa applications, required by overseas higher education students, were introduced. Further restrictions were imposed by the Immigration Act 2014 which reduced appeal rights, introduced a surcharge to access NHS services, required private landlords to check tenants' immigration status and increased the scope for government to raise fees for visas and immigration services (Universities UK, 2014: 9). In light of the economic contribution made by overseas students, universities have argued for changes to immigration legislation in relation to this group. A recent report by Better Futures/ Universities UK recommended that the UK Government should:

- remove international students from any net migration target
- launch an international student growth strategy, backed by investment, to promote British universities overseas, build new international partnerships and attract more international students to Britain
- make a renewed effort – through its words, actions and policies – to communicate a consistent message that Britain welcomes international students
- enhance opportunities for qualified international graduates to stay in the UK to work and contribute to the economy (Better Futures/Universities UK, 2014: 27)

Within the UK, immigration is a reserved power controlled by Westminster, although within this overall framework it is possible for different immigration rules to apply in different UK jurisdictions. For example, between 2004 and 2008, the Fresh Talent scheme allowed recent Scottish university graduates to stay in the country for two years after completing their degree to seek employment, but, to the annoyance of English universities, did not apply to graduates in the rest of the UK. During the course of the Scottish referendum, pro-independence campaigners argued that control over immigration policy would be beneficial to Scotland, since an increase in skilled migrants would boost the economy by contributing to 'healthy population growth' (Scottish Government, 2013: 267). In particular, there was a need to reinstate the post-study work visa scheme.

In the context of post-referendum negotiations on further devolution, a particular case has been made for a more liberal immigration regime in Scotland. The submission to the Smith Commission by Universities Scotland drew attention to Scotland's low population growth and the need for a more highly skilled workforce. Arguing for the reintroduction of the post-study visa, the submission noted that countries such as Canada allowed individual provinces to set their own priorities in relation to high-talent migration and that a similar arrangement could apply in the UK. In addition, it pointed out that countries offering post-study visas such as the USA and Canada have experienced greater increases in the number of international students compared with the UK. The UK Government Command Paper published in January 2015 suggested that the Scottish and UK Governments

> should work together to . . . explore the possibility of introducing formal schemes to allow international higher education students graduating from Scottish further and higher education institutions to remain in Scotland and contribute to economic activity for a defined period of time. (Her Majesty's Government, 2015: 84).

However, English universities would be likely to oppose the institution of a post-study visa for Scottish graduates only, on the grounds that this would give a market advantage to institutions north of the border.

KEY INFORMANTS' VIEWS OF IMMIGRATION POLICY

Senior university managers interviewed during the course of the project noted that current immigration policy was a significant problem in relation to the recruitment of international students. One Scottish key informant pointed to different attitudes to immigration in England and Scotland, which might warrant the application of different immigration rules:

> opinions about immigration are so different in Scotland compared to South East England [it would make sense] if . . . England and Scotland were to go their separate ways on that one, it might make life easier for everybody. (Senior university manager, Scotland)

Another key informant argued for a common approach across the UK:

> I would see that as an entirely common agenda, north and south of the border . . . We're all across the UK conscious of working against a migration regime that isn't as supportive as we would like it to be for the migration of high talent . . . if there's a regional argument in this, it's that policy is designed for an overcrowded South East . . . not the policies that support the interests of the rest of UK. But I would genuinely say throughout the UK, everybody is looking entrepreneurially to make sure their international engagement is as wide as possible. And everybody is striking against similar barriers of regulation and perception. (Senior manager, Universities UK)

One of the English key informants suggested that there was an over-reliance on international student recruitment, and that efforts to expand this market were hampered by negative messages on immigration:

> When I was on the HEFCE board there was a constant worry about those institutions which seemed to be over dependent on income from international students and sometimes rather optimistic [in their] projections of growth. But then of course there is . . . what I call this xenophobic anti-immigrant issue . . . that is a major issue and the message is going out quite loudly that we are not actually particularly welcoming. We are sending a very mixed message. (Senior academic, England)

It is clear that the financial solvency of UK universities is increasingly based on their ability to recruit international students. University managers are concerned that attempts to expand the number of international students studying in UK universities will be stymied by growing restrictions on overseas recruitment and the inclusion of international students in immigration caps. Tindal et al. (2014) note that this poses particular challenges for the Scottish university sector, since the number of 18-year-olds in the Scottish population is set to decline until 2023. In order to sustain the size of the sector, it will be necessary for Scottish universities to increase student numbers from the rest of the UK, the EU and internationally, which may become increasingly difficult. In the next section of the chapter, we summarise messages from the literature on the factors driving students to study overseas, before drawing on a case study of Chinese students studying in a Scottish city to shed light on their motivations and experiences.

MOTIVATIONS AND EXPERIENCES OF CHINESE STUDENTS IN UK UNIVERSITIES

Researchers have investigated the attraction of British universities for Chinese students. Lowe (2007) found that Chinese students valued the independence and new experiences provided by studying abroad, which would enable then to benefit from 'the broader range of social and cultural opportunities that are emerging [in China]'. They did not have a specific job in mind but believed that future work opportunities would be enhanced by studying abroad. Before deciding on a university and subject, students studied international league table rankings and took advice from others. The UK was often a second choice of destination, but visa regulations frequently meant that students were unable to take up a place at a US university, their preferred option. Given the high cost of international student fees, students without the benefit of a national scholarship had to rely on their families for funding. Some Chinese parents who had gained wealth through entrepreneurial activities rather than education were using their economic resources to enhance their child's social mobility. According to Lowe, Chinese society is in a state of flux and parents are very anxious that their children should benefit from its rapid development.

A more recent study by Bamber (2013) focused specifically on Chinese women's motivation for doing a postgraduate course in Accountancy and Finance at an English Russell Group university. The main reason for postgraduate study was to improve their labour market outcomes. The author noted that Chinese women are expected to complete their studies early so that they can get married. Masters programmes in the UK are typically shorter than their equivalents in China and the US, and were therefore regarded as more attractive. Students interviewed by Bamber reported that some Chinese parents regarded the UK as a safer place to study than the US because of its gun culture. Australia was also a popular destination and was regarded as offering a more welcoming environment. Overall, research suggests that a particular range of factors is currently encouraging students to study in the UK. Push and pull factors are likely to vary over time and from one country to another.

CHINESE STUDENTS STUDYING IN SCOTLAND: CASE STUDY FINDINGS

This case study examines the choices made by twenty-one Chinese students studying at Scottish universities in one city in Scotland. Sixteen of the twenty-one were female and most came from mainland China. Seventeen were studying at Masters level, two for a PhD and two at undergraduate level. Eleven of the students were undertaking a TESOL (Teaching English to Speakers of Other Languages) Masters level course, two of the students were doing Accounting and Finance and the remainder were on a range of different courses. Eighteen of the students were studying at an ancient university, two at a pre-92 university and one at a post-92 institution. Four of the students had scholarships for Chinese or overseas students, whilst the rest were sponsored by their parents. Parents worked in the civil service, school or university teaching, medicine and business. The yearly tuition fees paid ranged from £10,000 to £22,500.

A range of factors had influenced these students to study abroad, but most importantly a postgraduate degree was considered to enhance their labour market prospects. This was particularly the case for students who had not attended one of the highly competitive top Chinese universities, as explained below.

> My primary motivation is a postgraduate qualification . . . an undergraduate degree in China is no longer as rare as it used to be, and a postgraduate qualification might make you more outstanding. (Xinxin Zhong, mainland China, female, Masters in Education)

> Another reason was that I did not get my first degree from a top university. In China, if your degree is not awarded by a top university, such as one of those in Beijing and Shanghai, it will be very difficult to get a well-paid job. Therefore, I hope to gain a postgraduate qualification at a top . . . [Scottish] university to enhance my skills and increase my competitiveness for a better career prospect. (Mingjun Lu, mainland China, male, Masters in Accountancy and Finance)

Some students also spoke of wanting to experience a different culture and approaches to teaching and learning. One student described the Chinese teaching approach as focused on 'memorisation . . . making learning very mechanical'.

English-speaking countries were preferred by the students as this was a language they already knew and was required in the labour market:

> It is important because I don't need to learn an additional language, and it's easier to study and settle in using a language I know. If I went to France, I need to learn a new language. Since I already know English, studying in an English-speaking country is simpler and quicker to achieve what I wanted. (Nan Zhang, mainland China, female, Masters in TESOL)

Some of the students spoke of the US as their preferred country of study but were deterred by the higher entrance requirements of high-status US institutions. A further benefit of UK study was that the Masters course took only a year to complete compared with courses which were typically two years in other English-speaking countries. This mattered particularly for women because of the gendered expectations of marriage in Chinese society:

> The term [length of] of study is very decisive . . . many Chinese students who have chosen to study in the UK rather than in the US . . . are female. In traditional Chinese thinking, the older a woman is, the more prudent she has to be in using time. Many parents prefer their daughters to minimise their time of studying because it's more important for them to find someone and get married. Therefore, one-year MSc programmes in the UK are preferred to three-year programmes in China and two-year programmes in the US. You can actually tell that female Chinese students in the UK are more than those in the US. Most male Chinese students choose to study in the US as youthfulness is less important to them. Even though it's much more expensive to study abroad, it's also much more time efficient. (Yuting Wang, mainland China, female, Masters in TESOL)

When it came to choosing the particular institution, students referred to the UK and did not distinguish between England and Scotland. The main issue was the ranking of the university and the course:

> My main concern was that it was a UK university, followed by the university itself. The city where it is located came last. (Yaobang Chen, mainland China, male, PG Artificial Intelligence)

The international ranking of the university was seen as more important than the status of a course:

> It was the overall ranking [of the university] . . . I didn't consider costs at that time. Being able to study at a quality university is all the more important because I want to work with academic staff of high standards and classmates with excellent academic performance. (Yuting Wang, mainland China, female, Masters in TESOL)

Interestingly, students interviewed before the referendum expressed concerns that if Scotland were an independent country its universities might become less attractive. One student said they would rather study in London than in an independent

Scotland but others thought that as long as Scottish universities were adequately funded they would be able to maintain their international ranking. Post-study visas were regarded as appealing, and possibly one reason for Chinese students' preference for the US:

> Many Chinese students tend to study in the US these days because the immigration policies of the UK are getting more stringent and the possibility to stay behind is getting smaller. In the past, the possibility for international students who graduated from UK universities to stay behind and get a job is higher compared with the situation nowadays. Everyone is under the impression that it is difficult to get a work permit in order to get a job in the UK, hence prefer to study in the US. (Chunhui Shen, mainland China, female, Masters in TESOL)

This case study explored Chinese students' reasons for studying in Scotland and the factors which might affect student choices in the future. It would seem that one of the push factors was limited opportunities for postgraduate study at prestigious Chinese institutions. For women, the length of Masters courses in China was also offputting. In line with Bamber's (2013) study, the most important pull factors were the opportunity to study at a high-ranking university, improved work opportunities and the shorter duration of Masters programmes. The fact that teaching was in English was also important, as was the reputation of UK institutions for innovative pedagogy. Interestingly, students were attracted by the UK, rather than the Scottish brand. The extent to which this constellation of push and pull factors will continue to benefit Scottish and UK institutions in the future is a moot point. As China develops its own higher education institutions, then the relative attraction of UK institutions may diminish. Availability of funding to support overseas study cannot be guaranteed, but will depend to a large extent on the buoyancy of the Chinese economy. Similarly, Chinese students' choice of institution depends on university ranking in international league tables and the extent to which the country is deemed to offer a safe and welcoming environment. Given growing competition within the global higher education market, there is a danger that UK institutions may become complacent, simply assuming that students will continue to come to the UK without paying sufficient attention to the quality of what is on offer.

CONCLUSION

The recruitment of international students to UK institutions is part of a global trend in cross-border higher education. China and India are major 'exporters' of students due to their growing economies, the need for a more highly qualified workforce as well as lack of capacity in their own higher education systems (Altbach, 2009). Vincent-Lancrin (2009) argued that high-ranking universities in OECD countries would continue to attract overseas students for the foreseeable future. The considerable economic benefit of recruiting international students was likely to act as a driver of further expansion. The positive impact on future earnings of holding an international qualification from a top university was likely to encourage students to seek opportunities to study abroad. According to Vincent-Lancrin, the development of the overseas campus was unlikely to have a major impact on student mobility since these are expensive to run and are therefore unlikely to be supported by governments.

Vincent-Lancrin suggested the following possible future scenarios for cross-border higher education: (1) sustained diversified internationalisation; (2) convergence towards a liberal model; and (3) the triumph of the (former) emerging economies. The first scenario could arguably be described as representing the status quo. In this scenario English-speaking countries and some Asian countries continue to market higher education as an export commodity and national qualification and quality systems are in place to coordinate mobility of students. In the second scenario, higher education becomes an export commodity and is treated as commercial trade, leading to competitive tension between traditional non-profit and profit-making institutions. The third scenario sees the 'emerging economies' such as India and China developing highly competitive systems, with India having the edge due to its widespread use of English. In this scenario, countries which previously dominated the scene see a reduction in international student numbers, with a negative impact on institutional funding. However, the most elite institutions in Western countries continue to attract international students due to their high rankings.

Given these future scenarios, what are the potential outcomes for growth in international student numbers in Scotland and the rest of the UK and what are the challenges relating to international student recruitment? According to the first two scenarios described above, the UK will continue to attract students due to the perceived quality of its universities and the fact that English is the international lingua franca. These were both factors which strongly influenced the students in our case study, although HESA data suggest that recruitment of Chinese students in Scotland may be declining.

The third scenario presents a far more uncertain future. Could it lead to fewer students opting to study abroad or perhaps studying abroad for shorter periods to gain overseas experience? Whilst both China and India are developing their higher education systems, Altbach (2009) suggests that they will not be able to compete globally for some time, especially in relation to having world-class research-intensive institutions. However, he suggests that China may become attractive to students in East and South East Asia and this could have an impact on numbers coming to the UK.

The international student market is clearly unpredictable and key informants were concerned that international students were viewed mainly in economic terms, with insufficient attention paid to the quality of their learning experience. A senior English academic commented:

> So the idea that international students can just be seen as an income stream rather than a significant cost, I think that can be dangerous. And then the big question is, how sustainable is this? After all . . . the UK has a very high market share of international students but it's a dwindling market share . . . there is competition from other parts

of Europe, who are teaching more and more English . . . the Chinese themselves . . . will want to become an importing country at some point. (Senior academic, pre-92 university, England)

Internationalisation of higher education is of growing importance across the UK and is clearly an area of policy convergence. Whilst the Scottish Government emphasises the importance of the Scottish brand, it would appear that this is less important to international students than the league table ranking of individual institutions. By the same token, negative attitudes to international students emanating from a confused immigration policy are likely to have serious consequences for Scottish institutions, as well as those in the rest of the UK.

REFERENCES

Altbach, P. (2004), 'Higher education courses borders: can the United States remain the top destination for foreign students?', *Change: the Magazine of Higher Learning*, 38: 2, 18–25.

Altbach, P. (2009), 'The giants awake: the present and future of higher education systems in China and India', in *Higher Education to 2030, Volume 2: Globalisation*, Paris: OECD.

Bamber, M. (2014), 'What motivates Chinese women to study in the UK and how do they perceive their experience?' *Higher Education*, 68, 47–68.

Better Futures/Universities UK (2014), *International Students and the Immigration Debate*, London: Better Futures/Universities UK.

De Wit, H., I. Ferencz and L. Rumbley (2013), 'International student mobility: European and US perspectives', *Perspective: Policy and Practice in Higher Education*, 17: 1, 17–23.

Gallacher, J. and D. Raffe (2012), 'Higher education policy in post-devolution UK: more convergence than divergence?' *Journal of Education Policy*, 27: 4, 467–90.

Her Majesty's Government (2015), *Scotland in the United Kingdom: an Enduring Settlement*, https://www.gov.uk/government/uploads/system/uploads/attachment_data/file/397079/Scotland_EnduringSettlement_acc.pdf (accessed 22 April 2015).

Higher Education Statistics Agency (2014), https://www.hesa.ac.uk/index.php?option=com_content&view=article&id=1897&Itemid=634 (accessed 10 March 2015).

Lowe, J. (2007), *Decision Making by Chinese Students Choosing UK and Chinese Universities: Full Research Report. ESRC End of Award Report, RES-000-22-0911*. Swindon: ESRC.

Marginson, S. (2008), 'National and global competition in higher education', in B. Lingard and J. Ozga (eds), *The RoutledgeFalmer Reader in Education Policy and Politics*, London: RoutledgeFalmer.

Organisation for Economic Co-operation and Development (OECD) (2014), *Education at a Glance 2014: OECD Indicators*, Paris: OECD.

Scottish Government (2013), *Scotland's Future: Your Guide to an Independent Scotland*, Edinburgh: Scottish Government.

Tindal, S., A. Findlay and R. Wright (2014), *The Changing Significance of EU and International Students' Participation in Scottish Higher Education*, Oxford: Centre for Population Change.

Universities Scotland (2013), *Richer for it: the Positive Social, Cultural and Educational Impact International Students Have on Scotland*, Edinburgh: Universities Scotland.

Universities UK (2014), *International Students in Higher Education: the UK and its Competition*, London: Universities UK.

Vincent-Lacrin, S. (2009), 'Cross-border higher education: trends and perspectives', in *Higher Education to 2030, Volume 2: Globalisation*, OECD, pp. 63–88.

8

Research Policy in Scotland and the Rest of the UK

Sheila Riddell

INTRODUCTION

Across the developed world, the UK is at the forefront of creating a competitive and marketised research system, driven by the belief that this will contribute to the overall effectiveness and efficiency of universities and the wider economy. UK Government pronouncements highlight the success of science and research policy, noting, for example, that 'the UK is already the most productive country for research in the G8 – both in terms of publications and citations per unit spend' (BIS, 2014: 5). The Scottish Government has made similar bold statements about the excellence of Scottish universities; for example, the White Paper on independence noted that 'when adjusted for population, Scotland has more universities in the Times Top 200 world universities per head of population than any other country' (Scottish Government, 2013: 7). Over the last two decades, research policy has had a profound impact on university values and ideology, since, particularly in research-intensive universities, staff have been compelled to adopt the guise of 'academic capitalists' in order to advance their careers and secure funding for their research (Henkel and Kogan, 2010). Universities have embraced the entrepreneurial research agenda on the grounds that independently earned income provides a certain degree of freedom from 'state dependence', although the majority of research income continues to come from government sources, with the Research Councils funding a third of all activity. At the same time, it is evident that efforts by the state to control research activity have intensified, driven by a range of mechanisms including research assessment initiatives designed to concentrate funds in particular institutions, the prioritisation of specific research programmes and themes often linked to business and economic agendas, and the promotion of knowledge exchange and impact activities to ensure that funded research produces practical social and economic benefits.

The broad approach to university research in Scotland, and the extent to which this differs from UK research policy, is the central focus of this chapter. We discuss the way in which research featured in the referendum debate, noting areas of agreement and disagreement between the Scottish and UK Governments and the universities. In conclusion, we consider whether research policy in Scotland is consistent with the Scottish Government's claim that higher education north of the border embodies a different set of social values from those which are found within the wider UK system.

AN OVERVIEW OF DEVELOPMENTS IN UK RESEARCH POLICY

As noted by Brown (2013) and Henkel and Kogan (2010), prior to the 1980s research activity in the UK was relatively unplanned and uncoordinated, with academics enjoying considerable freedom to pursue their own research agendas and interests. The University Grants Committee (later Council) (UGC) distributed a block grant to institutions to cover both teaching and research activities, with little transparency as to how funds were allocated or should be used. In 1988 the University Funding Council took over from the UGC, and was replaced in 1992 by funding councils for each of the four UK nations following administrative devolution. During the 1980s and 1990s, universities across the UK experienced significant pressures, as a previously elite system of higher education with relatively low rates of participation (about 15 per cent of the age group) was transformed over a very short period of time into a relatively high participation system, with a doubling of participation rates. The rapid growth in the demand for places, accompanied by 'efficiency savings' imposed by a cost-paring Conservative government, placed a great deal of stress on research activity and infrastructure (Georghiou, 2001), leading to greater state intervention in the management and governance of research. Research assessment initiatives became an increasingly important part of the 'dual support' system for the allocation of research funds to institutions (see below for a discussion of the role of the Research Councils, which formed the second wing of the dual support system). Research assessment exercises, the first of which took place in 1986 and the most recent in 2014, used peer review as the basis for judging the quality of research produced by 'units of assessment' in different institutions. These judgements were used to inform the block grant allocated to particular disciplines within specific institutions, and institutional performance was considered extremely important in terms of both funding and reputation. Research assessment has played an increasingly important role in tightening state control over university research, particularly in terms of concentrating research funds in certain institutions and disciplines. Academics have generally supported the principle of research selectivity, but critics have pointed to a number of unintended and perverse consequences. For example, there has been growing pressure to publish in high-impact journals, reinforcing trends towards ideological conformity in areas such as economics (Harley and Lee, 1995). The Universities and Colleges Union (UCU) has also been critical of the managerial and sometimes bullying culture associated with research assessment exercises, which has led to the division of staff into 'research active' or 'non-research-active' categories. This has been accompanied by a tendency to privilege research over teaching activities, which might work to the detriment of students as well as staff (Copeland, 2014). Finally, research funds have become so concentrated in a small group of universities that academics in non-research intensive institutions may find it virtually impossible to engage in research, due to a lack of space and time. This may in the long run damage the UK research base by robbing the system of hybrid vigour and new thinking.

As noted above, research assessment represents one aspect of the dual support system for the distribution of government funds to universities, with the funding councils of the four UK nations deciding on the funding formula to use following a shared UK research assessment exercise. The second way in which government funding is distributed is via peer-reviewed research proposals submitted to the seven UK Research Councils. With a £3 billion budget, these bodies play an increasingly important role in steering university research activity. The Research Councils were established in 1965 as non-departmental public bodies and ostensibly distribute funding according to the Haldane Principle. The Haldane Report, published in 1918, suggested that research required by government should be designated as either basic or applied, with the former funded by the Research Councils. Academics, unencumbered by government interference, should be the arbiters of scientific merit. Applied research, by way of contrast, should be commissioned by particular departments to meet their operational needs. Whilst still adhering to the Haldane Principle, the UK Government argues that 'it is legitimate for Government to have goals and to take a strategic view on large capital investment'. Furthermore, it is suggested that:

> every Government will have some key national strategic priorities such as addressing the challenges of an ageing population, energy supply or climate change. The research base has an important role to play in addressing such priorities and the Research Councils, with the support of independent advice, have proposed research programmes to tackle them.

By the same token, it is acknowledged that 'ministers should not decide which individual projects should be funded nor which researchers should receive the money. This has been crucial to the international success of British science' (BIS, 2014: 57). Foresight areas identified by the Research Councils, in consort with government, include global food and farming future, land use futures and global environmental migration. In addition to the funding of policy-orientated research programmes and the identification of strategic themes and Foresight projects, funding mechanisms are used to lever additional funds from business and charities. For example, knowledge transfer funds have been used to support research that industry is willing to co-fund. Overall, the relative power of government and academics in decisions regarding research priorities, funding methods and grant allocation is contentious, and the UK Government has recently reiterated its commitment to the Haldane Principle in the light of academic concerns that political influence was growing and academic control weakening (BIS, 2014).

THE TECHNOLOGY OF RESEARCH MANAGEMENT

A number of commentators such as McGettigan (2013) have noted the growing commodification and financialisation of universities, and the way in which they increasingly mirror private corporations in their modus operandi. Changes in the management of university research over time illustrate his argument. In order to capitalise on research, universities have set up central and subject-based research and commercialisation offices staffed by a growing cadre of administrators. Subject groupings have research officers and knowledge exchange officers, and most universities have at least two vice-principals dedicated to the management of research, one focusing on academic research and one on commercialisation and knowledge transfer. The UK and Scottish Governments have attempted to encourage the formation of spin-out companies and the licensing of patents, so that universities may drive efforts to make the UK a 'key knowledge hub in the global economy' (HM Treasury, DfES and DTI 2004). However, Henkel and Kogan (2010) argue that some of this effort may be misplaced. They note that whilst the majority of UK universities have licensing agreements in place, most earn either nothing or very little from these agreements. Only 8 per cent of universities earned more than £1 million in licensing agreements in 2006, and even in successful universities economic gain from the exploitation of intellectual property rights is restricted to a small number of examples. The Lambert Report (2003) was highly critical of the financial value of spin-out companies, and there continues to be little evidence that universities are reaping financial rewards in relation to the amount of money invested.

In order to address anxiety about the costs and benefits of university research, a variety of management technologies have been utilised to monitor and control the use of academic time. For example, to investigate the way in which full economic costing (fEC) of research is operating, lecturers are required to provide information on the proportion of time spent on teaching and research. The Wakeham Review of Financial Sustainability and Efficiency of Full Economic Costing of Research in UK Higher Education Institutions reported in 2010. The report recommended that the best way to constrain burgeoning indirect costs within full economic costing regimes was to apply tighter constraints to those institutions with relatively high overhead rates. The report also expressed concern that academics were spending time paid for by teaching on research, but recognised institutional autonomy in relation to issues of cross-subsidy. It was suggested that governing bodies should take more responsibility for scrutinising the division of academic labour between teaching and research. The report did not question the accuracy of the information gathered in time management studies, nor did it acknowledge that universities' focus on research is driven in large part by the reputational and financial incentives of research assessment.

SCOTTISH RESEARCH POLICY

So far, the discussion has focused on the UK context, and the elements which appear to be common across all four UK jurisdictions. We now turn to the important question of the extent to which Scottish research policy has developed along different lines from the wider UK pattern, particularly in the context of the referendum and clear efforts to establish Scottish higher education as a bastion of social justice values.

As noted above, research assessment exercises have played a significant role in underscoring differences between universities, reinforcing a hierarchy which subsequently becomes reified in league tables. Since 1986, Scottish universities have participated in successive research assessment exercises, although there have been important differences across the UK in the formulae used by higher education funding councils to allocate funding. As noted by Gallacher and Raffe (2012), following the 2001 Research Assessment Exercise, England took the lead in concentrating funds on the highest-performing institutions and disciplines, whilst both Scotland and Wales opted for a less selective approach, spreading the funds more widely. Following the 2008 Exercise, all UK countries adopted a formula geared towards ensuring that the highest-rated disciplines and institutions received the lion's share of the funding. More recently, the UK government declared its intention to protect the science and research base, but also to ensure that funding was directed towards 'internationally excellent' work (BIS, 2010). The Scottish Funding Council followed suit, announcing in its funding letter of December 2010 that it would 'protect in real terms funding for the very highest rated research . . .' (Scottish Funding Council, 2010).

Some efforts have been made in Scotland to encourage institutions to work together by, for example, collaborating on bids for research funding and on research assessment submissions. However, most collaboration and pooling has involved pre-92 institutions, for example, Heriot-Watt and Edinburgh Universities put in joint submissions to the 2014 Research Excellence Framework (REF2014) in areas such as Physics and General Engineering. The concentration of research funds as a result of successive Assessment Exercises is illustrated in Table 8.1, which shows that in the academic year 2014–15, the University of Edinburgh attracted a third of research and knowledge exchange funding from the Scottish Funding Council.

Despite recent convergence in research policy, funding decisions announced in March 2015 following REF2014 appear to signal some cross-border divergence. Before demitting office as Cabinet Secretary for Education and Lifelong Learning in November 2014, Michael Russell requested that the Scottish Funding Council recognise 'emerging excellence' in research in its future allocation of research funding. Table 8.2 shows Research Excellence Grant allocations from 2014–15 to 2017–18. The University of Edinburgh continues to receive the lion's share of the Research Excellence Grant and was rated fourth in the UK for research power in REF2014. However, in 2017–18 its annual Research Excellence Grant allocation was scheduled to fall to £75.213 million, £10 million less than was awarded in 2014–15. This coincides with the withdrawal of Global Excellence

Table 8.1 Summary of Scottish Funding Council grants, academic year 2014–15 (all figures in £)

Institution	Teaching funding	SSI funding	Research and knowledge exchange funding	Total of these grants 2014–15
Aberdeen	44,745,344		27,135,000	71,880,344
Abertay	16,962,735		1,059,000	18,021,735
Dundee	40,848,780		24,994,000	65,842,780
Edinburgh Napier	38,152,481		2,793,000	40,945,481
Edinburgh	71,194,872		100,896,000	172,090,872
Glasgow Caledonian	48,470,546		3,175,000	51,645,546
Glasgow School of Art	7,438,018	2,820,000	2,326,000	12,584,018
Glasgow	84,368,306		56,010,000	140,378,306
Heriot-Watt	26,126,624		13,277,000	39,403,624
Highlands and Islands	30,620,398		2,630,000	33,250,398
Open University	20,741,055		141,000	20,882,055
Queen Margaret	12,134,498		937,000	13,071,498
Robert Gordon	32,569,750		2,903,000	35,472,750
Royal Conservatoire of Scotland	3,951,523	5,588,000	390,000	9,929,523
SRUC	10,078,035	1,014,000	1,718,000	12,810,035
St Andrews	15,290,181		22,454,000	37,744,181
Stirling	23,002,343		7,497,000	30,499,343
Strathclyde	64,607,442		23,380,000	87,987,442
West of Scotland	42,831,117		2,425,000	45,256,117

Initiative funding. Other institutions which have lost funding over this period include the Universities of Aberdeen, Dundee and St Andrews. Institutions which have significantly benefited from an increase in research funding include Heriot-Watt University, the University of Stirling and the University of Strathclyde. Glasgow Caledonian University, the University of the Highlands and Islands and the University of the West of Scotland have also seen a growth in their research funding. SRUC, Scotland's rural college, was included in the REF for the first time and will receive an allocation of £3.5 million annually by 2017–18. By way of contrast, the formula applied in England ensures a greater concentration of research funding in top-rated institutions such as Imperial College London, Oxford and Cambridge.

RESEARCH AND THE REFERENDUM DEBATE

As noted in Chapters 1 and 3, the distinctive character of the Scottish approach to student funding became one of the flagship policies of the Scottish Government during the referendum debate, used to indicate Scotland's adherence to the principle of universalism in the delivery of public services. However, in the area of research, the policy discourse adopted by the Scottish Government was somewhat

Table 8.2   Indicative Research Excellence Grant allocations for Scottish institutions, 2015–16 and 2017–18 (£ per annum)

	2014–15 excluding Global Excellence Initiative	2015–16	2016–17	2017–18
University of Aberdeen	21,144,000	20,829,000	20,408,000	19,987,000
University of Abertay Dundee	532,000	585,000	635,000	685,000
University of Dundee	20,857,000	20,437,000	19,913,000	19,388,000
Edinburgh Napier University	1,544,000	1,623,000	1,683,000	1,744,000
University of Edinburgh	84,017,000	81,363,000	78,289,000	75,213,000
Glasgow Caledonian University	1,826,000	2,136,000	2,437,000	2,738,000
Glasgow School of Art	1,870,000	1,641,000	1,402,000	1,164,000
University of Glasgow	44,793,000	45,276,000	45,535,000	45,793,000
Heriot-Watt University	9,934,000	10,699,000	11,414,000	12,129,000
University of the Highlands and Islands	1,368,000	1,862,000	2,350,000	2,837,000
Queen Margaret University Edinburgh	363,000	520,000	676,000	831,000
Robert Gordon University	1,891,000	1,707,000	1,513,000	1,319,000
Royal Conservatoire of Scotland	153,000	186,000	219,000	251,000
SRUC		1,181,000	2,363,000	3,544,000
University of St Andrews	17,732,000	17,656,000	17,490,000	17,325,000
University of Stirling	5,289,000	5,928,000	6,540,000	7,152,000
University of Strathclyde	16,426,000	17,095,000	17,681,000	18,267,000
University of the West of Scotland	910,000	1,091,000	1,268,000	1,444,000
Total	230,659,000	231,815,000	231,816,000	231,811,000

different, drawing on evidence from higher education league tables to illustrate the success of Scottish universities in the global higher education market.

Endorsing the position of Universities Scotland, the Scottish Government stated that, following independence, Scottish universities would remain part of a UK common research area, in order to ensure the continuation of collaborative research, access to facilities and peer review for researchers throughout the UK. This, the White Paper suggested, was in the interests of both Scotland and the rest of the UK (Scottish Government, 2013). The Scottish Government proposed that it would contribute to the funding of the UK Research Councils, based on population share. This optimistic scenario was contested by the paper on science and research published by the Department of Business Innovation and Skills (BIS, 2013) as part of its Scotland analysis series. Data on Scotland's share of Research Council funding were used as an example of the way in which Scotland benefited from membership of a shared UK research area. For example, in 2012–13, institutions in Scotland were awarded 10.7 per cent of UK Research Council funding, against 8.4 per cent of population (see Table 8.2).

The BIS paper argued that there would be no guarantee that Scotland would continue to be part of a UK funding area post-independence, because national governments fund national research programmes. Reflecting different economic and social priorities, the Scottish Government would almost certainly wish to develop a distinctive research agenda, making it very difficult to agree a joint research programme and funding share. The BIS paper also suggested that significant difficulties would emerge with regard to the funding of research by UK charities post-independence, pointing out that in 2012, Scottish universities received about 15 per cent of their total research income from charities, most of which are UK based. If Scotland left the UK, the BIS paper argued that most UK charities would wish to concentrate funding within their own territory, and Scotland would have to look to Scottish charitable sources, leading to fragmentation and duplication.

Following pressure from Scottish academics to clarify its research policy, the Scottish Government published a paper entitled *Scotland's Future: Higher Education Research in an Independent Scotland* (Scottish Government, 2014). The central argument of this document was that independence would allow Scottish universities to maintain existing collaboration across the UK, whilst developing stronger international collaborations, establishing clearer national research priorities and having greater influence on the operation of the UK Research Councils. Throughout the paper, reference is made to the importance of the Haldane Principle, whereby academics decide on the scientific merit of research proposals unencumbered by political influence. However, the paper suggests that the Scottish Government would wish to invest in a greater number of innovation centres to undertake work in areas of centrality to the Scottish economy, and would also consider setting up a Scottish Research Council to run alongside the UK Research Councils. Overall, it appeared that Scottish academics, particularly those in science and engineering, were unimpressed by these proposals. An online survey conducted by the Times Higher Education Supplement before the referendum suggested that 55 per cent of university staff were in favour of remaining in the UK, a result which mirrored the outcome of the referendum in September. Attitudes of university staff to Scottish Government research policy are explored in greater depth in the following section.

KEY INFORMANTS' VIEWS OF RESEARCH FUTURES

Ongoing membership of a common UK research area was seen by almost all interviewees as the most important area to maintain post-independence. However, Michael Russell, the Cabinet Secretary for Education and Lifelong Learning, had some criticisms of the way in which the Research Councils operated, believing that they imposed decisions on Scotland without adequate discussion:

> Very often if you look at the structures of the Research Councils it's done on the basis of decisions, major decisions made elsewhere and Scotland going along with them. The doctoral and post-doctoral research hubs . . . I think that's an interesting example where it's a policy that can be agreed on but it's not been agreed on, it's been imposed. (Cabinet Secretary, Education and Lifelong Learning)

He felt that, post-independence, excellent research in Scottish universities would continue, but there would be benefits with regard to greater equality in international collaborations and the establishment of a Scottish Research Council. He dismissed the UK Government's warnings that the common UK research area was unlikely to continue if Scotland became independent:

> I don't see why this is impossible at all. I think we could probably negotiate it in a weekend if we chose to do so in a sensible and meaningful manner ... There is scope for aligning existing [Scottish] Government research funding for Medicine, Environment and elsewhere into a mini-Research Council which might well operate out of the Scottish Funding Council to take forward some particularly Scottish research priorities ... I just think this is within a subset of the question, 'What should the relationship be between the two countries?' I'm a believer in a modern relationship between the two countries, that we can collaborate on all sorts of things and we can be the best of friends on a whole range of things but we will be able to have our own say and make our own decisions on key things which presently we cannot speak on. (Cabinet Secretary, Education and Lifelong Learning)

An interviewee with a civil service background was less sanguine about the automatic survival of the UK research area in the event of Scottish independence:

> The big area where you could see a really substantial potential difference structurally is around research or research funding. Obviously at the moment it's a UK matter with the volume of research funding, in terms of the government funding and also the big charities, tending to be UK based. So the debate about what the future might be for research funding is absolutely vital, you've got various models and it remains perfectly feasible that you could have an island-wide set of Research Councils. The question is politically 'How likely is it to be?' Because the call on that ultimately has to be London's, you'd have to assume. And they would probably call that very much on the basis of what the English universities said to them. And I don't know what the English universities would say. But if I was an English university looking at the percentage share of Research Council funding going to Scotland, which is disproportionately high on population share terms, though not on sector size necessarily, I might be inclined to be a little bit protective about funding ... The alternative is of course that you have your own research council in Scotland. And I would guess the academic sector here would be immensely nervous about that as an outcome. I think it's interesting that they're being very quiet about all that and it tells you a lot about their relationship with government that they're not making a bigger fuss about this in public. (Key informant, civil service background, Scotland)

University interviewees almost all believed that existing shared services, particularly the UK Research Councils, should be preserved:

> Access to RCUK – terribly important on what happens on that front. The maintenance of competitive funding throughout whatever system our government operates. The capacity to maintain open doors across the UK borders. (Senior manager, post-92 university, Scotland)

This interviewee also believed that it was important for Scotland to continue to participate in the Research Excellence Framework (REF):

[The REF] is bound up, I think, with RCUK. The capacity of Scotland to really present itself to the outside world on a peer based review process that is contained within Scottish borders I think would be not so good as operating within a UK system . . . You'll want actually the cement to be there as much as possible. (Senior manager, post-92 university, Scotland)

Senior managers of ancient universities were particularly likely to recognise the benefits of a common UK research area, which might even be broadened to include other countries:

Well I think the position on Research Councils [is very important]. It is good for English universities to be able to work with Scottish researchers. And it is good for Scottish researchers to be able to work with English universities. Now we have that at the moment in what you might call a single research area across the whole of the United Kingdom. It seems to me you would not want to lose that. So first point, maintaining a single research area is absolutely critical. To do that you have to have, it seems to me, some potential buy-in which could be arranged if people wish to be sensible with the Research Councils. However, you might also want to look at the potential for a single research area with other countries. And so you might not want to restrict yourself to buy-ins with the Research Councils in England. One might want, for example, to look at Scandinavia. (Senior manager, post-92 university, Scotland)

The thing one has to be clear about is that the UK Research Councils are a success. And they deliver success for Scotland. And they deliver success for the UK. And they deliver success for Europe. And it would seem to me that once one got into any detailed thinking, one would be wanting to maintain and build on that success. And . . . so and I would hope, and I'm very Pollyanna-ish, I would hope that post-referendum, whatever the outcome, people would say that the UK Research Councils benefit Scotland, benefit Britain, so what can we do to strengthen them? (Senior manager, post-92 university, Scotland)

However, the positive view of the UK Research Councils was not unanimous. A senior manager of a new university believed that Scotland would be better served by developing its own funding council, with research funding much more tightly geared to addressing the country's economic needs:

I'm probably the only university principal that actually takes a somewhat different view on this one. I am not a huge fan of the role of UK Research Councils . . . My view on the whole is that if . . . we see a need to develop Scotland as an economy, a society, a community with its own decision-making powers, if you see it in those terms then the research funding framework should have some connection with that . . . When you see it in England, that's a big enough society, big enough country and economy where you could actually say, 'We will determine who gets research funding solely on the basis of excellence. We'll ask no other question'. And when you look at it in a smaller economy you do need to ask those questions. You need to say, 'Well what is this actually doing for the country? What is the tax payer getting from that other than a glow of satisfaction?' (Senior manager, post-92 university, Scotland)

This respondent also questioned the utility of a number of other shared activities including research assessment:

> I do not believe [the REF] is a good . . . mechanism. I think the main impact of that has been to allow the proliferation of very mediocre research, encourage it. And in fact to deprive high-value research performers of the kind of support that they need because it's all going to sustain what's actually been mediocre research . . . So there are certainly things that we should be doing together with England and together with anyone else who makes sense. But that should be because it's the right thing to do or because it adds value. But just to maintain all these bureaucratic mechanisms, I don't think so. (Senior manager, post-92 university, Scotland)

English academics differed in their views on the future of a common UK research area in an independent Scotland, with a fairly even split between those who thought that negotiating a shared research area would be relatively straightforward, and those who felt that such negotiations would quickly founder. The representative of a UK higher education organisation believed that sharing of research capability and funding should be extended across Europe to challenge US supremacy:

> Of course, I would go further than that and say I think we should have a European Union research area if we're going to really challenge the United States as a powerhouse . . . It would not be sensible for Scotland to try and establish [a Scottish Research Council] and to think they could fund world class research with a scaled down version of the RCUK . . . I think that the BIS thing [suggesting that Scotland would be excluded from a UK-wide research area post-independence] is a bit of a bluster . . . (Spokesperson, higher education-related organisation, England)

A less rosy view was taken by one of the English senior managers who thought that academics in England would be unlikely to wish to share resources if Scotland had just voted for independence. He believed the attitude would be:

> 'Go fish in your own pond, more for us' because that's the way those research intensives tend to behave . . . (Senior manager, post-92 university, England)

As is evident from the views of the key informants quoted above, the consensus amongst the academic community was that universities north and south of the border benefited from operating within a common UK research area, which should therefore be preserved irrespective of Scotland's chosen constitutional future.

CONCLUSION

To summarise the points made in this chapter, whilst research policy may have ratcheted up research performance in Scotland and the rest of the UK over the past two decades, the methods by which this has been achieved have caused a number of problems. Henkel and Kogan suggest that:

> the degree of surveillance, performance management and competition for resources is now so high in the United Kingdom as to raise serious doubts about its implications in the longer term for academic capacity and motivation. In particular, there are concerns that it leaves insufficient space for diversity and nonconformity in academic inquiry and

that the balance between reward and punishment may inhibit the academic ambition, risk-taking, and tolerance of uncertainty needed to produce innovative work. (Henkel and Kogan, 2010: 379)

They also express concerns about research concentration, which deprives some institutions and disciplines of funding, as well as the focus of resources on patent applications and spin-out companies, which is only cost-effective for a small minority of universities (Guena and Nesta, 2006). Henkel and Kogan conclude that the measurement of research performance may be delivering diminishing returns, not least because of the resources absorbed by the REF including the time of senior academics and administrators. Overall, an 'unbridgeable gap' may be opening up between the relatively small number of individuals and institutions who success-fully exploit the rules of academic capitalism, whilst the majority of universities and academic staff are marginalised from the international changes in the produc-tion of knowledge.

Research policy in Scotland has been broadly in line with the direction of travel in the rest of the UK, although the distribution of funds following REF2014 indicates the re-emergence of a different approach to the concentration of research funding. The analysis in this chapter underlines the practical and ideological similarity across the UK in the fostering of an ultra-competitive ethos, the adop-tion of commercial language and practices and the development of a performative management culture. As in the rest of the UK, there has been growing government involvement in the establishment of research priorities geared towards the achieve-ment of economic growth and a focus on economic and behavioural rather than social structural problems.

REFERENCES

Brown, R. (2013), 'The funding of research', in R. Brown and H. Carasso (eds), *Everything for Sale? The Marketisation of UK Higher Education*, London: Routledge.

Copeland, R. (2014), *Seeing the Bigger Picture: The Future of UK Research and Development – a UCU Policy Statement*, London: University and College Union.

Department for Business, Innovation and Skills (BIS) (2010), 'Higher education funding for 2011–12 and beyond', https://www.gov.uk/government/uploads/system/uploads/attachment_data/file/32406/10-1359-hefce-grant-letter-20-dec-2010.pdf (accessed 10 March 2015).

Department for Business, Innovation and Skills (BIS) (2013), *Scotland Analysis: Science and Research*, London: BIS.

Department for Business, Innovation and Skills (BIS) (2014), *The Allocation of Science and Research Funding 2015/16: Investing in World Class Science and Research*, London: BIS.

Gallacher, J. and D. Raffe (2012), 'Higher education policy in post-devolution UK: more convergence than divergence?' *Journal of Education Policy*, 27: 4, 467–90.

Georghiou, I. (2001), 'The United Kingdom national system of research, technology and innovation', in P. Laredo and P. Mustar (eds), *Research and Innovation Policies in the New Global Economy: An International Comparative Analysis*, Cheltenham: Edward Elgar, pp. 253–96.

Guena, A. and L. Nesta (2006), 'University patenting and its effects on academic research: the emerging European evidence', *Research Policy*, 35: 790–807.

Harley, S. and F. Lee (1995), *The Academic Labour Process and the Research Assessment Exercise: Academic Diversity and the Future of Non-Mainstream Economics in UK Universities*, Leicester: Leicester Business School.

Henkel, M. and M. Kogan (2010), 'The United Kingdom', in D. D. Dill and F. A. van Vught (eds), *National Innovation and the Academic Research Enterprise: Public Policy in Global Perspective*, Baltimore, MD: Johns Hopkins University Press, pp. 337–86.

Her Majesty's Treasury, Department for Education and Skills (DfES) and Department of Trade and Industry (DTI) (2004), *Science and Innovation Investment Framework, 2004–2014*, London: Her Majesty's Stationery Office.

Lambert, R. (2003), *Lambert Review of Business-University Collaboration, Final Report*, London: Her Majesty's Stationery Office.

McGettigan, A. (2013), *The Great University Gamble: Monet, Markets and the Future of Higher Education*, London: Pluto Press.

Scottish Funding Council (2010), 'Indicative main grants to colleges and universities for academic year 2011–12', http://www.docs.sasg.ed.ac.uk/GaSP/SFCFunding/201112/Main/_SFC_Circular_Main.pdf (accessed 10 March 2015).

Scottish Government (2013), *Scotland's Future: Your Guide to an Independent Scotland*, Edinburgh: Scottish Government.

Scottish Government (2014), *Scotland's Future: Higher Education Research in an Independent Scotland*, Edinburgh: Scottish Government.

Wakeham, W. (2010), Wakeham Review of Financial Sustainability and Efficiency of Full Economic Costing of Research in UK Higher Education Institutions, London: Her Majesty's Stationery Office.

9

Devolution and Higher Education Policy: Negotiating UK and International Boundaries

Sheila Riddell

INTRODUCTION

In preceding chapters, we examined the impact of devolution on various aspects of Scottish and UK higher education systems, including institutional governance, approaches to tuition fees and student support, cross-border student flows, widening access, internationalisation and research policy. Evidence from policy documents and administrative data is interspersed with the voices of central actors within the higher education system, including university managers, prospective students in Scotland and the north of England, and international students. This mixed-methods approach has helped us understand the social significance and impact of government policies, as well as the trends revealed by official statistics. Throughout the book, higher education is used as a lens through which to interrogate critically the Scottish Government's claim that devolution is leading to the growing marketisation of the public policy arena in England, whilst Scotland remains a bastion of collectivism and social democracy (Scottish Government, 2013). In the sections below, we begin by summarising the central findings, before discussing cross-cutting themes emerging from the analysis.

The first over-arching theme concerns the implicit and explicit understandings of social justice informing higher education policy in Scotland and England, and the extent to which either jurisdiction appears to be delivering fairer outcomes. This involves a critique of the policy of free tuition in Scotland and the extent to which universal social services inevitably deliver more equal outcomes. Secondly, we consider the nature and extent of marketisation within higher education in Scotland and the rest of the UK. We argue that, prior to the changes of 2012, there were already strong elements of competition across the UK, particularly in areas such as international student recruitment and research funding. Whilst acknowledging the major changes introduced by the Browne reforms, we agree with Marginson (2013) that they have promoted a pre-existing quasi-market in higher education rather than establishing a full-blown economic market. Furthermore, their impact has not just been restricted to England, but has been felt across the UK. Finally, in relation to higher education, we consider the vision of further devolution as set out in the Command Paper entitled *Scotland in the United Kingdom: An Enduring Settlement* (Her Majesty's Government, 2015).

UNIVERSITY GOVERNANCE AND DEVOLUTION

The relationship between universities and the devolved governments is still evolving, with key informants pointing to both upsides and downsides of the closer relationship which is a consequence of operating within a smaller jurisdiction. Since the establishment of the Scottish Parliament, Holyrood politicians have developed a much closer knowledge of the workings of individual institutions and a stronger sense that universities' activities should support government priorities. In areas such as widening access, the Scottish Government has adopted a particularly hands-on approach, with the Scottish Funding Council steering activity through outcome agreements. The metrics used to define and measure social disadvantage have proved particularly controversial, with ongoing tensions between universities and government as to whether performance in this area should be based on self-review, or whether performance indicators should be externally specified and used to compare performance across institutions. The Universities Scotland response to the Scottish Government consultation on the Higher Education Governance Bill clearly expresses the sector's concerns, stating, 'At the level of general principle, we are concerned that the Scottish Government is proposing to legislate about matters which are properly for autonomous institutions to manage, and doing so without evidence that the proposals would bring benefit' (Universities Scotland, 2015: 1).

Through their representative body, Scottish universities have tried to speak with one voice, and appear to have had greater success in influencing policy than the more fragmented college sector. Indeed, college key informants believed that, whilst the college sector had borne the brunt of public sector cuts, universities had been over-privileged and unfairly shielded from public accountability. Since devolution, universities have made considerable efforts to comply with Scottish Government political goals, demonstrating their contribution to the country's economic, social and cultural well-being, and are aware that they are in a strong bargaining position. However, universities believe that their prized autonomy is under threat, and, as noted by David Raffe, over coming years, considerable political skill will be required on both sides to ensure that the relationship remains productive.

TUITION FEES AND STUDENT SUPPORT

For more than twenty years, tuition fees have been hotly debated in both Scotland and the rest of the UK, whilst considerably less attention has been paid to the equally important area of student maintenance. Alone in the UK, Scotland has preserved free tuition, but non-repayable grants have declined. As a result, within Scotland student debt is skewed towards those from the most disadvantaged backgrounds. By way of contrast, student debt is on average much higher in England, but in general students from poorer backgrounds receive greater support compared with those from wealthier backgrounds. In Wales and Northern Ireland the level of debt is similar to Scotland, but again students from less affluent backgrounds receive higher levels of support.

Tuition fees policy in Scotland, as in the rest of the UK, is highly politically charged and as a result its presentation has often been over-simplified. During the referendum campaign, it was implied that, whereas tuition was free in Scotland, in England young people had to pay up front, thus making it impossible for students from poorer backgrounds to take up a place at university. As noted by Lucy Hunter Blackburn in Chapter 3, some political journalists presented the Scottish Government's policy on tuition fees as reflecting quintessentially progressive Scottish values, with the implication that questioning the policy was inherently un-Scottish. As a result, there has been little consideration about the material effects of the policy, with all major political parties at Holyrood falling in with the government's position. There has been little examination of the data to determine the extent to which the policy of free tuition is actually progressive in its effects, with political rhetoric trumping evidence.

In Chapter 4, Sarah Minty reported on the views of prospective students in Scotland and the north of England who were interviewed as part of the ESRC project. Young people in Scotland were often under the impression that their counterparts in England had to pay tuition fees up front rather than taking out a loan. They were often unaware that tuition fee loans were available to Scottish students at English institutions, and to young people from the rest of the UK studying in Scotland. They were also unaware of the principles underpinning income-contingent repayment systems, so that student debt would only be repaid when income crossed a specific threshold. There was little understanding of the different loan repayment thresholds and interest rates applied to loans in Scotland and England, and the implications of these permutations on future loan repayments. In England and Scotland, students from poorer backgrounds had less understanding of the student loan system compared with those from more affluent backgrounds who generally had a family tradition of higher education participation.

Interestingly, and possibly counter-intuitively, prospective students from the north of England were generally resigned to incurring high levels of debt, having received the message that they would be rewarded through a handsome graduate salary premium once they began work. They had little understanding that additional lifetime earnings were likely to depend to a considerable extent on the institution attended and the course studied. Prospective students in Scotland, by way of contrast, were strongly debt averse and appeared unaware that those from poorer backgrounds were likely to finish a four-year honours degree course with high levels of debt. To avoid debt, those from less advantaged backgrounds were likely to choose an institution close to home to reduce living expenses, irrespective of institutional status and its impact on future earning power. Those from wealthier backgrounds were more likely to see student debt as an investment, and therefore be willing to incur the higher costs of studying away from home.

MASSIFICATION AND WIDENING ACCESS FOR UNDER-REPRESENTED GROUPS

Patterns of university participation are broadly similar in Scotland and England despite different fees regimes. Following the rapid expansion of higher education from the 1990s onwards, it was widely predicted that the introduction of much higher tuition fees in England in 2012 would lead to a significant decline in the proportion of the age group entering university. Table 1.2 shows university entry rates between 2010 and 2013 in each of the four UK jurisdictions. Between 2010 and 2013, somewhat counter-intuitively, university admission rates rose in England (by 2.48 per cent), Wales (by 5.3 per cent) and Northern Ireland (by 7.7 per cent). By way of contrast, the university admission rate over this period fell in Scotland by 2.3 per cent, although this was the only jurisdiction without tuition fees for home students. Figure 1.2 shows that when England and Scotland are compared, the university participation rate for under-21-year-olds is broadly similar, standing at around 25 per cent of the age group. However, Scotland has a higher proportion of the under-21 age group studying higher education courses, generally at sub-degree level, in colleges (about 6 per cent of higher education participants study HNCs and HNDs in Scottish colleges, compared with less than 1 per cent in England). A number of these courses lead to degrees through articulation arrangements, often with post-92 universities. Scotland also has higher numbers of over-21-year-olds in higher education compared with England.

Higher education participation rates of young people from the 20 per cent most deprived backgrounds in Scotland and England have risen only marginally over the course of a decade. The Social Mobility and Child Poverty Commission (2014) noted that, whilst in England there had been small increases over the previous decade in participation by students from the poorest neighbourhoods, the gap in participation was falling slowly and, on current trends, by 2020 students from the most advantaged backgrounds would still be twice as likely as those from the poorest backgrounds to enter higher education. Despite the absence of tuition fees, the situation in Scotland mirrors that in England. As shown in Table 1.3, in 2004–5 only 14.9 per cent of Scottish people living in the lowest Scottish Indeix of Multiple Deprivation (SIMD) quintile entered higher education, compared with 15.8 per cent in 2012–13. There was virtually no growth in the proportion of students in ancient universities drawn from the poorest Scottish neighbourhoods (the proportion increased from 7.9 per cent in 2004–5 to 8.2 per cent in 2012–13). By way of contrast, students from the poorest Scottish neighbourhoods continued to be over-represented on sub-degree programmes in the college sector, increasing from 21.3 per cent of the total in 2004–5 to 22.8 per cent in 2012–13. This raises concerns that colleges may be used as a means of diverting students from poorer backgrounds to a form of higher education which is cheaper for the government to fund but in general delivers less in terms of labour market opportunities (Gallacher, 2014).

The slow increase in participation rates by students from socially deprived backgrounds calls into question the value of widening access programmes, although of course it is important to remember that we do not know what might have happened in the absence of such initiatives. Whilst these are undoubtedly of value to participants (Riddell et al., 2014), they are likely to make only marginal difference to the overall proportion of students from socially disadvantaged backgrounds in higher education, particularly in more selective institutions. In a highly competitive context, the most important factor affecting the success of students from different social class backgrounds is prior school attainment, which is strongly associated with social class background (Riddell and Weedon, 2014). The Scottish Government's policy choice of funding tuition fees for Scottish-domiciled and EU students means that universities in Scotland have been largely protected from public spending cuts, whereas funding for colleges and schools has fallen. Between 2010–11 and 2012–13, school funding reduced by 5 per cent in real terms (Accounts Commission, 2014). Scottish local authorities have tended to allocate education funding on a per capita basis, with only 5 per cent of funds allocated to areas of social deprivation. As noted by Sosu and Ellis (2014), across Scottish local authorities there appears to be no clear link between deprivation and per-pupil expenditure. By way of contrast, initiatives such as the London Challenge channelled funds into the most deprived schools accompanied by clear targets for improved outcomes. This initiative led to marked improvement in the performance of pupils from the poorest backgrounds in London schools compared with slower improvements elsewhere, which was subsequently translated into improved higher education participation rates (Vizard, 2015). There is strong evidence to suggest that if Scotland wishes to improve university participation by students from the poorest backgrounds, the most effective way of doing this is to target resources on schools in the most deprived neighbourhoods. This may call for a re-examination of funding priorities across the entire education sector, a theme picked up by the Holyrood administration at the time of writing.

CROSS-BORDER STUDENT FLOWS

Over recent years, the distinctiveness of higher education in Scotland has been at the forefront of public debate, with less focus on the extent of systemic interdependency. Figure 9.1 illustrates the importance of cross-border flows to the different countries of the UK, highlighting the fact that students from the rest of the UK make up more than a third of the undergraduate degree entrants to Welsh universities and more than a tenth of undergraduate degree entrants to Scottish universities. By way of contrast, students from the rest of the UK make up a very small proportion of undergraduate degree entrants to Northern Ireland and England (about 2 per cent in both cases, although England has by far the largest number of border crossers). Wales has the highest proportion of international undergraduate degree entrants (about 13 per cent of the population) followed by

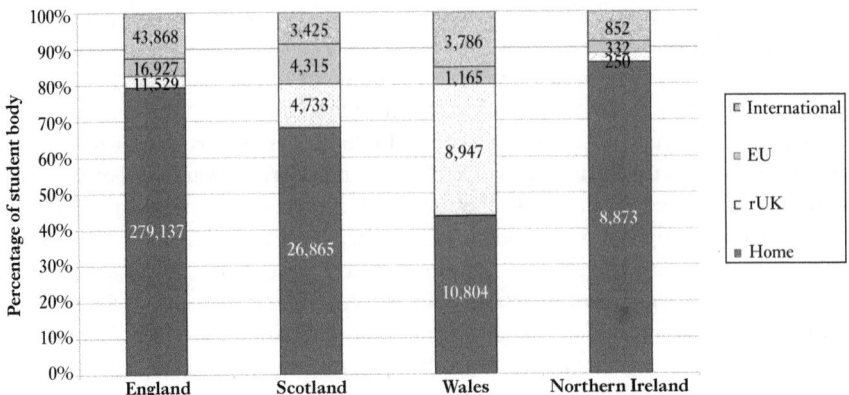

Figure 9.1 Full-time first degree entrants to higher education institutions in England, Scotland, Wales and Northern Ireland, 2012, by domicile

Source: Author's analysis of HESA data, 2013–14

England (about 12 per cent) and Scotland (just under 10 per cent of all undergraduate degree entrants).

These cross-border flows are extremely important not just in terms of individual institutional budgets, but also because changes in fees regimes affect students across the UK, not just the particular jurisdiction in which they are enacted. Hunter Blackburn (2015) has pointed out that Scotland and Northern Ireland have been 'surprising laboratories for unregulated fees'. Following the introduction of £9,000 fees in England in 2012, there were fears that 'fee refugees' would make their way to Scotland from the rest of the UK, thus denying places to Scottish students. The Scottish Government's response was to pass legislation allowing Scottish universities to charge those without a 'relevant connection' to Scotland a different fee from Scottish students. International students were already outside the fee cap set for domestic students. Scottish universities have chosen to limit fees for students from the rest of the UK to £9,000, but in principle they could charge much more than this, as is the case for international students. About a third of the undergraduate student population at universities such as Edinburgh and St Andrews are drawn from the rest of the UK, and these universities also have a high proportion of international undergraduates. As a consequence, in classrooms and lecture halls across Scotland, students taking exactly the same course are either studying for free or paying different fee rates depending on their country of origin, throwing up issues of fairness and citizenship entitlement across the UK. Such issues also crop up in Wales and Northern Ireland where students pay different fees depending on where they are defined as normally residing. It is somewhat ironic that, whilst vigorously opposing tuition fees for Scottish students, Scotland (along with Northern Ireland) has acted as a trailblazer in the introduction of unregulated fees for students from the rest of the UK.

The policy of free tuition for Scottish students studying in Scotland has had a number of perverse consequences which have often been ignored. For example, the Scottish Government is obliged under the terms of the Bologna Agreement to pay the tuition fees of students from other EU countries, in order to treat them in the same way as home students. As a result, EU students are in direct competition with Scottish students for university places, which are capped by the Scottish Government. The proportion of EU students has increased over recent years, making up more than 10 per cent of first degree entrants in Scotland, the highest proportion in the four UK countries. The Scottish Government would prefer EU students to pay fees and has made representations to Brussels to be allowed to do this, but so far has not found a feasible way of doing so.

The analysis above illustrates some of the tensions associated with the management of cross-border flows. The devolved administrations have become increasingly focused on ensuring that home students remain in their country of origin during their university years, but at the same time are increasingly dependent on recruiting students from the rest of the UK. For Scotland, increasing recruitment from the rest of the UK and the EU is essential if the size of the university sector is to be maintained. Some institutions are drawing a growing proportion of their income from the (unregulated) fees of students living in other parts of the UK. EU students studying in Scotland are extremely important in cultural terms, but are currently a financial cost rather than benefit to the sector due to the knock-on effect of tuition fees policy for Scottish students.

INTERNATIONALISATION, RESEARCH POLICY AND THE GLOBAL HIGHER EDUCATION MARKET

Overall, Scotland is highly dependent on international fee income, generating more than 52 per cent of its total fee income from international students, compared with 31 per cent in the rest of the UK. As shown in Figure 9.2, four Scottish universities (Edinburgh, Heriot-Watt, Glasgow and St Andrews) derive significantly more of their income from international students compared with home and EU students, whereas the reverse is true for all other Scottish universities. The University of Edinburgh is currently earning around £90 million annually from international fee income, compared with about £63 million from home and EU students.

University strategic plans suggest that international student recruitment at both undergraduate and postgraduate level will become even more important over coming years. This shift towards international recruitment has implications for the relationship of these universities with the Scottish Government, in particular the extent to which government continues to have the power to regulate their activities.

Scottish universities' reliance on the recruitment of international students has highlighted tensions between UK higher education and immigration policy. The UK Government has attempted to place a cap on the number of non-EU immigrants, including international students, entering the UK. Universities across the UK have argued that this policy is damaging for higher education, since growing bureaucracy is likely to deter international students. In addition, the

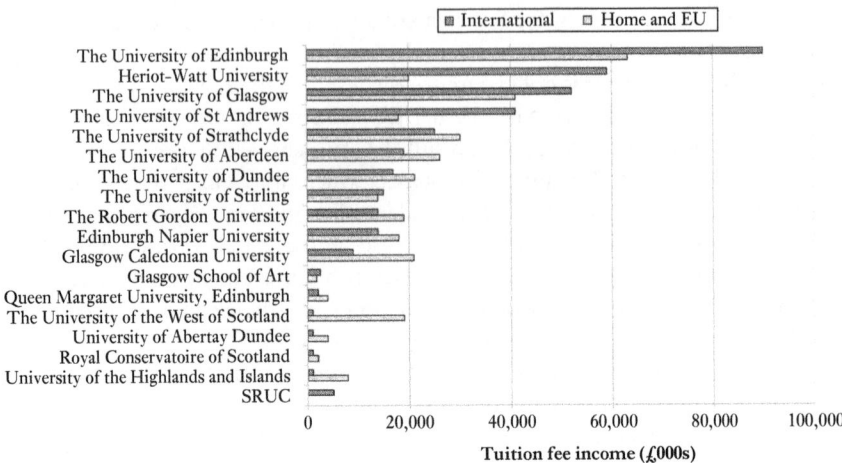

Figure 9.2   Tuition fee income by international, home and EU students, by higher education institution, 2012–13

Source: Tindal, Findlay and Wright, 2014

withdrawal of post-study work visas has made the UK a less attractive destination than other major recruiters of international students such as Australia. Scottish universities have made a strong case that post-study work visas should be made available for international students studying in Scotland, where overall levels of immigration are much lower than in London and the south-east of England. The Smith Commission recommended that the Scottish and UK Governments should discuss the feasibility of these proposals, although institutions in the rest of the UK might well object to Scotland having a market advantage in this area. Overall, international student recruitment highlights tensions between immigration and higher education policy at UK level, but also tensions between the Scottish and UK Governments. Nonetheless, it is likely that over coming decades at least a subset of Scottish institutions will see their principal market and frame of reference as international rather than local, with implications for autonomy and governance.

Research is another area where a subset of Scottish institutions regard themselves as operating within a global rather than local arena. Successive research assessment exercises have based their judgements of academic merit on evidence of international rather than local impact, and there is a growing emphasis on the recruitment of international academic staff and research students. Scottish Government research policy has, until recently, aimed to concentrate financial support on centres of excellence, in line with policy across the UK. Decisions following REF2014, however, indicate some degree of departure, with funding spread across the university sector, to the consternation of some of the ancient universities. Despite this variation, the broad trend in the area of research and the recruitment of international students is for policy convergence between Scotland and the rest of the UK, with a small number of Scottish institutions regarding their main competitors as international rather than local. Balancing national and international institutional identities presents challenges for government and for institutions. The Scottish Government often refers to international league tables as providing evidence of the excellence of particular institutions, but at the same time has an interest in maintaining the integrity and distinctiveness of the Scottish university sector. By the same token, Scottish universities, particularly those with a high proportion of international students, have to strike a balance between their local and international missions, which may at times pull in different directions. For example, efforts to promote a more diverse student body encouraged by the Scottish Government may be undermined by pressures to recruit wealthy international students who are able to pay unregulated fees.

Having summarised the main findings of our research, we now provide a brief overview of the overarching themes.

CONCEPTUALISING AND PROMOTING SOCIAL JUSTICE IN HIGHER EDUCATION POLICY

The first overarching theme concerns the conceptualisation of social justice informing Scottish higher education. As discussed above, changes in tuition fees policies in Scotland and England have had little impact on social class divisions within the university sector, where institutional hierarchies appear to be remarkably stable and resistant to change (Raffe and Croxford, 2015). Young people from private schools and middle-class backgrounds continue to be over-represented in more selective institutions, with little change over the last decade despite the promotion of widening access initiatives. This is an uncomfortable finding for the Scottish Government, which has based its higher education policy on the assumption that universal free tuition would automatically produce more socially just outcomes, and suggests that there is a need to examine the pros and cons of universal service provision more closely.

In countries like Sweden, with strong social democratic traditions, inclusive public services based on principles of universalism appear to have produced more equal social and economic outcomes (Green and Janmmat, 2011; Øverbye, 2012). It has been assumed that adopting a Nordic model of welfare provision in areas such as higher education and social care for older people is the best way of making Scotland a more equal society. However, as noted by Bourdieu and Passeron (1977), simply treating individuals the same in areas such as education may have the paradoxical effect of reproducing or even strengthening social inequality, because this approach fails to take account of existing economic and cultural disadvantages. To break the link between social class background and university attendance, efforts would need to focus on eliminating wider social and economic inequalities. As noted by Hills et al. (2015), since the economic crisis of 2007, despite rising levels of qualification, the economic position of young adults has deteriorated. Intra-generational differences have also widened as a result of the unequal distribution of inherited wealth. Whilst it is often assumed that Scotland is a more egalitarian society compared with England, the evidence on educational, health and economic outcomes does not support this belief (Hills et al., 2010). A progressive graduate tax, as well as means-tested student support, might be a more effective way of promoting social equality in higher education. However, this would involve greater critical scrutiny of universal free higher education and, for reasons discussed earlier, this has not been encouraged.

MARKETISATION AND HIGHER EDUCATION IN SCOTLAND AND ENGLAND

The second overarching theme concerns the operation of the market in England and Scotland. The White Paper on Scottish independence (Scottish Government, 2013) reflected the view that English higher education was becoming increasingly marketised, whilst the Scottish system was assumed to be immune from such influences. Our analysis suggests that the emerging picture is more complicated than this. Institutional competition is long-established in all UK jurisdictions, as students compete for scarce places and universities compete for research and commercial contracts and international students. The devolved administrations have become increasingly anxious to ensure that local students are encouraged to study in their home jurisdiction, whilst seeking to recruit fee-paying students from the rest of the UK to fill available places.

The stated goal of the Browne reforms in England was certainly to promote a marketised system. It was anticipated that, following the lifting of the fee cap in 2012, only a minority of institutions would charge the full £9,000 with students shopping around to find the best courses at the most competitive price. In fact, the envisaged market failed to materialise for a variety of reasons. As might have been expected, almost all institutions chose to charge the full £9,000, since it was assumed that students would regard a lower fee as signalling an inferior product. This was also the case in Scotland, although some institutions reduced the annual fee to reflect the additional costs associated with a four-year, rather than a three-year, honours degree. The Browne reforms also assumed that students would have access to market information with regard to the costs and outcomes of particular courses. Our interviews suggested that prospective students had little awareness of differences in the cost of particular courses, levels of student satisfaction or graduate salaries. Most appeared to be relying on recommendations from family, friends or the school, rather than information gleaned from league tables or websites such as Which? University. Prospective students, particularly those from poorer backgrounds in Scotland, had very little understanding of the student loan system either in Scotland or the rest of the UK and choices seemed to be driven by factors such as the need to avoid debt by studying locally rather than future employment prospects. Despite the market rhetoric, the 2012 changes to university funding were only ever likely to produce a quasi-market, with services free at the point of delivery and loans underpinned by government.

Finally, the extent of cross-border student flows between the different parts of the UK, the EU and internationally means that national boundaries have become increasingly porous, and changes to fees regimes in one jurisdiction have a much wider impact. As a result, the Scottish Government's rhetoric, suggesting a polarisation between a marketised system in England and a non-marketised system in Scotland, fails to encapsulate the complexity and interdependence of higher education systems across the UK.

HIGHER EDUCATION AND THE DEVOLUTION SETTLEMENT: FUTURE DIRECTIONS OF TRAVEL

The third theme weaving through the various research strands concerns the ongoing impact of constitutional change on the Scottish and UK higher education systems. As noted by Raffe (2013) and Trench (2009), constitutional debate has focused on the nature and extent of powers to be held by the Scottish Parliament, and has neglected to provide effective mechanisms for policy coordination across the four administrations. This is particularly marked in the field of higher education, where there is a history of each jurisdiction introducing changes to tuition fees regimes with little or no regard for its impact on its neighbours. The Smith Commission recommended closer collaboration between the respective UK governments, but this will require greater trust than has been evident over recent years. For example, despite their UK-wide impact, the Browne reforms were introduced with little consultation with the devolved administrations. Subsequently the devolved administrations have developed their individual approaches to student funding with little sector-wide consultation.

At the time of writing, there are a number of changes underway or under discussion, which, despite originating in one jurisdiction, would have a profound effect across the UK if implemented. For example, the Labour Party's proposal to reduce the cap on university fees to £6,000 would impact on university finances across England, but also on particular institutions in Wales and Scotland. Assurances have been given to universities that the fees shortfall would be made up from alternative sources of government funding and transferred to the devolved administrations via the Barnett formula. However, there is no guarantee that additional funding would be available and that it would find its way to the relevant institutions. The reduction of tuition fees might also have an impact on widening access bursaries provided by individual universities, since across the UK these are funded via variable fee income. Another change in the pipeline concerns the decision to remove the cap on student numbers in England from 2016. If pre-92 universities in England decide to expand the number of places available, this could mean that fewer students decide to study in another UK jurisdiction. In Wales, as part of its review of university funding, the Diamond Committee is examining whether the tuition fee grant should continue to be paid to Welsh-domiciled students studying in another UK jurisdiction. This might have an impact on flows of students out of Wales, the majority of whom study in England. Alternatively, it might lead to Welsh border crossers shouldering much larger debts than their counterparts studying at home, as is the case in Scotland. Clearly, changes to tuition fees across the UK are likely to continue, with each jurisdiction having the power to interfere with the policies of its neighbours. Much greater cross-jurisdiction policy coordination would be desirable, but there is little indication to date that this is likely to happen.

CONCLUSION

This study of higher education policy across Scotland and the rest of the UK has revealed some uncomfortable truths and a number of paradoxes. The rapid growth of higher education across the UK has led to the inclusion of more students from socially disadvantaged backgrounds, but institutional hierarchies have remained intact. Despite political rhetoric surrounding free higher education in Scotland, the system has failed to produce more egalitarian outcomes compared with the rest of the UK. However, the policy has become very difficult to challenge and is likely to survive for some time. Universities in Scotland have flourished over the past decade, but the fact that they have been prioritised for funding over schools and colleges has had some unwelcome consequences in terms of reproducing existing social inequalities. The devolution settlement is currently under intense discussion and constitutional arrangements will undoubtedly continue to change. However, with higher education systems increasingly interlinked, not only within the UK but internationally, policy approaches based on the permanence and inviolability of national boundaries are no longer tenable.

REFERENCES

Accounts Commission (2014), *School Education*, Edinburgh: Audit Scotland.

Bourdieu, P. and J. C. Passeron (1977), *Reproduction in Education, Culture and Society*, London: Sage Publications.

Gallacher, J. (2014), 'Higher education in Scotland: differentiation and diversion? The impact of college-university progression links', *International Journal of Lifelong Education*, 33: 1, 96–106.

Green, A. and J. G. Janmmat (2011), *Regimes and Social Cohesion: Societies and the Crisis of Globalisation*, Basingstoke: Palgrave Macmillan.

Her Majesty's Government (2015), *Scotland in the UK: An Enduring Settlement Cm 8990*, London: Her Majesty's Stationery Office.

Hills, J., J. Cunliffe, P. Obolenskaya and E. Karagiannaki (2015), *Falling Behind, Getting Ahead: The Changing Structure of Inequality in the UK, 2007–2013*, London: London School of Economics and Political Science.

Hills, J., M. Brewer, S. Jenkins, R. Lister, R. Lupton, S. Machin, C. Mills, T. Modood, T. Rees and S. Riddell (2010), *An Anatomy of Economic Inequality in the UK: Report of the National Equality Panel*, London: London School of Economics and Political Science.

Hunter Blackburn, L. (2015), *Scotland and Northern Ireland: The UK's Surprising Laboratories for Unregulated Fees*, http://adventuresinevidence.com/2015/03/04/scotland-and-northern-ireland-the-uks-surprising-laboratories-for-unregulated-fees (accessed 18 March 2015).

Marginson, S. (2013), 'The impossibility of capitalist markets in higher education', *Journal of Education Policy*, 28: 3, 353–70.

Øverbye, E. (2012) 'Deconstructing universalism', Paper presented at Trygdeforsker-seminaret, 26–7 November 2012, Oslo and Akershus University College.

Raffe, D. (2013), 'Was devolution the beginning of the end of the UK higher education system?', *Perspectives: Policy and Practice in Higher Education*, 17: 1, 11–16.

Raffe, D. and L. Croxford (2015), 'How stable is the stratification of higher education in England and Scotland?', *British Journal of Sociology of Education*, 36: 2, 313–35.

Riddell, S. and E. Weedon (2014), 'Changing legislation and its impact on special and inclusive education in Scotland', *British Journal of Special Education*, 41: 4, 363–81.

Riddell, S., S. Edward, E. Boeren and E. Weedon (2014), *Widening Access to Higher Education: Does Anyone Know What Works? A Report to Universities Scotland*, Edinburgh: University of Edinburgh, Centre for Research in Education Inclusion and Diversity (CREID).

Scottish Government (2013), *Scotland's Future: Your Guide to an Independent Scotland*, Edinburgh: Scottish Government.

Social Mobility and Child Poverty Commission (2014), *State of the Nation 2014: Social Mobility and Child Poverty in Great Britain*, https://www.gov.uk/government/uploads/system/uploads/attachment_data/file/367461/State_of_the_Nation_-_summary_document.pdf (accessed 11 March 2015).

Sosu, E. and S. Ellis (2014), *Closing the Attainment Gap in Scottish Education*, York: Joseph Rowntree Foundation.

Tisdal, S., A. Findlay and R. Wright (2014), *The Changing Significance of EU and International Students' Participation in Scottish Higher Education*, Oxford: Centre for Public Policy Change.

Trench, A. (2009), 'Un-joined-up government: intergovernmental relations and citizenship rights', in S. L. Greer (ed.), *Devolution and Social Citizenship in the UK*, Bristol: Policy Press, pp. 117–36.

Universities Scotland (2015), *Universities Scotland Response to the Scottish Government Consultation on a Higher Education Bill*, Edinburgh: Universities Scotland.

Vizard, P. (2015), *The Changing Anatomy of Economic Inequality in London, 2007–2013: Social Policy in Cold Climate*, Research Report 6, London: London School of Economics and Political Science.

Appendix 1: Research Methods

Much of this book draws on findings from an Economic and Social Research Council (ESRC) study conducted by a team of researchers at Moray House School of Education, University of Edinburgh in 2013 and 2014: 'Higher education in Scotland, the devolution settlement and the referendum on independence' [ES/K00705X/1]. The project was led by Professor Sheila Riddell, and the team consisted of Professor David Raffe, Dr Elisabet Weedon, Dr Linda Croxford, Sarah Minty, Dr Grace Kong and Susan Whittaker. The project involved both primary research and knowledge exchange activities and Table A.1 below summarises the different data collection methods which were used. Further details of research methods and findings are summarised in a series of briefings and working papers published on the CREID website (http://www.ed.ac.uk/schools-departments/education/rke/centres-groups/creid/projects/he-in-scotland).

Table A.1 Summary of data collection methods for different project strands

Type of data gathered	Details
Review of policy and administrative data	Analysis of policy developments on widening access and student support in the four UK nations
Analysis of data from the Higher Education Statistics Agency from 1996 to 2012	Analysis of cross-border student flows by student characteristics and institution attended
Key informant interviews	Semi-structured interviews (twenty-eight in Scotland, twenty-two in the rest of the UK and beyond) with academics, policy-makers, representatives of higher education-related organisations including union representatives
Interviews with young people in schools and colleges	Semi-structured interviews with 148 young people aged 14–19 (121 in Scotland, twenty-seven in England)
Interviews with international Chinese students in Scottish universities	Semi-structured interviews with twenty-one postgraduate students from Hong Kong and mainland China from three higher education institutions in Scotland

REVIEW OF POLICY AND ADMINISTRATIVE DATA

Policy developments in widening access and student support were analysed in the four nations. Findings from this strand of the research are reported in Weedon (2014) and Hunter Blackburn (2014).

ANALYSIS OF DATA FROM THE HIGHER EDUCATION STATISTICS AGENCY FROM 1996 TO 2012

This strand of the study compared the patterns and trends among students domiciled in England, Wales, Northern Ireland and Scotland, who entered higher education in 1996, 2004, 2010, 2011 or 2012. Data supplied by the Higher Education Statistics Authority (HESA) on full-time undergraduate students in their first year of study in UK higher education institutions in each of these years were analysed. The analysis explored patterns for entrants of all ages to full-time first-degree programmes, as well as young people (aged under 21), among whom entry to higher education is closer to an annual flow, such that year-on-year data reveal the main impacts of changes. Ideally Universities and Colleges Admissions Service (UCAS) data based on the year in which students applied to higher education, rather than HESA data based on the year of entry, would have been used, but a change of UCAS policy meant that its data were not available to the project. The analysis and interpretation of the data provided by HESA is that of the researchers alone. HESA does not bear any responsibility for the findings, inferences or conclusions of the analysis. The findings from this strand of the research are published in Whittaker (2014), Croxford and Raffe (2014a), and Croxford and Raffe (2014b).

POLICY-MAKER INTERVIEWS

Semi-structured interviews were conducted with 50 policy-makers from Scotland and the rest of the UK, as well as a small number of interviews with participants from Europe and the US. We sought to include respondents who were experts in higher education either because they were involved in research in this area or because they had served on committees relating to higher education policy.

Table A.2 provides an overview of participants which included senior academics and university managers, senior college managers (Scotland only), politicians and civil servants, trade union representatives and representatives of higher education-related organisations. Whilst the findings represent the perspectives of significant individuals in higher education they should be seen as a snapshot of opinion from this group and not as fully representative of the whole sector.

Each interviewee was contacted personally and half of the interviews were conducted face to face, with the other half conducted by telephone. In two cases people from the same organisation were interviewed as a pair, since they were

Table A.2   Overview of key informant participants

	University senior academic		University senior manager		College manager	University lobby group	Higher education-related organisation	Civil servant/politician	Total
	Pre-92	*Post-92*	*Pre-92*	*Post-92*					
Scotland		1	5	2	4	1	6	9	28
England	2	1	1	2		2	6		14
Wales	2								2
Northern Ireland				1					1
Republic of Ireland		1							1
Germany		1							1
Malta		1							1
Sweden		1							1
US		1							1
Total		11		11	4	3	12	9	50

able to comment on higher education policy from slightly different angles. The interviews were recorded and each interview lasted between forty and ninety minutes. They were all transcribed and the transcripts were returned to those interviewees who had requested a copy to check for accuracy. The main areas explored in the interviews were: policy formation and core values of higher education, university and/or college governance, interest group influence, student funding, cross-border flows of students, widening access, international and postgraduate students, policy futures and systemic stability. Interviewees were asked to focus initially on their own jurisdiction and then to reflect on the relationship between it and the rest of the UK and Europe. The data were analysed thematically; the Scottish findings are reported in Riddell (2014), while Weedon (2014b) is concerned with key informants from the rest of the UK and the Republic of Ireland.

RESEARCH WITH YOUNG PEOPLE IN SCOTLAND AND THE NORTH OF ENGLAND

In the final strand of the study, young people's views of higher education in Scotland and England were sought using semi-structured interviews conducted with 148 school and college students aged 14 to 19 from Scotland and the north of England. The interviews covered participants' views of the different funding systems within the UK and their attitudes to debt, as well as the pros and cons of higher education, issues around widening access and their thoughts on the referendum and the lowering of the voting age.

The research was conducted in two stages. In the first stage, eighty-nine

Table A.3   Overview of school-based research participants

Country	School pseudonym	Higher education progression rate[a]	% eligible for free school meals	SIMD/IDACI quintile of school[b]	No. of interviewees in each school	No. of participants		No. of BME pupils
						Boys	Girls	
Stage 1:	Edinburgh 1	18%	27.1%	5	3	1	2	1
Scotland	Edinburgh 2	67%	3.6%	5	8	2	6	1
	Independent school	Unknown	Unknown	3	11	7	4	0
	Fife 1	18%	27.8%	2	11	7	4	1
	Fife 2	20%	34.4%	1	9	4	5	0
	FE college	N/A	N/A	1	8	4	4	0
	Glasgow 1	21%	40%	1	10	7	3	0
	Glasgow 2	20%	47.6%	1	15	6	9	2
	Western Isles	32%	9.2%	2	6	2	4	0
	West Lothian	27%	24.5%	2	8	1	7	1
Stage 2:	Aberdeenshire	29%	9.1%	4	14	3	11	0
Scotland/	East Lothian	58%	5.3%	5	8	1	7	0
England	South Lanarkshire	34%	24.1%	2	10	5	5	0
	Lancashire	N/A	N/A	1	8	3	5	1
	Tyne & Wear 1	N/A	N/A	1	11	4	7	1
	Tyne & Wear 2	N/A	5.8%	3	8	4	4	3
Totals					148	61	87	11

[a]   Note that for Scotland, this figure comes from the school leaver destination statistics for each school. In Scotland an average of 36 per cent of school leavers go on to higher education. These data were not available at a school/college level for the English institutions.

[b]   SIMD is the Scottish Index of Multiple Deprivation. IDACI is the Income Deprivation Affecting Children Index. In both cases, the lower the quintile the higher the level of deprivation.

young people in nine Scottish schools and a Scottish college were interviewed on film in pairs or threes with each interview generally lasting about twenty minutes. Film clips from these interviews formed the basis of a short YouTube film, 'Our Future: Young people's views on higher education in Scotland' (https://www.youtube.com/watch?v=Alc1XzblgpE&feature=youtu.be). Along with a set of accompanying teaching materials (http://www.ed.ac.uk/schools-departments/education/rke/centres-groups/creid/projects/he-in-scotland/he-in-scotland-teaching), these were intended to stimulate discussion among young people in the run-up to the referendum and were sent out to all Scottish secondary schools in January 2014. In the second stage of the research, a further fifty-nine young people (thirty-two in Scotland and twenty-seven in the north of England) from six secondary schools/sixth-form colleges took part in in-depth interviews. Pupils were interviewed either in pairs or groups of three and each interview lasted around an hour. Table A.3 provides an overview of the participating schools and interviewees.

Participating young people were selected by school and college contacts. Three-quarters of interviewees said they planned to go to university upon leaving school, while a further one in ten were considering college. Due to the selection process, the interviewees cannot be considered representative of the wider 16 to 18 school and college population, but should be seen as representing the views of a particular sub-group of young people who are considering pursuing higher education.

Consent was obtained from all young people, and the parents of those who appeared in the film. In both stages of the research, interviews were recorded and transcribed and entered into NVivo. Data were analysed thematically. Emerging patterns and differences were explored by country, gender and social background. Pseudonyms are used throughout the book. Findings are reported in Minty (2014).

RESEARCH WITH CHINESE INTERNATIONAL STUDENTS IN SCOTLAND

The ESRC project included a small case study of Chinese students studying in Edinburgh. Semi-structured interviews were conducted with twenty-one full-time Chinese students studying in one Scottish city. The interviews took place during the pre-referendum period between December 2013 and February 2014. The main topics in the interview related to:

- their family and education background
- motivations for choosing to study at the current higher education institution
- the sources of funding and range of annual household income
- their current study experience, including their views towards their courses, classmates and university staff
- their living experience, including their views on accommodation and social life
- their future plan after completing their current course
- their views on working or studying in Scotland with reference to visa policy should it become an independent country

Table A.4 provides an overview of the Chinese students who participated in this strand of the research.

The students were recruited through a number of university contacts, the personal network of one of the researchers, the Confucius network and Chinese student groups. All interviews were conducted face to face individually, except one interview on Skype with an alumnus of the University of Edinburgh who had returned to China. The interviews were conducted in Mandarin Chinese, Cantonese or English. They were recorded and then summarised into English. Each interview lasted between forty and ninety minutes.

Table A.4 Overview of participants in Chinese international student research

Gender	Pseudonym	Current/highest degree	Current higher education[a]	Home country	Previous degree	Overseas study experience	Previous work experience	Only child in the family	Other family studying in the UK?
M	Qingming LIANG	Alumnus of MSc in TESOL	1	Mainland China	BA in English Language	No	No	Yes	No
F	Meili ZHENG	MSc in TESOL	1	Mainland China	BA in English Language	No	No	Yes	Yes
F	Yuan GAO	MSc in TESOL	1	Mainland China	BA in English Language and Foreign Affairs	No	No	Yes	Friends
M	Yaobang CHEN	MSc in Artificial Intelligence	1	Mainland China	BEng in Biomedical Engineering	No	No	Yes	No
F	Nan ZHANG	MSc in TESOL	1	Mainland China	BA in English Language and Literature	No	Yes	Yes	No
F	Shuwei LI	MSc in TESOL	1	Mainland China	BA in Business English	No	No	Yes	Yes
F	Lihua LUO	MSc in Economics	1	Mainland China	BA in Economics	Singapore	Yes	Yes	Yes
F	Xinxin ZHONG	MSc in Education Studies	1	Mainland China	BA in International Business Management	Sino-British university in China	No	Yes	Friends
F	Ling LIU	MSc in TESOL	1	Mainland China	BA in English and Translation	No	No	No	Yes
M	Guozhi HE	MSc in Accounting and Finance	1	Mainland China	BA in Accounting	No	No	Yes	Yes
M	Mingjun LU	MSc in Accounting and Finance	1	Mainland China	BA in Auditing	No	No	Yes	No

Table A.4 (continued)

Gender	Pseudonym	Current/highest degree	Current higher education[a]	Home country	Previous degree	Overseas study experience	Previous work experience	Only child in the family	Other family studying in the UK?
F	Fengyi HU	MA in Interpreting and Translation	3	Mainland China	MA in Interpreting	No	No	Yes	No
F	Wenhua KE	MSc in TESOL	1	Mainland China	BA in English Language	No	No	Yes	Yes
F	Chunhui SHEN	MSc in TESOL	1	Mainland China	BA in English Language	No	No	Yes	Friends
F	Hui HUANG	MSc in TESOL	1	Mainland China	BA in English Language	No	No	Yes	No
F	Xinyi LIN	MSc in Linguistics and English Language	1	Mainland China	BA in English and American Literatures	No	No	Yes	Friends
F	Sum Wai HO	BA in Music	2	Hong Kong	BA in Policy Studies and Administration	No	Yes	No	No
F	Yuting WANG	MSc in TESOL	1	Mainland China	BA in English Language	No	No	Yes	Yes
F	Yawen DAI	MSc in TESOL	1	Mainland China	BA in English Language	No	No	No	No
F	Mei Fong LEE	PhD in Clinical Psychology	1	Hong Kong	MA in Clinical Psychology	UoE	Yes	Yes	No
M	Dezhi LU	PhD in Microwave Communications	3	Mainland China	MEng in Mobile Communications	HW	Yes	No	No

a   1 = ancient university; 2 = post-92 university; 3 = pre-92 university

REFERENCES

Croxford, L. and D. Raffe (2014a), *Working Paper 4 – Student Flows Across the UK's Internal Boundaries: Entrants to Full-time Degree Courses in 2011*, Edinburgh: University of Edinburgh, Centre for Research in Education Inclusion and Diversity (CREID).

Croxford, L. and D. Raffe (2014b), *Working Paper 8 – The Impact of the 2012 Tuition Fee Changes on Student Flows Across the UK's Internal Borders*, Edinburgh: University of Edinburgh, Centre for Research in Education Inclusion and Diversity (CREID).

Hunter Blackburn, L. (2014), *Working Paper 3 – The Fairest of Them All? The Support for Scottish Students in Full-time Higher Education in 2014–15*, Edinburgh: University of Edinburgh, Centre for Research in Education Inclusion and Diversity (CREID).

Minty, S. (2014), *Working Paper 7 – Young People's Views of Tuition Fees and Their Attitudes Towards Debt*, Edinburgh: University of Edinburgh, Centre for Research in Education Inclusion and Diversity (CREID).

Riddell, S. (2014), *Working Paper 5 – Key Informants' Views of Higher Education in Scotland*, Edinburgh: University of Edinburgh, Centre for Research in Education Inclusion and Diversity (CREID).

Weedon, E. (2014a), *Working Paper 1 – Widening Participation to Higher Education of Under-represented Groups in Scotland: The Challenges of Using Performance Indicators*, Edinburgh: University of Edinburgh, Centre for Research in Education Inclusion and Diversity (CREID).

Weedon, E. (2014b), *Working Paper 6 – Key Informants' Views of Higher Education in the Rest of the UK and the Republic of Ireland*, Edinburgh: University of Edinburgh, Centre for Research in Education Inclusion and Diversity (CREID).

Whittaker, S. (2014), *Working Paper 2 – Student Cross-border Mobility Within the UK: A Summary of Research Findings*, Edinburgh: University of Edinburgh, Centre for Research in Education Inclusion and Diversity (CREID).

Appendix 2: List of Acronyms

BIS	Department for Business, Innovation and Skills
CI	Central Institution
DA	Devolved Administration
EHEA	European Higher Education Area
ESRC	Economic and Social Research Council
EU	European Union
FE	Further Education
HE	Higher Education
HEFCE	Higher Education Funding Council England
HEFCW	Higher Education Funding Council Wales
HEI	Higher Education Institution
HESA	Higher Education Statistics Agency
HM Gov	Her Majesty's Government
IDACI	Income Deprivation Affecting Children Index
MP	Member of Parliament
MSP	Member of the Scottish Parliament
NUS	National Union of Students
OECD	Organisation for Economic Co-operation and Development
OFFA	Office for Fair Access
PG	Postgraduate
POLAR	Participation of Local Areas
QAA	Quality Assurance Agency
RAE	Research Assessment Exercise
RCUK	Research Councils UK
REF	Research Excellence Framework
rUK	Rest of the UK
SAAS	Student Awards Agency for Scotland
SFC	Scottish Funding Council
SFEFC	Scottish Further Education Funding Council
SHEFC	Scottish Higher Education Funding Council
SHEP	Schools for Higher Education Programme
SIMD	Scottish Index of Multiple Deprivation
SLC	Student Loans Company
SNP	Scottish National Party

STEM	Science, Technology, Engineering and Maths
TESOL	Teaching English to Speakers of Other Languages
UCAS	Universities and Colleges Admissions Service
UCU	University and College Union
UGC	University Grants Council
UK	United Kingdom
US	United States
UUK	Universities UK

Index